A VILLAGE **BEFORE TIME**

Beyond An Age of Innocence

T N VENUGOPALAN

BlueRose ONE
Stories Matter
NewDelhi • London

BLUEROSE PUBLISHERS
India | U.K.

For permissions requests or inquiries regarding this publication, please contact:

BLUEROSE PUBLISHERS
www.BlueRoseONE.com
info@bluerosepublishers.com
+91 8882 898 898
+4407342408967

ISBN: 978-93-7139-554-0

Cover Design: Aman Sharma
Typesetting: Manisha Rawat

First Edition: October 2025

Dedication

Dedicated to three extraordinary individuals who have profoundly influenced my life: my father and mentor, the Late Natarajan Thaiveettil, who ignited my creative spark and whose guidance and wisdom continue to inspire me;

my loving mother, the Late Mrs. Janaky Natarajan Pullyadath, whose unwavering love and affection remain etched in my heart and

Suvarna, my steadfast companion, soulmate, and partner of 36 incredible years, whose love, presence, and care enriching life every day.

Oh! My Sweet Memories.

OH! My sweet memories, stay with me
Now and forever more
For you are my companion, my life, my everything
You bring me joy, comfort, and solace
You inspire and energise me as no one else can
In your soothing hug I experience peace and serenity
May you for ever be carved in my mind and soul
A treasured possession of beauty and love
That life has bestowed on me.

Author's Note.

While lost in thought today, I began envisioning a sequel to **Kerala Kaleidoscope***, my debut book. The notion arose from the fact that I had to omit several engaging articles on various subjects from my initial work due to obvious reasons. A sequel would allow me to tell those untold stories, share more insights and explore further into the rich tapestry of Kerala's culture, history, and experiences. During many sleepless nights, my restless mind would delve deeper into the past, mining a thousand memories worth telling to recreate the past. The story of my village before modernity swept in. Before roads were paved and streets got crowded. Chasing those timeless childhood memories that shaped the rhythms of village life. These are memories that are time capsules for generations who may never know what life felt like without electricity, life illuminated by the smouldering kerosene lamps. These memories explore the subtle details of village life, its curious inhabitants, and the everyday moments that linger long after. With a pen in hand and a heart full of passion, I began writing as the dazzling panorama of an eventful and hilarious past – brimming with innocence, wonder, secrets, mesmerising experiences, and cherished friendships – unfurled before my eyes. I selected a few of those resplendent ones that I'm sure will delight you. And the end result was* **A Village Before Time***, the book you are reading now. I tried as best as I could to avoid biases, to cut on exaggerated details and resisted the tendency to under-report to make the narrative as realistic as they happened. I have deliberately opted for a straightforward and accessible writing style, avoiding complex terminology and jargon to ensure that the content is easy to understand and engaging for all readers. To convey the nuances effectively without losing their essence, Malayalam words and phrases are liberally used, accompanied by their English* *translations. This book is a nostalgic pilgrimage through my memories, beautifully etched in the depths of my heart. I would like to share those precious memories before they vanish for ever untold. I'm reminiscing about those cherished stories from a life I once lived, which I have secretly and carefully preserved in the deepest recesses of my heart, untouched and unblemished. Within these pages, cherished moments are revived in all their splendour. I hope* ***A Village Before Time*** *will transport you to the vibrant and eventful past of Kerala, an age of innocence. Wish you a happy reading experience.*

Kochi 25th March,2025.

Contents

1.

Introduction.

"Kousalya supraja Rama poorva sandhya pravarthathe

Uttishta Narasardula karthavyam dhaivamanhikam," Venkateswara Suprabhatham, the enchanting hymns from the temple, the *Azaans* from the nearby mosque, and the sweet chime of the church bell, they were indeed the wake-up music for me, the symphony of religious tolerance, the *shantimantra* of secularism. I grew up in a rustic environment, surrounded by the sounds of faith, all those sacred resonances have captivated and influenced me. In those uneventful days, our dawns were heralded by the crowing of roosters in our yard, soon joined by their companions in neighbouring homesteads, creating a gentle symphony to start a day. In moments of joy, the cows mooed in the barn, and the calves responded with a cheerful tone that echoed through the air-the siren of the village that people believed to be a sign of good fortune. As the golden glow of the rising sun bathed the eastern horizon in a radiant sheen, the towering trees stood silhouetted against the sky, composing a truly breathtaking scene. I had a hilarious childhood packed with lots of exciting fun, frolic, adventure, and games that I loved. My marvellous childhood days in Palluruthy, then a nondescript village in Kochi, are filled with nostalgia, memories, innocence and hidden tales of growing up in a village. The allure and charm of the remote land was mindboggling. Those years bring to my mind vivid images of childhood games I played with my neighbourhood friends, many secrets we shared under the shade of the huge neem tree, childhood reveries, fearsome tales weaved and shared by friends, foolish believes and absurdities. Time stands still as I recollect those resplendent days. Under the serene full moon nights, a silvery cascade of moonlight poured down like a gentle shower of milk. The sight of a thousand fireflies floating through the air, dancing under a moonlit night sky was breathtaking. The glowing flies illuminated the night with their mesmerising dance. Some flitted playfully among trees, others mated coyly, while a few just drifted lazily, leaving behind trails of shimmering brightness that created an ethereal atmosphere.

Sunlight has faded as the setting sun cast long shadows. I day-dreamed of a fascinating, self-exploratory journey revisiting the village. The village paths lined with coconut palms that swayed back and forth in the twilight wind. The village alleys meandered through the length and breadth of the land, often its continuity maintained through the courtyard of others in the village. The landscape was lush, air fresh, and atmosphere quite refreshing.

The village was predominantly inhabited by the poor and marginalized working class, who lived in stark poverty. A few middle-class families resided there as well, and the rich were fewer still. Yet, all coexisted in remarkable harmony. The wealthy never flaunted their affluence - their assets remained well-guarded secrets - while it was the poor and middle class who occasionally put on airs, eager to appear more prosperous than they truly were. The villagers' needs were limited, so were their desires. They found pleasures in little things that made their days enjoyable and life happier. A sense of simplicity and naturalness pervaded the rustic atmosphere. Time seemed to stand still. The rural landscape would be cloaked in peaceful silence, only to be broken occasionally by the rustle of the leaves, chirping of birds or the whooshing wind. I cherish the fantastic scene of flocks of birds flying silently under the endless blue sky searching for their feasts early in the morning and returning unhurried to their nest, silhouetted against the golden evening sky. Every morning, herds of untethered cows would roam freely through the village's narrow lanes, searching for fodder without their owners in sight while buffalos would take rest in the mud-filled canals and village ponds. As the day drew to a close, they would make their way back, following the same winding path. Their daily routine a familiar sight in the village. In the hollows of the palm tree a few parrots found their home where they lived happily. After heavy rains, when the sun shone briefly, we built sand castles in the damp soil. We never vacationed in exotic locations, instead, we explored the amazing birds, rare butterflies, and uncommon plants in our backyard. The naturalists in us had a penchant for discovering the unknown creatures. Our childhood curiosities were endlessly fascinating. The mesmerizing sight of rain in the woods, the wonderful view of the full moon through the canopy of a sprawling mango tree on full moon nights and the late-night view of the setting moon in the western horizon were equally spectacular. Those full moon nights were truly magical, with moonlight cascading down through thick canopies like a gentle shower, illuminating everything in its path - these are some of my most treasured memories. The village, brimming with hidden wonders and untold secrets, beckons discovery. Within its heart lie the villagers' love, loss, lust, passion, ambitions, dreams, beliefs, revenge, friendships, and innocence—all waiting to be explored.

The grand spectacle of a medium-sized *kettuvallom* (wooden cargo boat) laden with coir, coconuts, river sand, and other freight gliding slowly through the placid backwaters was captivating. The gentle breeze that carried the sweet and distinctive aroma of the paddy in full bloom, caressed me softly. As small canoes leisurely ferried people across the lake, women who made a living from coir-making walked modestly along the narrow path separating the plots of adjoining paddy fields. The lagoon flowed slowly only to be merged with the sea somewhere, not far away. The sea, beneath the calm and serene surface, conceals a multitude of arcane creatures, many mysteries and rare gems.

On scorching summer afternoons, flocks of parrots would appear in the courtyard from nowhere and after a grand feast of ripe mangoes and seeds of *mandaaram* (dwarf white orchid), would vanish into the verdant landscape. In those idyllic times, house sparrows (*angaadikkili*) flitted happily through village markets, pecking at grains spilled from open bags. However, when village markets (*angaadi*) gave way to modern supermarkets, these birds were deprived of their staple food source, imperilling their very existence. Consequently, the once-familiar sight of house sparrows has become a rare and nostalgic treat. A few blue kingfishers (*Neela ponman*), once peaceful residents of the *njaaval* in the homestead (Indian blackberry tree), the lone woodpecker, whose incessant pecking on the dead coconut stem in the courtyard was a familiar sound, and the squirrels, who relished the cocoa fruits, have all vanished from the landscape. When the old family pond in the northeastern corner was filled in, the snakeheads (*varaal)* and climbing perches (*karooppu/kallathy)* that had thrived in the muddy depths below along with many tortoises became a cherished part of our collective memory.

The narrow and shallow canals meandered through the land, in which innumerable panchax fish(*maanathukanni*) merrily swam searching for their prey. Among the plants that grew along the water's edge, the riparian vegetation, tiny fishes took shelter to escape the scorching summer heat. Those canals served the twin purposes of irrigating farm lands and controlling floods. In many places, the villagers had carefully bridged these canals using the sturdy stems of coconut palms, which they crossed with practiced ease. Where the canals were wide and deep enough to accommodate small canoes, two palm stems would be placed side by side, occasionally supplemented with a stretched coir rope for added protection that served as arm support. This intricate network of waterways formed the lifeblood of the village. The village paths wound their way along the periphery of these canals, lined with screw pine trees, wild flowers and bushes that provided refuge for the shadows and snakes. The scene was nothing short of captivating. However, as the village underwent transformation into a small town, these canals were filled in to make way for roads. Ironically, the zigzagging roads that now characterize the city suburb were once the very canals that formed the artery of the landscape.

As my mind wandered through the rural landscape, I enjoyed the rustic blues of the old *koprakkalam*, located along the banks of the lake in a small tile-roofed shed, the plastering of the wall peeled off in several places, exposing the red bricks beneath. Laseenth Chettan was briskly de-husking coconuts using a wooden de-husker, fitted with a sharp metal blade on top. Laseenth was a middle-aged man struggling to make ends meet, his mobility being hindered by swollen legs caused by filariasis. His de-husking was so fast paced that I gawked in wonderment. While his assistant *kurudan* Joseph, who was completely blind, left me mesmerised as he de-husked coconuts briskly. Occasionally we used to collect sweet coconut water in copper pots that was later mixed with dough to make soft appam. During scorching summer days, Amma would bathe me in coconut water as a treatment for boils. It was believed that coconut water has the power to heal boils. Split coconuts would be dried in the yard under the serene hues of a blue sky. The dried kernel, the copra, would be extricated from the shell deftly with a long knife and the dried copra would be used for the extraction of coconut oil. The evenings spent with friends in the yard enjoying the cool breeze were part of my memorable memories. During rainy days when the sky would be overcast with dark clouds, the blue river would turn dark grey which would disappoint and frighten us at the same time. The riverbanks were lined with dense mangrove thickets, providing a shelter for fish to spawn and lay their eggs.

During peak monsoon periods, when the rain poured down incessantly, brief moments of sunshine would prompt women to wash their clothes by the family ponds. The sounds of wet clothes being thrashed against the washing stones would reverberate through the atmosphere, creating a symphony of rural life. The teenaged boys swam in the village ponds in gay abandon, in a carefree manner. During annual vacations, the hot summer afternoons were times of revelry as children would dive into the murky depths of mud-filled ponds. Tragically, drowning was a common risk associated with their adventurous water play.

We treated the minor injuries from our adventurous childhood games with the juice of the ubiquitous devil weed—*communist pacha.* It was our *ottamooli,* a trusted panacea for every bruise and scrape. Quick, accessible, and always at our fingertips, it came to our rescue in countless little emergencies. To arrest bleeding, we would successfully apply the fibrous, dusty powder scraped from the *konjatta* of coconut frond, often called *porippal* - it was our natural first aid, summoned straight from the backyard. To heal open wounds with pus, we applied the white, latex-like sap of the *Kuruttupala* tree - a remedy passed down through generations, trusted and close at hand.

How can I forget those rain-soaked days when we splashed through flooded village alleyways, revelling in the rhythmic patter of the raindrops? Or the languid summer days when we immersed ourselves in traditional village games and plays? The coldest winter mornings, (*makaramaasa kulir*), too, remain etched in my memory, when we'd gather around campfires lit with fallen dry leaves in the front courtyard, basking in their warmth. The breathtaking beauty of picturesque mangroves, babbling brooks and calm seas that hides many mysteries, wonders, and rare gems in its depths left me spellbound. Even the serene evenings spent bedridden due to childhood maladies became transformative experiences, teaching me the art of introspection and creative dreaming. In hindsight, I realize that those challenging days didn't aim to break me; instead, they strengthened my confidence, alchemised my dreams, and stirred overwhelming emotions that continue to inspire me. The famous words of Moliere, French playwright and poet that "**the greater the obstacle, the more glory in overcoming it**" proved true in my case.

We chased the colourful kaleidoscope of butterflies through the yards as they fed on the nectar of flowers in the gardens. Village boys, misled by the notion that chameleons suck blood, brutally stoned them. This unfounded fear proved disastrous for the harmless creatures' survival. They could change their colour to match with the surroundings – a ploy to escape the prying eyes of their predators. Once common in our courtyard, these days becoming an increasingly rare sight.

How can I overlook those wonderful memories of Vishu, when we would eagerly await the *Vishukaineettam* with great excitement and anticipation, dreaming of elaborate plans to buy countless articles with our modest amount? A marvellous, once-in an-year occasion. So are the fun-filled days of the *Utsavam* at the nearby temple. And Onam was yet another unforgettable festival, marked by the excited anticipation of new clothes, the cherished *Onakkodi.*

During their leisure hours, teenagers from middle-class homes devoured magazines like *Poompatta* and *Ambili Ammavan,* enthusiastically recounting the stories to their friends in class. The quintessential cartoon series, *Bobanum Moliyum,* by legendary cartoonist Toms, was a particular favourite, tickling their sense of humour and leaving them in stitches, struggling to control their laughter.

The villagers led a simple life without pretensions- a life full of contentment and delight. They never carried a heavy aspirational baggage over their shoulders that could burden the carrier for a lifetime. In the evening, after a long day of physically demanding work, they would take delightful breaks and gather in their courtyards. Neighbours would join in, sharing their pleasures and pains, hopes and fears, dreams and despair, triumphs and tragedies, gossips and hearsays. These informal gatherings were a source of rejuvenation for them.

Evenings would often see long lines of women waiting outside ration shops, enduring lengthy waits. To pass the time, they would engage in lively gossip under the faint glow of electric bulbs as the golden glow left long shadows. Cletus Pothampilly, the ration shop owner, always attired in a spotless white *mundu* and shirt, would sit in a wooden chair behind a wooden table scattered with a few thick registers and bill books. As a local Congress leader of good standing and an ardent fan of Indira Gandhi, he would often brag about his political career and contributions to the illiterate village women. The ration shops supplied worm-infested rice mixed with pieces of stones, and other items such as sugar, wheat, and kerosene at subsidized prices. In those days kerosene appeared in its original colour – a colourless, clear liquid. Later, when use of kerosene as an adulterant in more expensive fuels like petrol became rampant, a blue colour was added to it making its presence noticeable. A ration card was more than just a record of grain purchases; it served as a vital document, akin to a passport, for the villagers. In times of financial emergency, they would pledge their ration cards to secure loans from local wealthy individuals. Driven by poverty, they would borrow modest sums, only to pay exorbitant interest rates.

4 O' clock tea habit has become part of the daily routine of the people. It was as popular as the morning tea. For some, coffee was really their cup of tea. As far as they are concerned, coffee was not just another drink, it indeed was an emotion. The elders in the locality, a lazy lot, would huddle there long hours, sipping hot tea, reminiscing their adventurous past that was pure hogwash and in the same

breath blaming the younger generation for their passivity. The villagers celebrated their lives, which bordered on innocence and innate honesty, knowing that pride and arrogance were both worthless.

2.

Snapshots From An Incredible Childhood.

Born as the youngest of the six children of my parents in November,1961, I had a privileged yet sickly and lonely childhood. I spent many days of my childhood bed-ridden, plagued by childhood maladies. Those diseases together snatched away a significant part of my childhood. I was forced to spent many weeks and months in bed, isolated from my classmates and friends. As I lay motionless on my cot, I saw through the open window the spectacular view of aeroplanes landing. During misty mornings I heard the long whistle of steam engines that traversed through Willingdon Island, and in quiet evenings, the sirens of ships filtered through the sea breeze. I often fought with Sheela Chechy, my third eldest sister. But she always had a curious mix of love and sympathy for me. During my pre-school days at Unni Aasaan's *kudippallikkoodam* and later in my primary school days, she cared and tended me with motherly affection. An otherwise splendid childhood days were marred by bouts of asthma that recurred with unerring regularity. When I was diagnosed with advanced pneumonia, I was just eight years old. Tragically the village doctors misdiagnosed my ailment and prescribed me the wrong medication. As my health deteriorated, my family rushed me to Dr. Clement, a renowned paediatrician with the Ernakulam general hospital. With his expertise he swiftly and correctly diagnosed my illness and suggested immediate hospitalisation warranting emergency treatment.

The next day I was wheeled to the operating room where Dr. Clement performed a life-saving procedure. I was made to lie on my side and then with precision and care, he inserted a few inches long needle through my right ribs to draw the fluid and puss accumulated in my lungs. I screamed as he and his team struggled to comfort me. Their hushed conversation totally unnerved me. I can still recall those painful moments as he sucked out the thick, yellowish fluid with a haunting wheeze- the noise still echoes in my mind. The timely diagnosis and effective treatment by Dr. Clement saved me from imminent death. Even after discharge I was under stringent care for over a month, with the painful routine of a daily dose of two injections. Vettezhath Sahadevan and his wife Sarala lovingly and selflessly took turns and cared for me. One of them would visit me every morning and evening with a steel injection box containing syringe and needles. Amma would sterilise them by keeping them in boiling water for a few minutes. Despite their best efforts, the old, worn-out needles often caused tiny wounds through which blood trickled out. I longed in vain for freedom and wellness. In those tormenting days books and *Mathrubhumi* daily were my dependable friends. The back volumes of *Mirror*, a popular magazine, which was among my second eldest brother Rajiv's prized possession, was a great solace for me in those days of solitude as I would immerse in the engaging stories. When left alone I indulged myself in daydreams and self-talks. I often indulged in flights of fantasy, imagining myself rubbing shoulders with celebrities from the socio-cultural and literary spheres of the country. These whimsical musings, though fanciful, breathed new life into my otherwise sagging self-confidence.

As asthma has proved a life-long companion, I was refrained by Amma and siblings from taking part in games and plays that needed physical exertion. My fragile health and frail frame-both were a constant source of concern for my family. Though my parents provided me the best possible medical treatments then available, my health deteriorated and condition worsened. All too soon, childhood maladies shattered my fragile happiness, and I withdrew into a little world of my own.

Later my childhood friends too treated me differently in view of my fragile health. When they played ball games and such other village games, I watched them with a mixed feeling of enthusiasm and despair. However, games that did not need physical exertion, I too joined them. There was boundless joie de vivre.

When the news broke about my discharge from the hospital after a month-long medical treatment for pneumonia, the entire locality came visiting. The visiting ladies would huddle around my cot. The curious glances of those villagers made me uncomfortable. I felt annoyed. While their chattering continued, I would lay supine gazing at the wooden ceiling, contemplating on the uncertainty of my existence. As the clamouring ladies take leave, I would be suddenly brought back from my reveries by the chorus of the cicadas. Long faced, Amma would narrate the harrowing story in her own characteristic way in great detail, spiced up with a bit of exaggeration. Without any hesitation she would recount the story umpteen times as new guests came in to know about my health. On many nights, when breathing trouble tormented me, I refused to take my evening snacks and modest supper fearing that a full belly would exacerbate my breathing trouble. Watching my predicament, Ammumma, my maternal grandmother, would warn in her gentle voice," *Monay, athaazha pattini kidannaal oru madapravinte thookkam erachy kurayum*", (little son, if you skip your supper, you will lose flesh equivalent to the weight of a pigeon). While Amma would coax by frightening me with the story of *anchukannan*, the five-eyed demon, that prayed on children who refused to eat. The story would send shivers down my spine as I imagined the demon in myriad terrifying forms, coming to attack me. I would, however, be unmoved by Ammumma's loving admonishment. Nevertheless, Amma's fearful tales of the demon, the mere thought, would prompt me to settle for a frugal meal of milk boiled with semolina (*rawa*). As I grew up so was my breathing trouble that refused to relent. Whenever my breathing problem worsened, it forced me to make frequent visits to the toilet. Each visit proved gruesome, as squatting on the Indian-style commode would leave me breathless. Adding to my woes, the toilet was located in a remote corner of the compound, far away from the main building. When the suffocation became unbearable, I would sit on the bed, cross-legged, leaning forward with my face buried in my cupped palms. Achan, Amma, brothers and sisters then would take turn as they would gently rub my back that would sooth me. As I would struggle, gasping for air, Amma would administer some syrup containing broncho-dilators into my mouth for quick relief. She would then wrap heated river sand in a piece of cloth (*kizhi*) and the hot pouch would be gently rubbed on my sides. This would provide some respite from agonizing shortness of breath. The strong medicine would make me drowsy and slowly I would fall into a deep stupor. During episodes of such sleepiness, on a few occasions I experienced an Out-of-Body Experience (OBE), where I felt as though my soul was slowly leaving my body and floating around. The hot poultice would provide some instant relief but only to recur with more severity and ferociousness later, when the effects of bronchodilators waned. In those days, Amma would stay up all night beside me. By morning, when I would be a bit better, an exhausted Amma would have a brief nap. In those agonizing days, the bulb in my room would remain aglow throughout night, prompting neighbour's curious queries in the morning whether my condition had worsened last night. Back then everybody would keep a vigilant eye and any unusual signs will not escape their watchful eyes. Whenever children of my age in our locality would fall ill with symptoms similar as mine, their mothers would always approach Amma and sought her expert 'medical advice'. Then she would happily share the prescriptions which the doctor prescribed for me. Such symptoms-based treatment was common. When in emergency Amma would even part with a few tablets from my medicine kit without ever realizing the implications, either by the provider or the recipient, on the ailing child. When afflicted with various ailments, people sought refuge in the government hospital, where overcrowding forced many to lie on the floor, wrapped in blankets. Such was Amma's care that even when I was in high school, she would gently dry my wet hair with a *thorthu* after a bath. Then she'd apply a pinch of *Rasnadi choornam* to the centre of my head—her trusted remedy to keep colds at bay.

Recurrent absence in my classes had impacted the continuity of my studies. Kumara Pillai Master, my class teacher, who knew my plight, gracefully exempted me from attending the morning assembly under scorching sun or braving drizzles during rainy days. I would watch the assembly through the open window of the school building with a sense of disappointment. Teachers would line up on the edge of the long veranda that ran the entire length of the building, while students stood in lines facing teachers on the ground. Back then, the National Discipline Service (NDS), a programme introduced by the Central Government, was implemented in our school alongside the NCC and Scouts. Unlike the latter two, NDS was compulsory, and every student was expected to participate. Due to my frail health, I was exempted from taking part in the drills that formed an integral part of the NDS training.

Kunnamveettil Raghavan Master was assigned the responsibility of training us. Each week, a couple of hours were set aside for NDS, during which he led mass drills aimed at promoting physical fitness and teamwork among students. Introduced in 1954, the NDS scheme sought to instil physical discipline and general well-being in students. S.D.P.Y. School, my *alma mater*, was one of the few institutions in the locality to adopt this programme.

With a long cane in hand, Raghavan Master was a figure both feared and revered. It was nearly impossible to escape his vigilant eyes, especially when students indulged in mischievous antics. Yet, through his strict methods, he instilled the values of discipline and self-control at an early age—lessons that proved invaluable in later life. Raghavan Master's training was rigorous, a bit terrifying, but ultimately formative.

During my school days, my breathing troubles were so severe that they occasionally prevented me from completing examinations. However, my benevolent teachers would always pass me and promote me to the next grade based on my performance in the exams I had already taken. This continued until my SSLC board exams. Fortunately, I was able to appear for all the papers in the final exams and performed impressively, passing with high marks. Once, when asthma prevented me from climbing the stairs to the exam hall, the school authorities kindly made alternative arrangements for me to take the exam in the ground-floor office, as a fine gesture of their compassion and understanding.

It's quite interesting that chapatis were not part of our village menu until the late sixties. However, Amma had been making them for several years prior to that, even before the culinary revolution took hold in our locality. Her friends from neighbouring houses would gather around, wide-eyed, as she expertly rolled out chapatis on a wooden rolling-board with a long wooden rolling pin. More than seven decades ago, Shirly - the neighbourhood girl and daughter of Divakara Panikkar, the village barber - would visit daily, drawn by the piece of chapati Amma would lovingly offer her. She fondly called my mother '*Chapati Amma,*' recalls my eldest brother. In those days, we didn't have pressure cookers, and electricity wasn't even available in the village. Amma used a separate earthen vessel, called a "*chatty,*" to cook non-vegetarian foods like meat and fish. To tenderize the meat, villagers would add small pieces of *chiratta,* the coconut shell - a practice that worked wonders, even if the exact reason behind it remained unknown. A nugget of timeless wisdom from Granny's treasure trove.

After retiring from the Indian Air Force, Achan shed much of the stubbornness he had acquired during his long years of service and became more amenable. He would often lend a helping hand to Amma with household chores such as cutting vegetables, de-husking and scraping coconuts, preparing wheat dough for chapatis, peeling shallots and potatoes, and running similar errands. In the morning, it was his responsibility to buy fishes from the market, his choicest ones being Pomfret, Mullet and Pearl spot. To prepare his favourite fish curry occasionally Amma procured dried *kudampuli* (Malabar tamarind) from Ummathara Pauly *Kochamma,* as it had a unique taste and hence popular in the locality.

Middle-aged Christian women, clad in traditional *chatta* and pleated *mundu* that neatly covered their bulky backs, adorned with a *naadan* over their bountiful bosom and large earrings called *mekka mothiram* hanging from their earlobes, would walk leisurely in small groups to the nearby church, a familiar sight on Sundays. In contrast, younger women would typically drape themselves in saris or wear full-length skirts and blouses. Amma once recalled that, many years ago, Ammumma, the matriarch, never wore a blouse, much like others of her generation. Later, the sight of Ammumma traversing the village paths—her upper body covered only by a folded *naadan/melmundu*—became a source of embarrassment for her educated children. During her month-long sojourn to Bombay in early sixties, her first long-distance journey to visit her two sons who had settled there, she was compelled to wear a blouse against her will. However, from that moment on, the blouse became an integral part of her daily attire, while her contemporaries in the neighbourhood remained blouse-less, enviously observing grandma's sartorial transformation. In this context, it's worth recalling the historic "*Maaru Marakkal Samaram*", the struggle for covering breasts. This remarkable episode in Kerala history is referred as Channar Revolt (1813-1859). In those days only upper-caste women were allowed to cover their upper body and women from Ezhava,

Channar, and Nadar castes denied such rights as it was the norm. The women from these marginalized communities, as well as tribal women, were forced into a way of life dictated by feudal lords, compelling them to remain bare-breasted even in the presence of men. Today, it is difficult for us to fully grasp the stigma and suffering these helpless women endured. The demand of the women was to allow them to cover their upper body, considered a privilege of higher castes. To wear upper garments, women from lower castes were forced to pay a tax known as *Mulakkaram* (breast tax). In a powerful act of protest against this oppressive rule, Nangeli, a woman from the Ezhava community, defied the Travancore State by cutting off her breasts—a sacrifice that became a symbol of resistance and dignity. In 1859, Maharaja Aayilyam Thirunal, the King of Travancore officially declared the women from Nadar/Channar/Ezhava community could wear *Melmundu* to cover their bosom. This was a glorious moment in the history of Kerala in the fight for women's rights.

The villagers relied on herbal remedies for treating minor ailments like the common cold and fever. For mild fever and body pain, a few peeled shallots and a handful of *Tulsi* leaves would be crushed into a thick paste. This paste was bundled in a piece of fine cloth, then gently squeezed so that the hot, fiery liquid dripped into each eye. This remedy was often accompanied by *Kurumulaku Kashayam*—a hot concoction made by boiling dried pepper and guava leaves in water. During my childhood, people in the village turned to such simple, self-made treatments—and surprisingly, they often worked.

People were generally superstitious and indulged in many activities that may seem quite baffling for the current generation. Villagers used to hang grotesque images or figurines from the four corners of the roof as evil breakers. Amulets (*Raksha)* and *yantra* (thin copper plates with inscriptions (*mantras*) and geometrical patterns) were commonly used to ward-off evil forces. Sorcerers, astrologers, and palmists exploited the superstitious believes of the credulous people. In the past, mental illnesses were frequently blamed on otherworldly entities such as *yakshis* and *gandharvas.* Treatment typically involved *mantravadis,* practitioners who employed forms of black magic that involved macabre rituals like animal sacrifice. The villagers spun scary tales about the blood-thirsty creatures and their victims who were killed by their supernatural powers. The fear of the unknown, the supernatural, and paranormal forces were always accepted by the rustic population with a mixed feeling of fear and curiosity. Such believes were so firmly entrenched in the mind of the people that they preferred divine miracles over truth.

To get rid of the drudgery of the rustic life, villagers eagerly looked forward to festivals in temples and churches that offered a cornucopia of pleasures. Social bonding was quite strong and long-lasting. Everything in the village belonged to everyone. They shared their pains and pleasures with equal warmth. Marriages were celebrations for the entire village. As marriage gifts, they gave cash, and the patriarch of the home would keep a written record of the details of such gifts he received. Later when the occasions come, he would reciprocate the gesture, definitely after verifying his records to decide on the amount to be gifted.

Same was the case with deaths in the village. The entire villagers would be gathered when someone is died and would be with the bereaved family till the funeral. Close relatives would continue to stay with family of the dead person sharing their grief and supporting them.

The rumour mills always functioned ceaseless weaving stories, manufactured gossips, half-truths and untruths on trivial issues. They fought with one another on minor issues. But those bickering never affected their ties which were built on mutual trust and respect.

Devastha Vili

During the late hours on hot summer nights, the serenity of the vicinity would be broken by the doleful singing by the few elders in the neighbourhood Christian families. This religious practice was called *Devastha Vili,* the songs about death, final judgement, punishment and hell fire. The prayer was sung presumably to ward off the evil spirit. It would be sung during the Lent, from Ash Wednesday to Easter. Kochu Vareed Chettan, his son Agassi, Anso Chettan, and a few other elderly men in my immediate neighbourhood, would perform *Devastha Vili* on Friday nights. Kochu Vareed would chant the prayer song loudly in his hoarse voice, by sitting on a bench in his small veranda, with a cross in hands, facing east.

His emotional chanting in his booming, high decibel voice at extraordinary hours would send shivers through me. *Devastha Vili,* indeed, was a reflection of a tradition, part of a culture and a long-held belief that was deeply embedded in the psyche of the Latin community of West Kochi. It was popular in Vypeen, Varappuzha, Fort Kochi, Gothuruthu, Mundamveli, Palluruthy, Chellanam and Andhakaran Azhi. Original script was in Latin, that was subsequently changed to Malayalam. They have inherited such a practice from the

Portuguese who ruled over the land several decades. The word *Devastha* itself is of Portuguese origin. Under the cover of night, *Devastha Sangham* groups roam the streets, their songs a haunting reminder of human mortality, final judgment, and the fires of hell, calling people to repentance and renewal

Those singing the *Devastha Vili* firmly believed that if they dare to look back during the chanting, they would see the Satan, the personification of the evil force, waiting behind. After finishing his *Devastha Vili,* Kochu Vareed would burst a few crackers, again to ward off the evil spirit. This ritual was active till the mid-seventies, since then the practice gradually ceased to exist, as the practitioners of this ancient ritual died one by one.

Coir Making

In the village, many women supported themselves by crafting coir, a traditional industry. The coconut husks would be kept immersed in the water along the sides of the lake, allowing them to ret. The huge mound of retting husks would be tied together along the periphery to prevent them from being drifted away by strong currents. One could sense the smell of retting husks from a distance. Many in the village made a living by *thondu thallal,* thrashing the retted coconut husks and separating coir yarns from them. The laborious job never guaranteed them a decent living free from penury. Many others were engaged in the braiding of coir ropes from the fibres which was once a common household activity for women.

Locally, it was a common sight to see women gathered around a *Raat* (spinning wheel) a simple hand-driven machine, weaving coir fibres into long strands. It's a traditional tool which consists of a large wooden wheel mounted on a wooden stand with attached bobbin or spindle. As one woman turned the *Raat*, her companions, typically four or five in number, would carefully weave the fibres while walking backwards, chatting as they worked. In the afternoons, they would use a heavy wooden frame to twist two strands together, creating thicker, double-stranded coir. The rhythmic creaking of the *Raat* became a familiar soundtrack to village life that echoed in the still village atmosphere.

Gulf Boom

The young men from the locality, whose families benefited from Gulf employment, would roam the streets, wearing polyester shirts and *lungis*. As they walked by, the scent of their perfume would linger in the air for a while. They would proudly display 100-rupee notes in the pockets of their see-through polyester shirts, catching the attention of passersby. Some of them would carry 'National' and 'Sanyo' cassette tape recorders, blasting music at full volume through the streets, in an awkward display of their newfound prosperity.

The Gulf boom of the late 1970s and early 1980s drastically transformed the socioeconomic status of the region and the way people lived. A sudden surge in income among the lower and lower-middle classes created economic imbalance in the region. Sceptics among the population struggled to accept the changes, blaming the extravagant lifestyle of Gulf migrants for the rising prices of everyday commodities.

During that time, migrants to Gulf countries were mainly skilled workers, including carpenters, plumbers, masons, electricians, and drivers. Migrant workers from Kerala played a crucial role in transforming the UAE into a renowned nation as we see today.

During nights under the cover of darkness, pick pockets and prostitutes roamed the narrow corridors of the town each waiting for their victims, the former waited patiently for the unsuspecting night travellers, while the latter the sexually starved, lustful lorry drivers and local rowdies. Their alluring beauty, the maddening fragrance of the perfume, and their colourful, revealing attire, all combined to ignite the lustful passions of their clients. After a brief, hurried intercourse, they would vanish before dawn. Kusumam and Anitta (names changed to protect their privacy), nicknamed "Rocket", were two village women in our neighbourhood with a dark past of living as sex workers. While "Rocket" was a fair skinned beauty Kusumam was dark, short in stature and she would sit in front of her hut, dressed in vibrant clothing with her hair adorned with jasmine flowers, patiently waiting for her clients. Her sparkling outfits presented a stark contrast to her humble surroundings. The unemployed village youths full of youthful lust envied the truck drivers, who seemingly satisfied their desires with secrecy.

There were a few police constables in our village, viewed by the villagers with a mixed emotion of fear, awe, and respect. They proved to be real terrors for the people around. However, their appearance was quite amusing, with loose, skirt-like shorts, that tapered to a point in the front just above knees, long, conical caps, and handlebar moustaches. From below, it was a comical sight to watch those policemen in their loose trousers climbing stairs.

In old Malayalam movies and dramas, they were perpetually portrayed as comical characters, always making them the subject of ridicule. Unfortunately, the police back then would often scare and punish people over trivial matters, and even extort money from habitual offenders and rowdies in exchange for not framing them in petty cases.

It was Ommen Chandy, the then Home Minister of Kerala who in 1981 modernized the police uniform, that they wear with pride and pleasure.

The nine-o'clock siren from the nearby Giovanola Binny Company served as our bedtime signal, beckoning us to surrender to the allure of sleep and traverse on fantastical journeys through the fanciful worlds of our dreams.

The vast front and backyards of my homestead would be swept daily in the morning by two women in the neighbourhood. Brigit and her daughter Philomina continued to do their work for many years for which Amma fixed a modest monthly salary and served simple breakfast that was an additional incentive. Kunjachan, Brigit's son, would often accompany his mother and we would play together. More than play, he was attracted by the wheat flour *appam* and *puttu,* which Amma would serve him. Now my front courtyard had been shrunk to a mere patch of tiled courtyard. Thus, I lost the pleasure of walking barefoot in the soil, enjoying the picturesque skyline, a thrilling experience indeed.

In the village markets and temples and places where people gathered, the beggars with twisted fingers and many deformities sat begging, a sight that was disgusting.

Marriages in the village were real celebrations where the relatives and neighbours would gather a couple of days before the wedding. The event would begin with the ceremonial fixing of the first pole of the makeshift Pandhal called *Kaalnaattu Karmam* in Malayalam. From then on everything from the construction of Pandhal, arrangements for the sumptuous feast to the grand finale of the ceremony, would be carried out by them. In those days marriages were occasions that were social celebrations involving the participation of everyone in the vicinity. In today's society, marriages have become grand celebrations staged by event management teams in luxury hotels and high-end convention centres, with the event live-streamed to accommodate friends and relatives in distant locations. Marriages are increasingly used as opportunities to showcase wealth, affluence, and social status. Nowadays, a marriage ceremony rarely lasts more than a few hours, during which time guests swarm around the newlywed couple, pose for a photo shoot with practiced smiles, and depart after a hurried meal. Neither the guests nor the hosts show an iota of sincerity. On the wedding day, the homes of the bride and groom remain locked. What a stark contrast to marriages of past decades, when homes remained vibrant and silent witnesses to the auspicious occasions. Today, unfortunately, on such joyful occasions, our homes-the private and unique spaces we often claim as our own-remain eerily silent, shrouded in a sombre stillness. This has become an integral part of the pretentious lifestyle of modern society, where la-di-da thrives.

Back then they mourned the death of their loved ones with loud wails, as women beat their breasts in anguish. The lamentations were intense, involving both tears and self-talks, (*patham paranju karachil*) vocal expressions of grief. To a modern generation accustomed to restraint, such raw emotional displays might seem uncivilized.

During the first four decades of my life, I witnessed the remarkable transformation of our quaint village into a thriving city, now an integral part of West Kochi, a city prides itself on its rich legacy and gentility.

The village's winding paths gave way to tarred roads, while hand-pulled rickshaws gradually made way for pedal-powered ones, and eventually, electric autos. The old beasts, fossil-fuel guzzlers of the kind of Bedford and Fargo buses, with their billowing smoke, were replaced by modern Volvo, Scania, and Bharat Benz vehicles. By early years of twenty first century the once ubiquitous Ambassador and its tiny rival Fiat totally disappeared from the roads of Kochi as in rest of the country. The space left by these automobile giants was soon filled by Maruti that led to cut throat competition in the sector paving the way for the arrival of many auto majors including Hyundai, Honda, Ford, Nissan and the desi Tata and Mahindra.

In those charmingly beautiful days, once in a while we enjoyed the pleasure of travelling in buses. I have an insatiable passion for travelling in buses. My earliest memories of a bus travel were when I was hardly four. Along with Amma, in the company of Bhavani *Kunjamma,* her husband Velayudhan and son Amrut, we travelled from Palluruthy to Mattancherry to attend a marriage in a match-box sized bus. As the bus journeyed zig-zag through the tarred road, I looked out with eyes wide open while Velayudhan *Elayachan* rendered a running commentary of the landscape and its landmark buildings which at once pleased me and Amrut. When I was tormented by asthma, Amma used to take me to Ernakulam General Hospital in the town bus. Though I laboured to breath, I deeply enjoyed the ride.

With child-like wonder, I watched the majestic train chugging past through Willingdon Island, smoke billowing, as buses paused momentarily at Venduruthy rail crossing. In those rare moments, a plane or helicopter would soar overhead from the nearby Naval airport. The roar of the engine would reverberate in the air. As the bus travelled at slow pace, unhurriedly through Thoppumpady bridge, I sat silently enjoying the beautiful landscape. As the bus moved past the Naval Base, children would crane their necks for a glimpse of the parked aeroplanes in the airport apron. On certain rare occasions, we would board buses that passed through Willingdon Island. This ride would provide an added incentive, as the bus would circumvent the Cochin Port Trust Office at the northern end, on the way moving alongside the Mattancherry and Ernakulam Wharves where there would be huge mountains of coals and sulphur, offloaded from ships, awaiting transportation to their final destinations by road and rail. The scenes of huge cargo ships and oil tankers berthed in the wharf were captivating. The spectacle of majestic ships carrying coal, sulphur and crude oil that passed leisurely through the Kochi backwaters bewitched the onlookers.

In those days there was a lone double-decker bus owned by KSRTC that plied the short distance between Willingdon Island and Palarivattom. Overhanging branches of gigantic trees, narrow and winding roads with sharp turns and many low-lying electric lines prevented the entry of the bus to Fort Kochi, the original route planned for the bus, much to our disappointment.

In those days roads were dominated by sturdy buses, their engine compartments were in the front of the bus, separate from passenger cabin. Leyland, Benz and Bedford were the iconic brands which had wooden interiors with seats arranged in two rows on either side with space aplenty in the aisle. Those buses used to stop wherever the commuters requested. The passengers enjoyed their unhurried rides in those slow-moving buses where they exchanged pleasantries. By late sixties, contemporary style line buses with engine well-integrated into the cabin near the driver seat came into existence. Those buses, however, were simple and quite different from modern, sleek, hi-tech vanity buses that ply today. Matador Van was the favourite vehicle of the people for large groups. The Van was indeed India's first Diesel Light Motor Vehicle being powered by a 1.8L engine. Bajaj Tempo Motors was the manufacturers of Matador which later became Force. The 10-seater van was widely used for picnic and family get-togethers, though it was more popular as school van.

Landing of aeroplanes at the old Kochi Naval airport was a marvellous experience, offering breathtaking views of the blue lagoons, seas, and mesmerizing beaches of Fort Kochi. The lush green paddy fields, majestic Chinese fishing nets, ancient temples, and churches, as well as the vast fish farms of Kumbalangi-Chellanam stretch, made for a truly remarkable sight that I fondly admired. With the turn of the century, the airport was relocated to a new site, at Nedumbasserry, far from its original location. As a result, those fantastic views, once glimpsed through the tiny windows of airplanes, became a cherished part of our collective memory.

The old Kochi airport was a military-civil, dual-use airport and it was under the operational control of Navy. It was from this tiny airport that I travelled for the first time in an aeroplane way back in 1985. The flight to Goa was booked a couple of weeks early in the Indian Airlines office in the city. Back then one had to undergo a process of "okaying" the ticket 48 hours before the journey, a kind of re-confirmation, an odium that took me once again to the airline office. The four-page ticket with a beautiful and colourful jacket with the insignia of the Indian Airlines contained several dos and don'ts for the passengers. Whenever I travelled by air, I had the strange hobby of keeping those ticket jackets and the piece of the boarding passes as mementoes.

The daily bus ride to Thevara en route to college and back was equally enjoyable. The Naval airport then was ill equipped to handle night flights. On rare occasions when there were night flights, Navy men would arrange oil lamps called Goose Necks, all around the airstrip. In the evening, on my way back from college I would crane my neck to have a glimpse of the wonderful view of the illuminated airport bathed in the golden glow of the setting sun. The twilight scenes were really captivating.

On Tuesdays and Fridays, the "market days," it was a familiar sight to see massive wooden handcarts, known as *bharavandy,* heavily loaded with groceries from Ernakulam market, moving hesitantly through the streets. The sombre-faced men who pulled these carts struggled under the weight, often causing traffic congestion at the busy Thoppumpady junction. As the cart approached the elevation of the bridges, the cart-puller laboured with the heavy loads. Commuters on buses would gaze down at them with impatience. However, some kind-hearted passersby would offer a helping hand. In contrast, smaller carts piled high with freshly cut grass from Willingdon Island would move obediently along the sidewalks. The grass would eventually be sold as fodder in Palluruthy and Mattancherry.

The old thatched shacks and tiled-roofed houses were replaced with huge concrete structures that boasted of best of modern amenities. The concept of a house has evolved over the years, transforming from a serene and elegant living space to a luxury structure, a symbol of extreme profligacy and upper-middle class opulence showcasing one's pride and wealth. Mammoth sized apartments touching the heavens mushroomed along the coast and waterfronts. The gated community lived in such residential complexes with restricted access where they often enjoyed amenities like Gyms, parks, swimming pools and club houses. Paradoxically, as house sizes increased, the emotional distances among occupants grew. Small single room shops gave way to larger ones, eventually making way for gigantic shopping malls. Today sitting in the air-conditioned rooms, we remain connected to the entire world 24x7 using our handy smartphones. The digital revolution has reduced human beings to digital victims being trapped inside a virtual world, a digital ecosystem, where everything, ranging from finances to entertainment and health needs are managed by smartphones. Home theatres with fantastic sound effects, 4K visuals, and acoustics ushered in a new era of cinematic experience. The Covid-19 pandemic has played a catalytic role in changing the work environment from office to homes. The migration of the urban youth to distant lands in search of better prospects is a recent phenomenon that has brought about the demographic shift. With fewer children to care for, a growing number of elders are becoming increasingly health anxious, beset by a multitude of real and perceived ailments. Young people who are not much well educated from rural areas too started migration into fresh pastures leaving a void in their homes and communities. These were some of the several significant changes that occurred during the turn of the century. The world indeed was changing in incredible ways, leaving us awestruck. The sudden deaths of a few close friends in recent years have left me shattered. The loss has prompted me to ponder the ephemerality of human existence.

3.

Village Whisperings.

A.Toddy shops

There were a few toddy shops in the quaint village where the villagers would assemble as the sun disappeared below the horizon, marking the end of yet another day of struggle and hardship. Those toddy shops were an integral part of Kochi which were famed not only for the typical milky white mild alcoholic native beverage, the *Kallu,* but were equally well known for the lip-smacking and flavourful curries which were a class apart. Even today *Shapp curry* has many devoted aficionados. Those are characterized by their simple recipe but highly delectable flavour and taste. Many would flock the toddy shops just to savour the appetizing curries. On certain evenings, fuelled by the local brew, the inebriated villagers transformed toddy shops into impromptu art centres. The high-spirited performances of *Naadan paattu,* the folk songs, filled the air accompanied by dances replete with improvised but unsteady steps. Thus, the toddy shops played a crucial role in popularizing *kallu paattu* and *kallu dance* which were frowned by the educated and the elites. In fact, they were the torch bearers of a lost culture, the cultural ambassadors of a bygone time. The time they spent there had enlivened their lives by alleviating the drudgery of village life. Housed in small thatched sheds, the *naadan kallu shaap* would be furnished with a few wooden benches and desks where the regulars, clad in *lungis* and often bare chested, would sit and unwind themselves freely exchanging news and gossips. Huddled around wooden tables, slowly tasting the native brew, they discussed everything; from the mundane to truly spiritual, covering topics as diverse as food, football and philosophy. It was not uncommon that the high-spirited talks often leading to passionate political debates which would escalate to raucous arguments and end up in slugfests. *Kappa* and fish curry were the staples of toddy shop food along with *chemmeen ularthiyathu, karimeen pollichathu, kanambu, kaada, kozhi,* and *thaaraavukari.* The patrons would sip low- alcohol toddy from large glass bottles, one after another, till they become high spirited. While many would become chatty and friendly, others would become pensive and retreated into a whimsical world detached from the clamour and commotion around them. The women of the village hesitated to pass by the toddy shops, fearing the unwelcome gesticulations and often vulgar remarks, as well as the piercing gazes of the inebriated patrons.

Nestled among the buildings near Thoppumpady there was a remarkable toddy shop, a refined version that stood out from the rest by the grandeur of its building. It was housed in an old tiled house with many small rooms, its walls echoing with history. Within those weathered walls, cosy small rooms welcomed a select clientele, eager to savour the native brew and mouth-watering food in tranquillity. During our long walks through the village alleys on way to Patel Talkies, we passed through the front yard of this magnificent toddy shop. The toddy shop stood as a silent witness to our journeys, a place where time stood still. Today there is a newfound love for *kallu shaap* curry, being promoted by Tourism Department and social media groups as a legacy which we inherited. Thanks to these efforts today the patronage for *kallu shaap* has increased tremendously among the youths and urban elites for the culinary magic cutting across genders, ages and social status. With several women clients flocking Kerala's *kallu shaap* for savouring the spicy *meencurry,* gender equality has finally taken shape in *kallu shaap.*

After a day's hectic and chaotic life, marked by stress and exhaustion, the villagers found time to relax and rewind in these village toddy shops.

B. Kumaran, Madan Mohan and the S N Auditorium.

Kumaran was a dark-skinned, tall and lean man, both his legs swollen with filariasis. He was always attired in a shirt and a white *mundu* which reached up to the bottom of his feet skilfully concealing his swollen legs. It was a pathetic sight- the way he moved, each step a silent struggle against discomfort. His physical discomforts never deterred him from performing his duty with punctuality and dedication as the peon of our school. He always wore black socks- thick layer of fabric to keep his enormously swollen legs from the curious eyes of both the children and teachers. A mild-mannered gentleman, as our faithful peon he earned the unspoken respect of the children and trust of the staff. His pathetic physical condition, however, had become the basis for the unkind nickname that the unruly children had cruelly bestowed upon the poor man.

In our school, we had a vintage cyclostyling machine that was lovingly operated by Kumaran. The machine was kept covered with a black leather cover atop a small, gleaming wooden table in a corner of the office. As the machine's custodian, he took great pride in his work, tending to it with utmost care and dedication. The Cyclostyle was invented by David Gestetner which was essentially a stencil copying machine. The working involves cutting stencil on wax paper to be followed by placing the half-perforated stencil sheet on a normal writing paper and an inked roller was rolled over it. The ink created impressions through the perforations onto the paper below. Apart from his routine duties of ringing the school bell in the morning and evening, Kumaran donned the coveted role of a cyclostylist, responsible for producing copies of important documents. During annual examinations, teachers would entrust him with typed templates of question papers, which he would meticulously convert into the required number of copies. We students would gather around, fascinated by the printing process, as Kumaran skilfully rotated the machine using a lever, producing copy after copy with ease. What impressed us most was his unwavering commitment to secrecy, ensuring that the question papers remained confidential throughout the process. Kumaran's dexterity and discretion made him an indispensable part of our school's examination process, and we revered him for his role in helping us navigate our academic journey. With the advent of Photostat machines and computers, Cyclostyles had faded into oblivion.

Before the cyclostyling process, Surabhi, the woman typist, would meticulously cut the template using her old typewriter. This task was more arduous than regular typing because she had to exert more force on each button to ensure clear impressions on the template. However, for question papers of Malayalam and Hindi, the language teachers themselves would write the matter on the stencil paper as in those days Malayalam and Hindi type writers were non-existent.

Madan Mohan was another revered peon of the school who commanded genuine respect and adoration from the students. He was a medium built, chubby man, his face adorned with a caterpillar moustache curving above his lips and a perpetual grin added elegance to his face. This unreserved respect sprang from his deft handling of the Public Address System of the school, which comprised a large amplifier encased in a metal case with several vents, four or five cone shaped loud speakers and a couple of oblong shaped steel microphones perched on sturdy steel stands- an intricate setup that fascinated us. During momentous occasions like Independence Day, and youth festival, it was Madan's duty to breathe life into the PA system which he performed enthusiastically. Raveendran master, our teacher, would keep a close watch as Madan Mohan worked, occasionally giving suggestions. We would gather around him, rubbernecking to catch a glimpse of his enviable role. Though the students' excited chatter might have irked him, he never expressed his displeasure, as a permanent smile adorned his face. Once the system hummed to life, he would strategically position a table fan near the *Ahuja* amplifier to cool the instrument - a guardian of sound waves. Before the beginning of the official programmes, he would play a few light music and film songs from the record player much to our delight. We looked wide eyed the magic of that contraption as it created melodies and the working of which left us wonderstruck. Madan Mohan's world indeed was fascinating where technology met artistry.

In the heart of our school compound stood the **S N Auditorium-** a huge edifice sandwiched between two school buildings. Built in 1965, this iconic structure was graced by none other than R Shankar, the then Chief Minister of Kerala, during its grand inauguration. The auditorium played host to numerous events and festivals. During school youth festival, competitions in light music. drama, mono act, elocution and many similar items were held inside the auditorium when it reverberated with youthful vigour. Interestingly, this venue was an open space devoid of confining walls. On either side, the building was flanked by graceful extensions, that stretched the entire length. Those asbestos roofed, open verandas were separated by wooden screens into several compartments where primary classes were held. After assigning simple tasks to their students, the teachers from neighbouring classrooms would gather behind the wooden screens, where they exchanged gossip and secrets in hushed tones. The setting sun filtered through, casting irregular patterns on the cement floors as young minds were engrossed in their lessons, in an air filled with chalk dust and the rustle of books. Once during a film screening, the entire façade was covered with tarpaulin sheets creating darkness. Seated on wooden benches inside the makeshift theatre, we watched *Muthassy* in quiet delight.

The frontage was elegant and ornately designed and when completed in 1965, the building stood out by its sheer size and magnificence from the rest. Despite its grandeur, from the very beginning the auditorium was plagued by its poor acoustics-due to echo the sound bounced back much to the disappointment of the performers and the audience which marred the sound quality. Supported on massive brick pillars, the auditorium was an impressive architectural structure. Madan Mohan, the unsung hero behind the scene, was the self-proclaimed "light and sound engineer" of the auditorium where two wooden, rectangular speaker boxes were hung permanently on sturdy metal clamps on either side. During the numerous functions, Madan's amplifier and other paraphernalia found their place in a discreet corner near the green room, ready to amplify every word uttered, every note played, every song sung. Change, however, is an inevitable part of existence. In 2023, this historic building, once witness to myriad performances, had been demolished by the school authorities to build a colossal airconditioned modern auditorium. On a rainy August morning in 2024, the new, splendiferous, structure was inaugurated, ensuring both continuity and transformation. This marked the rebirth of S N Auditorium, one where comfort met tradition, and Madan's wooden speakers gave way to sleek, high-tech sound technology. Yet, memories of the magnificent old structure, a fine example of architectural brilliance, despite its many flaws and imperfections, is permanently etched in our memory. So are the memories of Kumaran and Madan Mohan, heroes of our childhood years. The charm and naivety of school days create a melange of memories.

C. Muthalaly's *Aluwa*: A Taste of Nostalgia.

Mittayikkaran Muthalaly's humble sweet shop, nestled beside SDPY School and Sree Narayana Guru's statue Mandapam, was a beloved institution decades ago. This unassuming hut, doubling as a stationery store, earned name and fame for its mouthwatering *aluwa,* a sweet treat savoured by students of all ages. Though basically a small shop selling stationary items like notebooks, pen, pencil and ink for fountain pens, the shop became popular for its irresistible sweet candy bars once relished by school students cutting across their ages and gender. The nondescript sweet meat shop housed in a tiny hut was a famous place frequented by school children several decades ago.

Every morning by nine Muthalaly would reach his thatched hut, carrying a heavy wooden table on his head. He would slowly and lovingly get to his work. The table provided with a glass topped lid would be kept on the ground in the front part of the shop. He would sit comfortably behind the table. In the many small compartments of the table, he would arrange his offerings; a number of sweets and fried foods. Colourful sugar candy, fired chickpeas, roasted ground nuts, *masala kappalandi, attani,* honey *mittay, naaranga mittayi, chukkunda, kolu mittayi* (Stick Candy), and peppermint *mittayi* would adorn the table. Seasonal gooseberries, paired with salt and chili powder, were a special delight. But the star attraction remained his signature *aluwa* bars, made from jaggery, coconut, and Maida flour. During intervals, when the sun shone brilliantly in the blue sky, children would huddle in the shop braving scorching heat and clamoured for *aluwa.* The *aluwa* had a unique flavour and incredible taste which still lingers in the air. Priced 2paise a piece, it would be neatly folded in a newspaper piece. Muthalaly did brisk business in the much sought after *aluwa* the recipe of which was a closely guarded secret.

The thatched walls on all three sides would be decorated with maps, note books, map drawings, and transcription books. On a stretched twine, papers and copies of *Vistruta Manappadam* would be hung. On one side inspirational posters of legends like Mahatma Gandhi, Subhash Chandra Bose, Nehru, Patel and Dr Radhakrishnan would be hanging in a row which captured the attention of the children. We used to refill our fountain pen with Bril ink and for each fill he levied a small amount. Those who had enough money often bought a bottle of ink filled in used injection bottles for 5 paise. Teachers used to buy red and green ink and the indispensable *chooral*. Interestingly the one who bought the cane would be often the first to get beaten up by his teacher making the proverb "*Vadi koduth adi medikkuka*" meaningful.

In the evening, marking the end of a hectic day of brisk business, *Muthalaly* would wind up and start his homeward journey carrying his table, dreams, and memories.

D. The Lazy Creep of Tortoises and the Feast of the Strangers.

Once a gentle creep of tortoises made their home in our family pond, moving in blissful freedoms under weeping monsoon skies. From time to time, one or two would rise from the depths and crawl laboriously along its sloping periphery-slow but with unwavering determination. Their movements were never rushed. Once ashore, they would spend joyful moments basking in the warm sunshine. With their heads and limbs retracted softly into their thick gleaming shells, they would sit in meditative stillness. However, whenever disturbed or threatened, they would let out a pungent, foul smell through their rear opening, an attempt to escape their enemies.

Once a band of wanderers (*paandikkar*), from a neighbouring state, had camped in our village. They stayed in temporary tents erected in the Palluruthy Veli maidan. Under cover of dusk, occasionally they would slip past Watcher, our trusted dog - ever drowsy, ageing sentinel unnoticed. Once sharp-eyed, alert, his spirit has softened with age. He no longer paced the perimeter or barked warnings to strangers and passerby. Most of the time, he lied under the mango tree, drifting between sleep and dream. Occasionally he would howl seeing invisible figures -that only he could see. The carefree wanderers would secretly sneak into our compound, slipping past the sleeping guardian and steal the tortoises from their quiet world. By nightfall, the intruders would be celebrating their grisly feast- fire would be burned, the innocent creatures of the little pond would be roasted. Tortoises flesh paired with bottles of illicitly brewed arrack would make a delightful dinner for the wanderers.

Later, the pond vanished and so are the lazy tortoises and the delicious dinner of the vagabonds.

E. On Parallel Colleges & Tuition Centres.

In the 70's and 80's the academically non-performing students found refuge in the several parallel colleges that mushroomed in the Ernakulam city for pursuing their dreams of higher education. Menon & Krishnan was a famous parallel college in the city well known for its high standards of teaching. Being run by two excellent retired professors named S. Krishnan and Sankara Menon the institution has carved reputation as a centre of excellence. Students of the college proudly proclaimed that they were the students of Menon & Krishnan. During its heyday, the tutorial college occasionally advertised in leading English and vernacular newspapers, using captivating visuals and compelling narratives that captured the readers' attention. By late eighties the once common parallel colleges stopped operations as they could not meet the increasing demands of the students for subjects such as medicine and engineering which those institutions were unable to afford.

Tutorials and Tuition Centres, as they were known, mushroomed in the nook and cranny of the village. My closest friends were groomed by one such famous tutorial college near our school. They strongly encouraged me to join them as it would compensate for my lost classes due to my medical condition. When I told him, Achan vehemently refused my request and instead advised me to remain confident steadfastly. In his opinion the classes provided in such tutorials by raw and inexperienced teachers were far below in standard and were no match for the classes taught by the learned teachers in the school. Though his decision disappointed me, later I realised that he was right.

A few of our teachers supplemented their income by moonlighting as private tutors. However, teachers like Thankamma teacher selflessly offered free tuition classes in their homes, benefiting academically weak and underprivileged students who couldn't afford private tutoring. Thankamma teacher's kindness extended beyond academics; she also treated her students to delicious foods.

4.

Annual Festival of Sree Bhavaneeswara Temple: A Vibrant Village Jamboree.

Sree Bhavaneeswara Temple of Palluruthy is a well-known place of worship consecrated by Sree Narayana Guru which is famed for its annual festival, the *utsavam,* the eleven-day long festivities commence on *Bharani* in Malayalam month of *Kumbham* (Feb.-March). The festivities were eagerly awaited and fervently celebrated as an occasion of great joy and excitement. It was not just another celebration for the people of Palluruthy, it indeed was an eclectic experience etched in our shared memories and dreams. An open-air jamboree full of merry and boisterous celebration marked by revelry and unrestrained frenzy. It played a role in shaping the secular credentials and culture of the land. During the eleven days, the entire village and its neighbouring localities would be drenched in festive spirit. The extended family would gather from far and wide to celebrate the *utsavam* in their ancestral homes. Achan and my two elder brothers, who served in the Air Force, would adjust their annual leaves to coincide with the temple festival. Likewise, my two uncles with their families, who were settled in Bombay (now Mumbai) for many decades, would get together in the old *tharavad,* the ancestral home of Amma, on the occasion.

The festival would begin with *Kodiyettam,* the ritualistic hoisting of the sacred temple flag. Till late seventies, the flag used to be hoisted on a massive betelnut palm stem, that would be implanted in the centre courtyard of the temple, right in front of the *Sreekovil* after an elaborate pooja. This would be followed by *Kodiyettam* in a reverent atmosphere amid ululations and chanting of Shiva mantras by women. By early eighties a permanent *Kodimaram* (flag pole) made of steel was erected which, a few years later was replaced with the present golden flag mast (*Swarna kodimaram*).

It was the *Para vazhipadu,* that used to be the star attraction of village boys and girls. On the day of the *Para vazhipadu,* elaborate arrangements would be made in our home to receive the idol of the presiding deity Shiva, considered to be an auspicious event that promised year-round prosperity and wealth for the family. Construction of a small rectangular, temporary platform marked the beginning of the preparations. My second eldest brother Rajiv would take the lead and in the arduous task he would be assisted his neighbourhood friends Josy, and Dhanappan. They would meticulously scoop white sugar-like sand from the depths of our family pond, using which the small rectangular *thara* (platform) of approximately 4*2 feet, would be constructed. It would then be covered with a clean white cloth, stretched between four wooden poles positioned at the four corners, that would be the roof. The narrow path leading from the entrance of the compound to the platform would be swept clean to get rid of fallen dry leaves and twigs. This would be followed by a purification ritual as Amma would sprinkle water mixed with cow dung. Either side of the path and all around the roof over the platform would be decorated with neatly trimmed and split *kuruthola,* the tender coconut leaves on stretched coir ropes that would add glory to the setting. Then begins the long and patient wait for the *parayeduppu* team to come. At the end of the long wait, the team would arrive led by an oracle (*velichappadu*) draped in red silk clothes with a shining ceremonial sword (*pallivaal*) in hand in the front followed by the caparisoned elephant, with the *ko'lam*, the golden metal shield with ornate design with the idol of Shiva fixed on the centre, on top of its head, secured by the priest. Chandra Mohan, a handsome, tall, young man, with a cash bag in hand, would walk ahead. He was entrusted with collecting money for the *para* and issuing receipt- a job that he performed with utmost dedication till he died a decade and a half back. Another team of a couple of persons would follow with *kathina,* (the dyna) in a basket that would be burst on request, of course a paid add on service. The *thara* would be covered with two or three large plantain leaves, on which the lighted *Nilavilakku* (ceremonial lamp), a brass *Kindy* (goglet) filled with water, a hand of ripe banana, a few lumps of jaggery and lighted incense sticks would be neatly arranged.

One in the group would place the *para* (the ancient wooden jar used for measuring paddy) in the middle of the *thara.* Another would empty the paddy from a gunny bag into an elongated bamboo basket with tapering end (*vaalan kutta*). The elder in the family, normally Amma, would transfer three handfuls of paddies initially into the *para* pray fully with reverence and the rest of the paddy would be transferred to the *para* through the tail end of the basket till the *para* overflows. This formed a *Nirapara* from which the *Velichappad* would take a little bit using his ceremonial sword and offer as prasadam. Amma would receive it in her cupped hands and in return give a coin as *dakshina.* As the *para vazhipadu* was performed, the accompanying percussionists would stage a brief *melam.* The mahout (*paappaan*) would gently put the banana and jaggery lumps into the open mouth of the elephant, who has been waiting impatiently for them. This marked the culmination of the much-anticipated, once-a-year *para vazhipadu.*

The *Kaavadiyattam* and *Pooram* processions drew massive crowds from all around. *Kaavadiyattam* indeed is a votive offering to Lord Muruga, the elder son of Shiva and Parvathy. The ritual involves devotees, young boys and youths carrying *Kaavadi,* wooden arch-shaped structures ornately decorated with colourful paper flowers, complemented with an opulent finish of embellishments. It's widely practiced in Sree Muruga temples to appease the god. The *Kavaadi* festival is celebrated as part of the annual festival at Sree Bhavaneeswara temple on *Pooyam* day in the Malayalam month of *Kumbham. Kaavadiyattam* involves rhythmic forward and backward movements of the performers and often spinning around madly with wild joy in tune with the accompanying symphony of *Nadaswara melam*. The young revellers, in an inebriated state, would dance and stomp in frenzied mood through the village roads leading to the temple, carrying massive *kaavadis. Kaavadi* came in an array of types such as *peelikkaavadi, kalabhakkaavadi* and *karpoorakkaavadi.* At peak of their performance, the performers would enter a state of trance. As a prelude, the pilgrims undergo a 41-day long *vruta,* that involve early morning baths, meditation and vegetarian foods to prepare the body and the mind of the devotees for the arduous and painful ritual. Crowds would gather on either side of the road to witness the ritual, often causing traffic disruptions for hours. The sight of devotees piercing *soolams*—thin metal tridents—through their tongues, cheeks, and chests was horrifying. In some cases, a single but long *soolam* would pierce through the cheeks of half a dozen people who would line up side by side, with a lemon fixed to the pointed end of each rod. They would be smeared with *bhasmam*, the sacred ashes on their faces and body, the frenzied devotees would move back and forth rhythmically according to the symphony of *Nadaswara melam*. Later, in early seventies the government banned this primitive and barbaric ritual, which involved self-inflicted injuries, as an offering to appease Lord Muruga. According to the lore, the weapon of Muruga is the *soolam* (Vel), which is why he is called Vel Murugan. In those days, fierce competition arose during *Kaavadiyattam* between the *Vadakke Cheruvaram* (the northern group) and the *Thekke Cheruvaram* (the southern group), often escalating into fisticuffs and violence. The *Pooram,* featuring a parade of 9 to 11 caparisoned elephants (numbers always limited to odd ones as even numbers were considered inauspicious) in the sprawling temple ground accompanied by the rhythmic ensembles of *chenda melam, nadaswara melam*, and *pancha vadyam,* marks the finale of the grand event. It would be held on the *Pallivetta,* the penultimate day of the festival and *Aarattu,* the final day. The pooram involving the parade of elephants adorned with golden caparison, colourful parasols, complemented with *aalavattom* (ornamental fans made of peacock feathers) and *venchamaram,* special type of royal fans, would be the crowd-puller, an event that would bring people even from neighbouring places. The one carrying the holy *thidambu* with the idol of Lord Shiva, would stand majestically in the centre with all others standing in a line on either side. The slow-paced movement of elephants accompanied by *chendamelam* and *panchavadyam* through the vast temple ground is a sight to be beheld. As the parade would come to a pause in a few pre-determined points, the ensemble of percussionists would present a spectacular *melam* that would thrill the *pooram* aficionados. There were occasions in the past when up to seventeen elephants were paraded for the pooram. However, now owing to government restrictions, the number had been reduced to seven. With escalating instances of elephants running amuck and causing damage to life and property, many temples have replaced elephants with mechanically operated elephants and *radhams,* the wooden chariots. As preached by Sree Narayana Guru several decades ago, future temple festivals might adopt elephant-free and cracker-free celebrations.

Cultural programmes, that were performed simultaneously in three venues, were the best and most enjoyable part of the temple festival. On the first day of the festivities, *kodiyettam* would invariably follow by a Kathakali performance as an indispensable item of entertainment. A traditional dance-drama of Kerala, where the drama unfolds in lyrical from. The language was a mix of Malayalam and Sanskrit, referred as *Manipravalam.* While traditional temple art forms such as *Kathakali, Chakyar Koothu,* Carnatic music, *Ottanthullal,* and *Vilpattu* were performed on the stage near the temple, the stages in the high school maidan hosted drama, ballet, *ganamela,* and *Kathaprasangam,* which drew a large audience. Renowned Carnatic music maestros of South India such as M.S. Subbulakshmi, D K Pattambal, K. Soundararajan, Dakshinamoorthy, K.J. Yesudas, Thrissur V Ramachandran and Charumathy Ramachandran had enthralled the audience with their electrifying recitals. Villagers once spent sleepless nights, enthralled by the *Kathaprasangam* performances of storytelling greats like V. Sambasivan and Kedamangalam Sadanandan. Renowned drama troupes such as KPAC, Kollam Kalidasa Kalakendram, Alleppey Theatres, and Viswa Kerala Kala Samithy—under the leadership of the legendary N.N. Pillai—also graced the stage during the Sree Bhavaneeswara temple festival. Back then, with few other sources of entertainment, these programmes brought joy, wonder, and a sense of community to everyday life. They unreservedly enjoyed the programmes. By evening, groups of people would gather on the temple grounds, carrying *paaya* (screw pine mats), bed sheets, and torches. Until a couple of decades ago, these cultural programs would run till daybreak, but with increasingly hectic lives and government-imposed restrictions, they now typically conclude by 10 pm.

The festivities would come to a close with a spectacular fireworks display that added to the razzmatazz of the celebration.

The sellers of balloons, vendors selling simple and inexpensive toys and colourful candies always caught the children's attention. Children would assemble around the balloon seller demanding apple shaped balloon and oblong shaped one with a long tail attached to its end. Almost always I would demand a toy, mostly a toy car or bus made of cheap plastic. Once my desire of owning a toy automobile is satisfied, I would add them to the growing pile of old toys. Unlike other children of my age, I never tried to dismantle my toy cars and bus to understand the secrets and wonders behind their functioning. This is partly because of the fear that I might not be able to reassemble them to their original glory and partly because of the reprimand from Amma. By the time I completed my high school, my toy collection has reached an astronomical proportion forcing me to share a few with my nephews and nieces.

A few astrologers and palmists occupied the far end of the vast temple ground. They foretold the future of the people by carefully reading their palms or predicted what lay ahead in life with the aid of *Pakshi Sastra,* that involved a trained parrot randomly picking a card from a pack and based on the card predicting the future. The satisfied customer would pay a good amount as service charge. The palmists and astrologers did brisk business by exploiting the foolish believes of the gullible villagers. Sellers of hot *paayasam,* tea, and coffee who waded through the milling crowd too did good business.

Since then, a great deal has changed in our socio-cultural milieu and lifestyle. What has remained unchanged is our passion for a festival that is deeply ingrained in our personality

5.

Remembering Obby: My Bosom Buddy In Life, Laughter, And Adventure.

It was the evening strolls along with close friends that really invigorated our days. Along with Obby, I journeyed through every nook and corner of the small town, occasionally accompanied by Rajeev Shenoy and Unnikrishnan. We were classmates in college and bosom friends. Obby was more than just a friend - he was my bosom buddy, my confidant, and my partner in every adventure. We shared a bond that dated back to our early childhood, and as we grew older, our shared passions for music and electronics only deepened. Our friendship was a tapestry woven from lively debates, good-natured arguments, and mutual inspiration. To seemingly complicated things he always suggested easy solutions that would be pragmatic and simple. He always used to say that it was the solution that came first and that the problem followed suit. I owe a great debt of gratitude to Obby, who constantly encouraged and inspired me to pursue my passion for writing. Irrespective of one's age or gender or social background, he endeared with one and all with equal respect and dignity. Playful, often mischievous and always affectionate and affable he personified friendship. Quick witted, his humorous remarks occasionally tickled our funny bones. On certain occasions when we emotionally overreacted, he remained calm and composed, a quality that surprised us. Many of my friends were his and vice versa. Obby's maturity and wisdom belied his age, and he was always the first person we turned to in times of trouble, seeking his sage advice and guidance. Tall, debonair, and handsome, Obby had always been a great hero and cheerleader among the girls in our college, much to my envy. As we walked together through the college's long corridor, his imposing presence overshadowed mine, my short stature and less-than-appealing appearance drew little attention from the girls. As I reflect on our time together, I vividly remember our evening bicycle rides through the picturesque village paths, narrow, dust-filled village roads and narrower clayey bunds (*nadavarambu*) that zigzagged through the expansive paddy fields that stretched infinitely. As Obby pedalled, I sat side-saddled on the horizontal frame in front of him, firmly clutching the handle bar. His breakneck speed through the narrow, rough, and winding village alleys both exhilarated and terrified me as he rejoiced- a scary yet exciting bicycle ride indeed. Our evening cycle journey became a familiar sight for our neighbours who might have wondered what secrets we exchanged during those rides. Often Rajiv and Unnikrishnan would join us on another bicycle. During our evening peregrinations very often, we would come across Fr. Xavier Karuvally, the parish priest. A tall, fair skinned, balded gentleman in white cassocks, he travelled endlessly through the village alleys on his bicycle. He befriended everyone he met and was adored by children. We would exchange pleasantries with the Father as we passed by. On some occasions our journey would extend as far as Fort Kochi beach where we would cluster and spend a magnificent evening. There were times when we spent the evening sipping a frothy, hot tea and hot vada in yummy coconut chutney at Hotel Vasant Vihar. Our conversations would be spiced up by the sharp observations and self-deprecating humour of Obby. As we travelled back along the narrow path flanked by paddy fields and narrow channels, the song accompanied by rhythmic drumbeats and the melodious tunes from Clarinet filtered through the gentle breeze from the other side of the lake where in some remote corner the rehearsal of a *Chavittunatakam* was in progress. The distant sound of the music and the air thick with the captivating scent of growing rice transported us into another world. The ducks, those delightful creatures, gleefully swimming in the canals were an enchanting sight. The sun cast long shadows across the waterlogged fields. Our leisurely evening strolls would stretch for hours, and upon returning, night would have already veiled the sky. Occasionally, the fading light would surrender to an eerie darkness, stirring primitive fears within us as we wrestled with the unseen demons that haunted the shadows. Those hilarious years we spent during the seventies and eighties are etched in my memory for ever. His presence was always comforting. As we travelled, we engaged in endless talks on practically every topic which may be known or unknown to us. We shared many crazy ideas and offbeat subjects which we always refrained from talking in the presence of other friends for fear of being branded us mavericks. One day our topic of debate was on life after death and both of us firmly clung to the belief of *punarjanmam,* the rebirth. Around that time, there were heated debates between atheists and non-atheists on the subject which attracted media attention. Are souls immortal? Do they continue to exist for many years, even decades after death? Would the souls of our beloved harm us? For majority of Indians death is not an end in itself, rather a door opening to another world. Eminent jurist and scholar late Justice V R Krishna Iyer was a staunch advocate of *punarjanmam-* and he claimed that he often spoke to the spirit of his dead wife. When testified by a person of Justice

Iyer's stature, we have no reason to disbelief him. His book *Death and After* offers a vivid portrayal of life beyond death. Afterall the nature's ways are mysterious. One evening we concluded with certainty the existence of *atma* and continuation of life beyond mortal frame. Before parting, we made a pact, that whoever departed this world first would attempt to reach out to the one left behind. Since then, years and decades slipped silently. When Obby decided to end his life prematurely one day in March, 2024, the news shattered me to the core. When he left, I wept inconsolably. The day my all-weather friend left me was one of the saddest days in my life. I still struggle to comprehend how someone with his remarkable courage, calibre, and maturity could choose such a path. Obby and I shared a deep and unconditional bond of love and affection. Obby was my *anam cara*; we shared the same passions, same dreams, same thoughts and same feelings and saw the world through the same lens. He was a social butterfly and, in the school, and college he could easily mingle with others and enjoy socialising. Today, his framed photo adorns the living room wall of his palatial house, looking down with a mischievous smile. Today Obby's magnificent house stands by a cul-de-sac, in a quiet neighbourhood, like a haunted house.

Will *atma* of my *atma mitra* ever fulfil our agreement and try to contact me as agreed? Who knows! Anyway, Obby, I shall patiently wait.

The memories of our beloved ones keep them alive in our hearts.

"OUR DEAD ARE NEVER DEAD TO US, UNTIL WE HAVE FORGOTTEN THEM."

-Alexander Smith. (Scottish poet)

6.

Jasmine-Scented Recollections of Village Games and Gambles.

During the formative years of life, our mind was a tabula rasa – fresh, unspoiled, and untainted by the harsh realities of an uncertain world. During those colourful childhood days, we would engage ourselves in myriad games. Our motto was "play with passion or don't play at all" and we played and played with remarkable passion, unravelling thrill, fun and excitement. Hide-and-seek topped our list of favourite games which we played whenever we had spare time. The sprawling school compound with several old and isolated buildings having innumerable nooks and corners gave us ample hiding places. The two-and-a-half-hour lunch break on Fridays was the eagerly awaited playtime which we used fully for games. There would be several groups of children, separate groups for boys and girls. While **hide-and-seek** used to be a timeless and ubiquitous game, other games like ***goli kali, kuttiyum kolum, panthu kali, pambaram karakkal,*** all are seasonal games which we used to play with amazing regularity year after year. During hot summer vacation days, in a quirky corner of the homestead we would play ***kasuvandi kali*** using dry cashew nuts. Spinning top was another favourite game of boys. Yesudasan, Henry and Judson were maestros who excelled in spinning tops on their palm tops by delicately balancing them which left me flabbergasted. The magical sight of wooden tops precariously balancing itself on needle point, twirling continuously for long was simply amazing and form cherished part of childhood memories. ***Pambaram kotthickal*** was a game of tops played by elder boys which involves one player twirling his top on a surface while the opponent would hit the rotating top with his own, often breaking the other top.

Many of those native games needed just the paraphernalia from the nature, unlike the expensive, high-tech modern-day vanity toys. The most commonly used ingredient for those desi toys was coconut leaves which the experts amongst us converted to an assortment of toys like fans, balls (*oala panthu*), snakes (*oala pambu*), flute (*oala peeppi)* and toy cars fitted with two *machinga (*young baby coconuts) as wheels. Green and thick leaves of *karingotta* was the raw material using which we skilfully made shoe, cap, belt and cross-belt of police to play the game of ***kallanum pooleesum.*** Only very few had toys and I was among the fortunate few to own several cars made of plastic and tin. During the local temple festival, Amma gifted me a black film-viewer made in metal with several film strips. Next day I took the new gadget to school and proudly presented to my friends. They huddled around me to view the films for which I charged a pencil bit. They enjoyed the captivating scenes magnified through the lens of the viewer. The hand-held device provided a fascinating visual experience for the children. Back then nothing was free and for every service we charged heavily for which we devised a wonderful system of barter deal. We bartered small things we had as service charge, for example, a broken piece of pencil for a couple of ink drops. To view the film, I charged a slate pencil piece for each viewing and in their anxiety to see it, they happily parted with their prized pencil bits. In the evening, I became wealthy with several pencil bits filling up my bags. But my contentment was short lived as the very next day I had to shell out a few to my friend Joshy to get a few pieces of *pacha* in another barter deal. *Pacha* are succulent leaves and stems of ubiquitous plants like peperomia (*mashy pacha*) and water hyacinth (*kula vazha)* called *motta pacha* which was used to erase the slates by rubbing over the letters. Those whimsical games and delightful childhood toys created a fantastical universe of nostalgia. Ganesh, the most creative among us once made a picture -viewer using discarded cigarette packets. The indigenous picture- viewer would be provided with a small window opened and closed by pulling a twine. Behind the window, small stamp sized pictures of gods and goddesses would be kept. As he entered the class, Ganesh announced in his feeble voice, *"padam kaananamenkil pencil"* which meant that to view the pictures, one need to give pencil pieces as service charge. Soon he was surrounded by his own class mates and also from adjoining classes. He made brisk business before the class teacher entered. Once Uthaman brought a mouth organ (Harmonica) to class and fascinated by the melodious sound produced by the tiny instrument, we surrounded him to try our talent. He, however, was indifferent and refused to part with his gadget. Finally, bowing to our requests he agreed to give us a try on the instrument and for this service we paid him in kind- broken pieces of pencils and worn-out erasers. While I looked wide-eyed at the instrument, Adrean was more interested to know how it produced a variety of sounds as the player blew out and blew in, creating a wonderful musical treat. However, when we played, it produced some jarring notes that was irritating. On one occasion, a friend of mine brought a kaleidoscope to class, much to our delight. As we tilted the gadget, it revealed mesmerizing patterns that captivated us completely. Then little did we realize that we were learning the basic lessons of barter trading. Andy, my closest friend, once astonished us by bringing a few coveted Carambola fruits, also known as Star fruits (*Karambola puli*). Children swarmed around him, their eyes widening with excitement and mouths watering in anticipation. Generously, Andy handed out star-shaped slices to his friends, a heartfelt gesture symbolizing his affection for us.

The rules of *Kuttiyum Kolum* bore striking resemblance to Cricket and it was a game which was enjoyed by the children and grown-ups with equal zeal and enthusiasm. Back home our favourite games were carroms and *ettukali* using shells. For *ettukali,* squares in a particular pattern would be drawn either on the ground or a wooden plank. The game can be played by two or four persons as team. For the paly eight pieces of shells or cowrie are used and hence the name. Each player would have four coins which had to be moved up till it reaches the centre square. The shells would be tossed in the air and points would be decided by the number of heads. Whoever reaches the centre square first with all four coins would be declared the winner. Once *ettukali* was a favourite pastime of village elders, however, with passage of time, the popularity of the game had waned with very few practitioners left behind. Nevertheless, the spirit and joy of the game still live in the hearts of the elders. ***Kili kali*** was a very popular outdoor game of our generation played by boys. The play field consists of a large rectangular box which was divided lengthwise into two equal parts within which five rectangular boxes are marked. One player was selected as *Kili,* who has a key role to play with special privileges and other members of the team act as per the instructions from *kili. Kili* is at liberty to move along any field and knock out the opponents. A player becomes *uppu* when he manages to escape without being hit by the Kili or other team members, while those standing in the inner boxes are *pacha*. The rule of the game being often bend by the mighty ones to suit their convenience. The more ingenious among us played for cashew nuts which the loser had to pay the winner. Swinging was more than a game, it was an entertainment of the villagers where men, women and children cutting across age participated with enthusiasm. ***Oonjalaattam*** was an integral part of Onam festivities when coir ropes would be deftly fashioned to make swings on the low-lying branches of trees. Tied to two tall adjacent coconut trees, there used to be a mammoth- sized swing in the homestead of Velayudhan *Chettan*, which we viewed with awe. An *udukku kottu* artist, Panampally Velayudhan as he was popularly known, was an expert in weaving coir cots. A friendly man, he always allowed the neighbourhood youths to swing which they made good use of. Often, they would swing in a competitive spirt, each stretch as long and high as to touch the top branches of the nearby tamarind tree with their outstretched legs which we watched with bated breath. For young girls, preparing *mannappam* in coconut shells using wet soil was a game they chose imitating their mothers, following stereotypic female roles in their families, while the boys would engage in more strenuous game like "driving" old cycle tires through the zig zagging village paths at breakneck speed, inviting the wrath of elders. The drivers beating their "wives" under the influence of "alcohol" was enacted as such scenes were common in many households, especially among the ill-bred, illiterate working class.

One day Joy, our neighbourhood friend and son of carpenter Chacko Mappila, who had a penchant for surprises, brought a square board with colourful squares interwoven with pictures of **snakes and ladders**. We looked in wonderment at the new game as he patiently explained the rules of the game. We were thus introduced to a game alien to the village. A game of unexpected ups and downs full of uncertainties, the game became an instant hit among us. We rolled the dices and waited with bated breath for our next move, sometimes a ladder would take us to unexpected heights or a snake might send us tumbling down, spoiling our hopes. Our fortunes rested on mere chances and there was the thrill of possibilities. For the following few days Snake and Ladder became our much sought after game however, the game lost its charm after a few days persuading us to look for new ones.

It was Joshy, son of our next-door neighbour Padmakshy, who once introduced me to the game of ***chaturangam,*** the game of squares. One day he approached us with an enigmatic smile waving a square board with 64 black and white squares. He introduced us to the enchanting world of chess and explained using his modest knowledge the different pieces like the Knight, Queen, Bishop, Rook, Pawn and King. The movement of each piece on the chess board was unique, and his explanation was incomprehensible for us and many of us showed a lack of interest in that intellectual game. The rules of the game were arcane. Soon we gave up the ancient game of India being played by Kings in the days of yore in favour of more native games.

When we had enough money to buy *'potass',* the small circular crackers, we would buy a packet and burst them by taking turns which provided unmatched enjoyment. Those mild explosives were made of sodium potash and hence the name *potass* which came in small, attractive round shaped boxes. A few among us had guns made of metal in which there were space for keeping *potass* and to crack them by releasing a lever, a rare luxury.

Goli kali was a quintessential game and an all-time favourite. We had several versions of the game which we improvised as per our imaginations. Rules were set by the elder boys and we were made to simply follow them unquestioningly. *Goli kali* was an all-season game which we played occasionally either in groups or with twin participants. With innumerable local variants the game never lost its appeal on us. The common among them is the one involving half a dozen pebbles which would be thrown into a rectangular paly area drawn on sand. The game involves flicking the pebbles using one with precision to knock down the other *goli* in the square. During summer months children huddle together in the dusty open spaces in the school yards, courtyard of homes and temple grounds, with pocket full of *goli*. This simple yet enchanting game was a favourite among village boys and girls, a celebration, a delightful tradition.

When we had nothing else to do, we would engage in riddles and proverbs for pastime. Then our armoury was full with innumerable Malayalam riddles and proverbs. At times when we had free time, just to kill time we engaged in the game of ***"who-will-wink- first"*** (*kannum-kannum-nokkal* or *imavetta malsaram*), a game which involved two players gazing directly into each other's eyes without blinking as time stands suspended, heart skipping beats. The one who winks first or looks away will be the loser. Senior students used to give us tips to win the game such as suggesting us to focus on the opponent's nose or forehead and to avoid thinking about blinking. This was a simple yet engaging challenge which put to test our power of endurance and focus.

"**Statue**" was another beloved outdoor game from our school days. Played with multiple participants, the game's rules were simple: when one player tagged another while saying "statue," the tagged individual had to freeze in place. They remained motionless until another player tagged them to "unfreeze." The playground would often be dotted with "statues," creating a humorous and lively spectacle. During our lengthy runs through the village paths, we would occasionally gather at the edge of the long canal and engage in a light-hearted, impromptu competition to see who could pee the farthest. This playful challenge added a dash of humour and camaraderie to our routine.

The game called pick-up sticks or **Mikado game** was a popular childhood game played in schools and homes. The game involves throwing a set consisting of a dozen or so thin *eerkkil* or sticks in a bundle. The task is to carefully remove each stick using a longer one without moving or disturbing other sticks. If in the attempt any stick moves, his/her turn ends and the one who successfully removes all the sticks is the winner. The players take turns and play the game which needs a lot of patience.

During my school days, some friends displayed exceptional skill with **catapults** also called slingshots, astonishing me with their unerring precision. The instrument comprised of a forked stick, to which an elastic or rubber strap was fastened to the two prongs. They would effortlessly bring down green leaves of the banyan trees that stood in the temple ground. This talent was put to use in a popular game among village boys - using catapults to knock mangoes off trees. However, local elders disapproved, concerned that stray shots might accidentally shatter roof tiles, much to their dismay.

Similarly, some of us would catch fish from lakes and ponds using homemade **bows and arrows**, a skill in which Michael, a neighbourhood youth particularly excelled. Resourcefully, we crafted both bows and arrows from discarded umbrella spokes. My elder brother was remarkably adept at catching fish from the placid waters of our family pond using these home-made arrows, showcasing his exceptional skill. As he shot his arrows from the bank, ripples were created in the calm water. Following days of relentless rain, the pond would overflow its banks, forcing the hidden inhabitants of the pond to emerge from the depths. **Angling** for snakeheads (*Varaal),* climbing perch (*Karoop*), and other fish in our ponds was another thrilling pastime. We'd use live earthworms, carefully extracted from damp soil, as bait, threading them onto hooks. This delicate art demanded immense patience and skill, and I often found myself disappointed. Only a select few could master the skill of angling, which was rewarded with prized catches.

Gambling was a favourite pastime of many in the village. In rural areas, gambling in its modest form was practiced by children. The most popular and the simplest involved a **game of luck** using a rotating circular board, painted with numerous small, triangular shapes in various colours. As the bard rotate, a plastic tongue cleaner, attached horizontally to an upright stem, would brush against the projecting needles fixed along the board's edge. The gambler would announce, "*onnu vechal pathu, pathu vechal nooru*", If you put in one, you get ten. If you put in ten, you get one hundred. The lure of the game was so irresistible that many would burn their fingers. To play, a child would select a triangle and place a coin on it. The gambler would then gently rotate the board. If the free end of the needle (tongue cleaner) stopped on the selected triangle, the child would win a payout ten times the value of their coin. However, in most cases, the child would lose, and the gambler would win.

Another gamble was the ubiquitous '***shodathy,***' an ancient and traditional practice of conducting lucky draw, primarily among children where each one would try his luck by paying a small amount as an entry fee. A large cardboard display was the centrepiece. The top part was attached with an attractive set of small, usually hand-made objects like tiny toys, sweets or trinkets wrapped individually each with a unique number. On the bottom part were several tiny, different-coloured paper pieces—the coins of the game—each enclosing a secret number. Participants would pick a coin, open it, and check the number against those displayed on the upper part. The lucky ones would receive the prize corresponding to their number. However, often there would be no number. I tried my luck a few times but to no avail. This game of luck is deep-rooted in the culture of Kerala and is played during temple festivals and celebrations. The element of surprise, the core spirit of the *shodathy,* added to the excitement, and continued to delight the children.

Tambola—also known as **Housie**—is a lively number-based game that's a staple at parties, family gatherings, and community events across India. The game appeared in our village by mid-seventies as a gambling by elders. To conduct the game, the organizers would set up a small tent near the church at Chirackal, inside which the managers of the game sat. The players would buy tickets with several squares with random numbers in each one. There would be a playing board with numbers 1 to 90 marked prominently. Once the tickets are distributed the game would start. A manager would randomly select a numbered coin from a pot after shaking vigorously and hand it to the caller, who would announce it through a microphone. Players marked matching numbers on their tickets with pencils or punched with small sticks. The one who match all the numbers, called full housie, first would be declared the winner and would claim the prize. A fun game, it soon became a favourite gambling replacing cards (*pannimarlathal* and Rummy being the most popular card games) among the youths and elders and when its popularity grew police intervened and put an end to *tambola.* Fascinated by the game, the children started an improvised version with numbers written on small pieces of papers and the hard cover of the game board was fashioned out using the hard cover binds of old note book. Under the shade of our compound's massive Cashew nut tree, we spent hours enthralled by this homemade *tambola.*

Several decades back, when I was still a kid, Achan once brought a used **Carrom** board which we used for many years. The game provided a peaceful escape from the hardships of life. Rajiv Chettan, my second brother and Achan mastered the game which they played with unusual ease and sleight of hand. During my teenage years carroms provided an easy escape from the drudgery and monotony of village life. Every evening after prayers and homework, Sivan Chettan, next door neighbour, Sheela, my elder sister, and I, we would assemble around the board and for the coming hour we would be engrossed in the game. (Though separated by seven years apart, the age difference did not matter much to Sheela Chechy, my third elder sister and me. During by growing-up years, Sheela regaled me with her colourful, made-up stories. She had a velvety voice but as aged it turned harsh.) When free, Amma would also join us, she has in fact considerable knack in the game. Once we replaced the old and worn-out coins with a new set and the faded lines redrawn thus giving the board a new lease of life. Later Sreeni, my nephew, took away the board much to my dismay.

Summer afternoons were spent watching my elder brother and his friends playing **badminton** on a makeshift court in the nearby compound owned by Bhavani *Kunjamma*, my father's younger sister. The court was created by clearing the bushy undergrowth. They enthusiastically played the game using homemade bats made of plywood while we, the children, rejoiced the game with incredible pleasure. During annual vacation days, our front courtyard transformed into a mini-stadium where children played football. Two pieces of coconut fronds kept a few feet apart formed the goal post.

By end sixties a few **cycle** shops came up in our vicinity, which used to give cycles for rent. Raleigh and Hercules were the two popular brands that dominated the streets. Different types of cycles were available including the smaller versions for children and the ones for ladies with arched bars instead of horizontal ones for easy embarking and disembarking. None had training wheels and consequently learning cycling without falling was impossible. The children would keep a part of their *Vishukaineettam* for taking bicycles on rent and during summer vacation it was a common sight of young boys and girls engaged in self-training in cycling. A few years later, as we reached high school, a few of our classmates had cycle and they commuted on them which made us envied. My own cycling adventure was short-lived. With my friend and relative, Asokan's encouraging support, I once gave it a try, but he suddenly released the handle, leaving me to wobble precariously for a few feet before crashing to the ground with a thud. That instant, I vowed never to cycle again. Thus, my crash course in cycling had a tragic end, while my friends became skilled cyclists.

However, I delighted in watching my friends learn to ride. Though they started on badly maintained bicycles without bell and brake, gradually they learnt the art of pedalling and slowly transformed into confident and seasoned cyclists. In later years, I often rode pillion with friends Obby and Rajiv Shenoy. During the frequent lightning bus strikes of those days, I relied on them for commuting to and from Cochin College, which was just a few miles from my home.

Kite flying was a beloved pastime among the older boys, who would eagerly take to the sprawling school grounds with their colourful paper kites. They crafted their own kites using coconut midrib (*eerkkil*) skeletons, carefully covering them with newspaper pieces. To ensure stability, a long paper tail was attached to either side of the kite. Open school grounds and beaches served as ideal spots for children to indulge in this joyful activity. On one memorable occasion, a group of kite enthusiasts crafted a gigantic kite from bamboo sticks and paper, and on a windy afternoon, they set it soaring. As the massive kite climbed slowly and unsteadily into the sky, the school's children gathered around, mesmerized by the breathtaking sight.

The landscape has changed, and the past feels like a distant era. The village boys I grew up with - Robert, Henry, Josy, Yesudasan, Mariakkuty's son Xavier, and many others - have transformed into wise and weathered men, tempered by life's trials and tribulations. In hindsight, I cherish the unique and wonderful memories of our marvellously beautiful childhood, filled with delightful games that brought endless joy. Then little did I realize that it was the most blessed period of my life. However, it pains me to see my grandson, Alekh, spending his free time glued to his mobile phone, a reminder of lost childhood. Unlike my generation, Alekh has neither friend of his age in our locality to play with nor the space for him to engage in such village games that once thrilled and rejuvenated young minds. Those cluster of young children playing around in courtyards and school playgrounds was a sight once so common, now so rare. The children of the present generations are denied many simple pleasures and joys of childhood that we enjoyed heartily. Are we humans becoming an endangered species after all.

Carry your childhood with you, and age disappears.

7.

Learning Beyond the Norm: Classes on Unconventional Days and Times.

In the bustling heart of the small-town at Palluruthy, there stands tall a school basked in glory that has etched a name for itself in the collective consciousness of the city. Sree Dharma Paripalana Yogam Boys High School affectionately known by the sobriquet S D P Y B H S needs no introduction to the citizenry of Kochi, as it is a well-known and largest Aided School in West Kochi. The century old school that wears a storied past has a modest beginning being inspired by the teachings of Sree Narayana Guru, the revered philosopher, saint, spiritual leader and social reformer. Inspired by Guru's philosophical teaching *"Attain enlightenment through education, gain strength through organization"* today the school has made a mark as a premier institution in providing education to the students from the marginalized sections- the ones who cannot afford plush private schools of the elites.

I had my secondary school education at SDPYBHS, Palluruthy during nineteen seventies. Coincidentally, this period marked the most tumultuous phase in India's political history, culminating in Indira Gandhi's emergency declaration in June 1975. The campus, already politicized, became even more volatile. Sixties and seventies have witnessed several violent student agitations and strikes for causes both genuine and politically motivated. Back then there were two strong political fronts who reigned the campus in Kerala: Kerala Students Union (KSU), the student wing of Indian National Congress and the Kerala Students Federation (KSF), owing allegiance to the left, which later became Students Federation of India (SFI) in December 30, 1970. Student agitations and struggles often took violent turns and the warring factions wantonly destroyed public properties in gay abandon. As a corollary, the campus politics has taken a heavy toll on the academic performance and reputation of the school with pass percentage plummeting. This has become a serious concern for the teachers and parents alike. In those stormy years, T P Peethambaran Master, our Head Master, introduced many pedagogical innovations. One such non-traditional teaching initiative was the introduction of night classes for struggling high school students, mostly senior boys who had failed and lost years. Unlike the present day, back then many seniors were much elder than the normal age expected for high school students as they failed and lost years. Then failure was the norm. The offbeat idea of the night classes gladdened the senior boys and they enthusiastically welcomed the concept. Classes in tough subjects like English, Hindi, Science and Math were thus arranged and teachers like Peethambaran Master, Pavithran Master, Vivekanandan Master, Mohanan Master, Parameswaran Elayathu Master, Velayudhan Master, Ramakrishnan Master and Hamza Master were joined the forces to conduct classes in challenging subjects. The under performers identified and were cohorted in assigned classes. Surprisingly, they showed keen interest in the new arrangement. For the night classes, the rooms in the upper level of the double storied school building were readied and a few bulbs were fitted which hung from temporary electric lines. Classes would commence by seven in the evening and would continue till late night, in those quiet hours enveloped in deadly silence as the world slept. The dedicated elder students huddled under the yellow glow of the naked bulbs and their curious minds happily unravelled many complicated mathematical puzzles, with equal fervour they delved into the mysteries of photosynthesis, the alchemy of life, and memorized the secrets of complicated chemical equations. After the classes the students along with teachers would sleep in the poorly lit, cramped class rooms, as wooden benches became makeshift beds. A fine chapter in the teacher-taught relationship was thus scripted – a camaraderie forged in dedication. Today we cannot even imagine this kind of dedication and commitment as we sit in cozy comforts of well-lit rooms, surrounded by modern gadgetry. By five in the morning everyone would wake up, as someone would make a *kattan chaya* for the teachers and the students. After rejuvenated by the hot tea, the students and teachers would reassemble in their respective classes for another round of fresh up session, which would continue till seven. As the clock strikes seven, it was an indication for them to stop that night class, disperse and rush back to home for a quick bath followed by a modest breakfast. The students and teachers have to reach again at 10 in the morning for normal classes. The teachers toiled as much as the students but nothing prevented them from their unwavering commitment. A rendezvous between teachers and pupils at unearthly hours transformed the classroom into a captivating space, creating mutual excitement and connection. Classes beyond the normal school hours were a thrilling and enchanting experience for them. Unconventional classes in unusual settings sparked the curiosity among students, teachers, and the entire village. Those unusual classes created an atmosphere where students enjoyed unrestricted freedom to ask questions, while teachers encouraged their individual talents. It was a marked departure from the outmoded educational system.

During that time, I was in the upper primary and the sight of elder boys coming on their bicycles to attend the night classes envied me. It was a familiar sight for the devotees who came for the *deepaaraadhana,* the evening ritual in the nearby Sree Bhavaneeswara Temple. From the long corridors of the school the seniors gazed us with pride as we looked back in wonderment. The thought of myself attending such classes in the night after a couple of years enthralled me. However, by the time we reached the high school the night classes were discontinued much to our disappointment. This became a necessity as one by one these elder boys completed their courses and bade farewell to the school. Thus, the need for the arduous night classes- the marathon sessions fuelled by determination- became unnecessary. Although I never got to attend these night classes the memory of elder boys attending them left a lasting impression.

By the time I was promoted to the high school; to compensate for the working days lost due to strike and student unrest, classes were often arranged on Sundays. Deviating from normal classes, on such special occasions teachers appeared less stringent, more affable and lovable which endeared us to them. Velayudhan Master's history classes, always laced with ambiguous remarks, thrilled his students, while Ramakrishnan Master's math lessons—once a virtual torture cell—gradually became more enjoyable. Before our disbelieving eyes, Elayathu Master conducted curious experiments in Chemistry with the ease and finesse of an alchemist.

Even teachers who normally appeared rough and tough would be quite lenient and, atmosphere unusually warm and congenial that made such classes more enjoyable and wonderful experiences for us. We were blissfully spared of the usual corporal punishment by Ramakrishnan Master, our math teacher, for our failure to do homework. In normal classes we would give poorly manufactured excuses to escape such punishments but of no effect. During those unconventional sessions we enjoyed a break from the strict discipline of everyday classes and we were mercifully exempted from the usual punishments such as being caned or having our ears tweaked. This transformed us into more responsible and well-behaved individuals. The *parippuvada* (lentil fritters) served by the teachers from the nearby teashop added to our enjoyment. Unconventional class hours during unconventional hours were an unforgettable experience which served to strengthen the teacher-student bonding. Students of the present generation could not understand the magical spell of those Sunday classes which were funday for us.

By the fag end of our Secondary classes yet another teaching innovation was introduced, this time students spread across four divisions were grouped into three clusters. The first group comprised high achievers, the second the average students, and the third the under performers. We belonged to the first category and looked down the other two groups with contempt and scorn which irked them. Though such classification with different orientation based on their calibre and intellectual level paid its dividend, it invited criticism from the parents of the third group. They expressed concern that this categorization has unfairly labelled their children as nincompoops, leading to emotional distress and mental trauma. Whatever be the reason, this kind of grouping was later abandoned despite its advantages in improving the academic performances of all the three groups.

Looking back, I feel the thrill and magical synergy of those unconventional classes held during fun filled nights and on upbeat Sundays. The rustic atmosphere alchemized a strong and unbreakable bond between the students and teachers. I salute the unwavering spirit of determination of those teachers who walked the extra mile, breaking barriers, to enable children from modest backgrounds to pursue their passions and chase their dreams. A testament to the pedagogical excellence in fostering learning experiences. We have taken those opulent days to an extreme of extravagance.

8.

The Thrill of Map Reading: Fun-Filled Days of Exploration.

It was when I was promoted to the 5th grade that I first encountered geography as a subject under Social Studies. These were also the days when we were introduced to the fascinating world of maps.

One afternoon, Prema, our geography teacher, entered the classroom holding a folded sheet of thick paper with wooden frames at the edges. As she gently unfurled it, we looked on with curiosity and excitement at the colourful geographical map of Kerala. It was printed on glossy paper, reinforced on the back with a layer of calico, and framed with sturdy black wooden strips at the top and bottom. With care, she hung it above the wooden blackboard.

As an introduction to map reading, she taught us how to identify the four cardinal directions on a map. Judging from our bewildered expressions, she realized her explanation hadn't quite landed. So, she simplified it: the top of the map was North, the bottom South, the right-side East, and the left West. This clarification was enough to dispel our confusion. She then went on to explain the colour codes—light blue for oceans, lakes, and water bodies; green for forests and vegetation; and brown for mountains and hills.

I remember that in 1971, Kerala had only nine districts. The remaining five were formed later through redrawing of district boundaries. After class, the teacher carefully folded the map and asked Joseph—the naughtiest among us—to accompany her to the office with it. Tucked away in an obscure corner of the office, beside a shelf lined with trophies and shields, stood a wooden rack filled with neatly arranged folded maps. That map, as a teaching tool, ignited an instant sense of wonder in us. I began yearning for one of my own.

To our surprise, the next day Uthaman arrived with a smaller but strikingly colourful map of Kerala. We all huddled around him, eagerly trying to identify geographical features using the colour codes we had just learned. He had bought this prized possession from *Aluwakkaran Muthalai*'s sweetmeat shop.

That evening, I told Amma about my desire to own a map. She initially declined, reminding me that a black-and-white version already existed in my textbook. She wasn't wrong—but I was relentless. Eventually, worn down by my persistence, she gave me money to buy a small, colour map of Kerala. I bought it the very next day and, for fear of it being damaged by my classmates, kept it hidden as a secret treasure.

In the following classes, our teacher trained us in the art of map reading—how to recognize landscapes, water bodies, main roads, rail lines, and airports using colours and symbols. She also taught us about the concept of scale. One day, to our delight, she asked us to bring a map-drawing notebook to the next class. That very evening, we rushed to Pai's stationery shop and bought our books.

In the weeks that followed, we drew maps of Kerala, India, and different continents. These weren't just routine assignments with paper and pencil—they became occasions for learning, creativity, and imagination. Some of the cleverest students traced outlines from textbooks using transparent paper and reproduced them in their drawing books. Others, with more flair, coloured the borders with precision and flair.

We spun stories around maps—tales of explorations, epic journeys, and legendary wars.

Back then, map reading and drawing weren't just classroom exercises. They were magical gateways to distant lands. Those colourful sheets didn't just educate us—they inspired awe and creativity. For me, they sowed the early seeds of curiosity and a lifelong passion for learning.

I can still picture Prema teacher unfolding those vibrant maps and unveiling new worlds to us.

Later that same year, during the Youth Festival, buoyed by our teacher's encouragement, we attempted something ambitious: a gigantic sand sculpture of India. Karthikeyan, our drawing master—who had six fingers on his right hand (we used to joke that God had granted him an extra one for his artistic talents)—helped us sketch a massive outline on the ground. The more artistic among us sculpted a detailed map out of damp sand, then coloured it using vibrant grains to match the geographical hues we had memorized.

We won a consolation prize for our efforts—and our hearts swelled with pride.

Each map back then was a treasure chest of distant lands, cloaked in mystery and brimming with adventure. And those splendid days—they were truly filled with wonder, laughter, and joy.

9.

Nilaamazha: A Longing For Moonlit Nights.

Have you recently basked in the splendour of a moonlit winter night? I haven't. In fact, I can hardly recall the last time I truly savoured a magnificent full moon.

There was a time in my life several decades back when I thoroughly enjoyed the full moon and its exuberance. Back then nights were dead silent, except for the occasional chirping of cicadas. I along with Amma and two elder sisters would sit under the canopy of the large *Moovandan* mango tree in the front courtyard on a large *thazha paaya* (the braided mat made of dried screw pine leaves). The cool moon light filtered through the thick canopy and rained on the ground creating white irregular shadows. At midnight the village mongrels howled loudly at the sight of the dark shadows dancing in the moonlight. As Amma and sisters would engage in lively gossips I would stare at the clear night sky studded with a million sparkling stars. As I sat there lost in a world of my own, I felt as if being transported to a different world, a distant one. The untethered joy was indescribable, a sensation that defied words.

During the silent transition of our sleepy village into a small town and later an urban suburb, we were blessed with many modern amenities such as electricity, banishing darkness and fear from the land. Yet, in the process, we lost the simple pleasure of witnessing full moon nights in all their natural glory. The generation that followed mine never experienced the serene beauty of moonlit nights. Though artificial lights have altered our lives in ways that are unimaginable, we have to pay a price for it. Light pollution, an oft-overlooked issue, disrupts the circadian rhythms of birds, animals, and humans alike. We recognise air, water, and sound pollution, but light pollution remains a blind spot which has failed to get the attention it deserves.

Occasionally we collectively observe the Earth Hour by turning off all lights and other gadgets, an initiative to save energy and reduce emissions. Why not replicate this locally? How about a **Moon Hour**? Let's turn off artificial lights for an hour during full moon nights, reducing energy consumption and allowing people to revel in nature's moonlit splendour. In those rare occasions of a Blue Moon, when we see two full moons in a month, the joy will get doubled. And the prospect of a Super Moon, when the moon is at its closest to the earth making it brighter and larger than usual, is really mind boggling, our joy would be trebled. Needless to say, about the fantastic full moon on Onam that illuminates the landscape with the spectacularly magical *Onanilaavu* when our joy would be multiplied. Who can forget those enchanting nights when moonbeams rain down upon earth like sandalwood-scented rain?

Quite interestingly, there is an association named the International Dark-Sky Association which in collaboration with The American Astronomical Society and similar organizations observe International Dark Sky Week (IDSW) an annual event in April during the week of new moon. The week is celebrated by arranging night walks along with family and friends to enjoy the beauty of the dark sky, and create awareness about the negative consequences of light pollution. IDSW is an idea proposed by Jennifer Barlow, a high school student in Virginia, USA. People around the world enjoy IDSW by turning off their lights to enjoy the beauty of the night sky without light pollution.

Dark night sky

It's absolutely essential to have Dark night skies to keep the harmony and rhythm of life on Earth. Light pollution from human activities has serious implications not only for humans but for many other species of birds and animals too. With all pervasive light pollution today hardly 20% of the world population have been blessed with the ability to see the Milky Way at night. Today we have mounting scientific evidence to support the adverse effect of artificial lights on wildlife, plants, human health, and energy consumption.

10.

Bhargavi Amma-The Unsung Midwife of Palluruthy.

Bhargavi Amma was a heavily built woman with a manly manner. She was the village midwife who had assisted many young mothers in their painful journey through life from the confines of the womb to a new world. She was tall and strong and I often wondered whether she was the personification of a man's spirit trapped in a woman's body. Bhargavi, an enigmatic woman, stood remarkably tall, her traditional *mundu* barely reaching her shins. Wearing only a *mundu* and long blouse she moved along the rough terrain of the village and attended to the women awaiting child birth. She was a chatterbox, endlessly loquacious and voluble, often sharing her wishful thinking and gossamer dreams. During those days her service was an indispensable one and the parents of pregnant women would often book her services well in advance. She was very much sought after for her exemplary service in child delivery at home at a time maternity hospitals were far too less and fell short of requirements. Moreover, the poor and illiterate women reposed tremendous trust in the obstetrical abilities of Bhargavi Amma. Naturally she was their preferred choice and they approached government hospital only for surgical emergencies related to birth control and sterilisation. Bhargavi would expertly deliver babies, using her simple yet effective tools using which she cut the umbilical cord. An elderly woman from the family would lend support, supplying the essential items she needed as rest of the family waited outside with bated breath. As she assiduously did her job, the screaming of the delivering women, the birth pangs of motherhood, echoed in the air. Finally, ending the anxious wait, Bhargavi would peer through the half-open door, announcing the birth of a baby boy or girl. Simultaneously, the family matriarch would meticulously record the precise time of delivery, essential for creating the child's horoscope later. Back then the government used to give cash incentives and a plastic bucket as gifts for men and women who had undergone sterilisation. It was an initiative aimed at population control. The motto of the Family Planning scheme was "We Two, Ours two". Attracted by the incentives and gifts many people had undergone sterilisation, even chronic bachelors and middle-aged men and women past their fertile years got themselves sterilised. Such was the lure of the cash incentive.

She not only took delivery but also gave child care during the first two or three months till the newborn had grown up for its mother or grandmother to take care. She had a well-developed procedure for post-partum care of the newborn baby and mother. The routine begins with a lavish bath of the mother and child in the morning. The child would be bathed in oil and would be kept for long hours in an arecanut spathe called *paala* in local parlance. The noisy wailing of the child would not deter her in any way from assiduously performing her tasks. Her mouth filled with betel nut; she would sing lullaby in her hoarse voice as if to pacify the wailing kid which in fact served only to further irritate the child. At the end of the oil bath the baby would be washed in lukewarm water using soap and bathing the head needed special care as there are every possibility of the water getting into the nasal cavities and suffocating the baby. Once the baby bath was over, she would wipe it with a clean towel, both the ear openings would be cleaned with cotton wicks, finally eyes and eyebrows would be lined with Kajol and a black beauty spot on her forehead and cheek.

Then comes the laborious job of bathing the mother for which she would have prepared herself a special bath liquid containing certain Ayurvedic medicines and leaves. *Pullani* leaves were the commonly used ones. This preparation for post-delivery bath was called *Vethu Kuli* (post-delivery herbal bath) which Bhargavi Amma has perfected. It was believed that child birth is associated with imbalances in the *Tridoshas* and the herbal bath helped to relieve such imbalances. *Vethu* normally had *naalpamaram, pullani* and guava leaves as main ingredients which along with turmeric are boiled the previous day and then cooled down to lukewarm before being used for bathing. In the open courtyard on a makeshift hearth, she skilfully prepared this *vethu* liquid in a large traditional copper vessel (*Chembu*). A thorough massage with Dhanwantharam *Kuzhambu,* a soothing Ayurvedic concoction, was a preferred option before *kuli.* Bhargavi Amma excelled in the preparation and mastered in the application of *Vethu Kuli.* Using either Soap or a paste of chickpeas flour, turmeric powder and milk the body of the mother would be washed thoroughly. It was widely believed that this kind of post- delivery Ayurveda regimen would rejuvenate the mother to her past self. She was also credited with the preparation of special diets for the mother.

Washing and drying the soiled clothes of the baby and mother was also a part of her routine job which she did perfectly. On the 28th day of delivery, which was considered an auspicious occasion when the naming ceremony of the new born was held, it was a special occasion for Bhargavi. The family of the mother and baby would bid farewell to her with a handsome amount and also gifts brand new clothes as token of their appreciation and affection. A widow, she made a living by the service charges she received from her clients but she never complained about anyone though she struggled to make ends meet. Despite the struggles in life, an outspoken Bhargavi always appeared happy and contended. She dared to walk alone through the deserted village alleys even at unearthly times as the village slept. During her solitary night walks, she was undisturbed by the several invisible ghosts, demons and supernatural creatures which the villagers were afraid of. In olden days, our village was roamed with ghosts of all kind- male and female alike. As night fell, fear gripped the villagers. Sivan, my neighbour once told us his spine-chilling confrontation with a female ghost several decades ago. With the arrival of electricity in our locality, light dispelled not only the darkness but also the deepest fears that had lingered in its shadows.

Amma and Achan had great respect for her. While they affectionately addressed her as Bhargavi *chedathy* the rest of us called Bhargavi *Maamma,* a respectful rural term used to address elder women. It was Bhargavi Amma who took the post-delivery care of my elder sisters though they delivered in hospitals. An outspoken woman, she never missed an opportunity to strike a conversation with others and often gave unsolicited responses much to the consternation of the family. She conversed freely without linguistic restraints. Profanity was a common part of her conversations with her clients and friends. When got provoked, a few choice abuses would escape her lips but she never felt guilty of lalochezia, a testament of her innocence. She never set boundaries in her life and mingled freely with others.

One day, while bathing my second sister Anandam's infant, Bhargavi's attention drifted to the lively gossip session unfolding in the kitchen. Engrossed, she accidentally poured water onto the wailing baby's face, causing him to inhale a few drops. Panicked, she loudly raised an alarm and vigorously shook the baby, who was now struggling to breathe.

Quickly taking charge, Bhargavi sucked out the trapped water and mucus from the baby's nostrils, reviving him. With cotton wicks, she skilfully cleared the nasal passages. As the baby began crying again, Bhargavi calmly wiped him down and walked inside, as if nothing happened.

Amma and Ananda Chechy were stunned by Bhargavi's quick response and amazing presence of mind.

Hers was an excellent service in our quaint village when hospital delivery was rare and did not find favour with the villagers. Life's twists and turns often left her bewildered and frustrated. Later when childbirth in hospitals became the norm, the villagers still depended on her for the post-delivery care which she did with pleasure and dedication till she became too old to undertake cumbersome tasks. When she passed away in the late 1980s, the elderly women and men of the village mourned the loss of a devoted village midwife who had guided a generation into the world. Bhargavi Amma was indeed yet another unsung heroine of our village.

11.

Home Deliveries and Postpartum Care: A Glimpse into the Past.

Long ago, home deliveries were the norm in our village, and very few women relied on hospitals for childbirth. Aristocratic families had designated rooms in their magnificent houses for women to give birth, known as *Eettillam,* meaning "room for childbirth." Adjoining the kitchen, these tiny rooms would have wooden cots made of *Kanjiram,* with their heights less than normal. Ordinary village women, on the other hand, gave birth in tiny, matchbox-like rooms, *Pettu muri* their floors plastered with cow dung paste for warmth and sanitation.

In those days, postpartum care was an elaborate process, typically lasting 56 days. During this period, the mother and newborn were kept in the delivery room, with limited access for guests and visitors. The mother and child were confined to poorly ventilated, dimly lit rooms—a practice that, despite its hardships, provided protection against infectious diseases.

I vividly remember how Amma cared for her three daughters with profound attention during the crucial postpartum period. Their thick and long tresses would be oiled with a specially prepared concoction. A body massage with *Kuzhambu,* an Ayurvedic oil, followed by a bath in warm water infused with medicinal plants, was compulsory. Later, Amma would serve them a unique Ayurvedic preparation with immense health benefits—the *Pookkula*

Rasaayanam. Made from medicinal plants, with tender coconut flowers as the key ingredient, this sugary syrup was believed to have remarkable healing properties, particularly in alleviating back pain after childbirth.

A few minutes before breakfast, Amma would serve a specially tailored preparation designed as a strong appetizer. About a month before the baby was due, she would prepare a rare concoction consisting of unadulterated arrack, in which dry grapes were left to cure for a month. To make this, she would buy a litre of high-quality arrack from a local man who brewed it using crude, illegal methods. The alcohol-and-dry-grapes mixture would be stored in a *Bharani*; its wide mouth covered with fine cloth to allow the fermentation gases to escape. By the time it was ready, the soaked grapes would have expanded to the size of a gooseberry. A spoonful of this liquid, accompanied by one of these grapes, was then served.

Throughout the postpartum period, Amma provided several small servings of food, along with herbal *Rasaayanas* such as *Ajamamsa Rasaayana* to strengthen the body. Mutton soup, prepared in the traditional village style with an abundance of peeled shallots and garlic, was part of the daily menu. After 60 days of this rigorous care, the mother would regain her health, glow of the skin and physical strength. This deeply rejuvenating regimen had a magical effect on a mother's well-being after childbirth.

12.

Tailor Gangadharan And My Archiac School Uniforms: Some Sartorial Ruminations.

Gangadharan's tiny tailor shop at Palluruthy, was a place where intellectuals of the village gathered and discussed politics every evening. After his retirement from Indian Air Force, this unremarkable village tailor shop became Achan's favourite hangout where he spent many uneventful evenings with Gangadharan and a few regulars. It's here that I have got my school uniform stitched. He was a bosom friend of Achan and he would give stern instructions to Gangadharan regarding the shape and patterns of my trousers and shirts. I had no control over the design or fit of my school uniform or in their sartorial style. My sartorial elegance solely depended on the archaic design and poor imagination of Taylor Gangadharan. As a prelude to stitching school uniforms Achan would purchase the clothes- Navy blue drill cloth for trousers and white cotton for shirts- from the nearby Mohan's Textiles. Unlike my friends, who wore sleek and skin tight trousers, mine was too loose that in those loose-fitting trousers I looked awkward with my skinny legs and limbs. Wearing them my reflection in the mirror was embarrassing, reminiscent of the Bhima Jewellery logo - a boy drowning in baggy pants. My brothers often jocularly remarked that my body was ideal for medical students to study the skeletal system as all bones could be visible, a living skeleton. Sitting in class was a challenge, as the gaping holes in my baggy trousers revealed more than I wanted. Self-conscious about my posture, I struggled to focus. Dressed in such loose clothes I appeared as a comical character out of a comedy film which made me a laughing stock in front of my classmates. My frail frame just floated inside those oversized outfits much like a scarecrow. A few were, however, kind and considerate who sympathized with me.

In those days villagers contemptuously called such loose-fitting baggies as "*kalasam*", the attire of a poor youngster. Quite funnily the young urban boys and girls of the current generation brought up in cities and towns wear similar outfits. But when being worn by the elite it ceases to be a *kalasam*, instead it incarnates as Bermuda, respectable and widely popular trousers quite suitable for our tropical weather. Now I feel how fortunate I was to be able to wear such Bermudas in a time the tight fits were the norm.

Those infinitely wearable, modest attires were not just a part of daily school life, but also a symbol of equality, as everyone wore the same clothes regardless of their background. The clothes, thus erased the difference between the rich and the poor. Indeed, for many children, having more than a pair of uniform was a luxury.

In primary classes uniforms were not enforced and some of us enjoyed the freedom to come in fanciful clothes. It's interesting that the uniform policy of our school changed as I progressed through the school. It was fun to wear colourful clothes gifted by my family on special occasions in primary classes. however, in high School, uniforms were made mandatory. Those simple school uniforms, consisting of only trousers, skirts, and shirts, lacked added embellishments like ties, belts, and shoes. Most students walked barefoot in their uniforms. We gazed with a mix of astonishment and envy at the few children in the locality who attended central schools, where they wore well-defined uniforms. Clad in navy blue pants or skirts and white shirts, complemented with tie, belts and boots, they exuded confidence in their neatly tied and polished attire. In our school teachers also had an unwritten dress code. Male teachers typically dressed in white *mundus* and white Terry cotton shirts. Although lady teachers didn't have a strict dress code, and most wore colourful sarees, a few like Thankamma teacher followed a uniform of white sarees paired with green blouses.

One day I reached high school wearing colourful dress but to my embarrassment, our class teacher Kumara Pillai Master, denied permission to enter class without uniform. I cut a sorry figure in front of my class mates. As the teacher sent me out, the suppressed smile of my classmates irritated me. I went back home and returned half an hour later in my trade mark uniform tailored by Gangadharan. This incident made me extra careful about wearing uniform. It's funny how these incidents, though awkward at that time, become memorable stories when we look back with a smile. Those shared laughs and inside jokes became some of the best memories from school days. Its moments like these that make school life so unique and memorable.

In the late 1970s, as I joined for my pre-Degree studies in college, I abandoned my traditional "*kalasam*" attire and embraced modern fashion. It was an era of vibrant style, characterized by bell-bottom pants, colourful shirts with oversized dog-eared collars, shoulder straps, and pockets with flaps. Many of my friends including several girls came to the college attired in such modern outfits. The intellectuals whom the rest of us called *buji*, an abbreviation of *budhi jeevi*, always wore long, loose kurta-pyjamas complimented with sling bags made of cotton. The aesthetic sensibilities of my college days were shaped by the western culture and the period witnessed the emergence of hippies. Characterized by their neglect of personal hygiene, hippies would roam the campus in their signature bell-bottom jeans and shirts, often sporting long hair that appeared to have gone months without a shower. Oversized sunglasses were an integral part of their distinctive look. In my youth, I had a bird's nest hairstyle, *kuruvikkoodu,* where my front hair was curled to resemble a nest. This style was trendy until the early seventies, when hippies popularized long, unkempt hair. I was fascinated by their look and wanted to grow my hair long, but Achan wouldn't allow it, fearing it would trigger cold-related health issues. Most of my friends had such long fashionable hairstyles. Despite hairstyle being a personal choice, I obeyed him to avoid reprimand. Achan instructed Peter, our barber, on exactly how to cut my hair, and Peter followed his directions precisely. Every month, Peter would give me a close crop, keeping my hair neatly trimmed. Quite funnily, 80's fashion in clothing, accessories and hairstyle are now on a comeback trail as they are warm-heartedly embraced by Genz. Cargo pants, (loose trousers with large external pockets); Overalls, (loose, sturdy trousers, usually with a bib or bib-like piece to which shoulder straps are attached); butterfly clips, newspaper print shirts, and choker are once again regained their lost glory. I had to contend myself with a pair of cotton pants that were tight-fitting attire called *"kuzhal"*, the pipe in local parlance. The bell-bottoms of the fashionists reached beyond their feet, often sweeping the streets, mine was correct-sized reaching to ankle level. However, after a couple of wash, the cotton shrank, reaching only up to ankle level. Adding insult to injury, I had a closely cropped hair while my compatriots had long hairs, chisel shaped sideburns and caterpillar moustache. Once again, I became the subject of ridicule by my friends for my obsolete dressing style. My teachers, however, were appreciative of the "decently dressed and well-trimmed' teenager for which I thank a disciplinarian father who mentored me and tailor Gangadharan who tailored my clothes. I am reminded of the sarcastic remarks of Oscar Wilde: "Fashion is what one wears oneself; what is unfashionable is what other people wear". The way one dresses has profound cultural, social, and personal significance, a means of identity and self-expression. It is said that the way you dress is the way you are addressed. A scantily clad Mahatma Gandhi, contemptuously addressed as a half-naked fakir by the coated, booted and tied British Prime Minister Winston Churchill, however, has proved to the world, that more than the dresses one wear, it was the values one believes and practices which are more important; that dresses have only underwhelming role in a person's personality. His modest way of dressing was not an obstacle in his becoming an iconic figure for them, the voice of the voiceless, the hopes of the hopeless. In our time, Dr A P J Kalam embodied simplicity, disproving the notion that wealth equals excess. Despite being able to afford a life of luxury, he famously owned and wore only three or four pieces of simple suites, inspiring generations with his sartorial preferences. In his inexpensive suites he walked with aplomb as a fine example of sartorial elegance. The right kind of dressing reveals one's true self.

13.

Celluloid Dreams: A Cinematic Journey.

Nostalgic memories of going for movies along with Achan, Amma, and my siblings form part of the memories of an eclectic childhood. Under the vast expanse of the bright blue sky, white clouds scattered like cotton tufts, forming irregular shapes. I wondered as who decides the shapes, sizes and movements of these clouds. Coconut fronds swayed gently in the southern breeze, as if rocked by a lullaby. Birds have not yet begun their return journey to reach home before sunset. Amma was still in the kitchen hurriedly finishing the household chores. We, my two elder sisters and myself, were excited about our imminent journey to Jayalakshmi Talkies as we got ready well before time. As time passed by, I became impatient while my youngest sister gazed into the mirror for another time ensuring that her modest makeup was intact. Soon we would begin our much-anticipated journey to Jayalakshmi Talkies to watch the film that we have been waiting for so long. And at last, Amma had emerged out from the kitchen, hurriedly washed her face, draped herself in a sari and applied a coat of Cuticura powder marking the beginning of our much-awaited cinematic journey. The thought produced goosebumps in my mind. "*Kumara Sambhavam*" was such an acclaimed film, its story being based on the epic, that missing to see it would be a huge loss for us. The film was noted for its cinematic brilliance and evocative songs with rich lyrical content. My classmates who saw the film bragged about its appealing visuals and star-studded characters in colour. They shared the story in bits and pieces which heightened my curiosity. The film was running houseful for the past few days. It was after too much pestering and persuasion that Amma finally agreed to see the film. The occasional advertisement from loudspeaker-fitted cars and the gist of the storyline she gathered from film notices served to arouse her interest too. And at last, we started our journey to the theatre that was located a mile away. In those days watching a film used to be a social event in which many people in the locality would come together, marching to the theatre to enjoy the film like a large family. The news was broken to my friend Robert's mother and she joined us along with her four children. On the way Bhargavi *Maamma*, the village midwife, joined us along with her two daughters and a couple of her neighbours. In the long procession, Tomy, our pet dog and a few of his friends joined surreptitiously. As we reached halfway of the long stretch, an elderly woman who came across informed Amma in a hushed voice about the death of someone in the village. She suddenly stopped walking, stood still as if sudden break was applied. Bhargavi *Maamma* followed suit. We, my sisters and I, looked at each other with concern. We feared that Amma might cancel our plans on hearing the news of the death of someone important to her. I cursed the dead man for choosing the wrong time to die, and uttered a few expletives for throwing a spanner into our plan. However, regaining her composure, Amma suggested us to go to the theatre and enter the hall after entrusting their tickets with the door keeper while she along with *Maamma* would join us later after paying the last respects to the dead man. We heaved a collective sigh of relief as we resumed our walk, quickening our pace to compensate for the lost time.

We were greeted by a huge crowd that thronged in front of the theatre. My sisters struggled to get into the long queue to fetch our tickets which was restricted to two per person as I waited with bated breath. Then the practice was to give tickets to everyone who the auditorium could hold, irrespective of the seats available. As we walked into the auditorium, it was filled to the brim. We squeezed into the crowded theatre. The earlier visitors occupied the seats reserved for the respective classes; others sat on steel chairs that were lined up in the aisle while the late comers stood in every inch of space available. Those who sat behind the wooden pillars in the auditorium strenuously stretched their necks to have an uninterrupted view of the screen. When we reached the theatre, the film had already been started. Standing in the crowd we watched *Kumara Sambhavam*. I could only glance at the scenes through the crowd and the rest I imagined. I tilted my head and stretched my neck to its limits, desperate to sneak a glance at the screen. The story earlier revealed by my classmates helped me to stretch my imagination. Some of my movie buff friends had a habit of spoiling the suspense, revealing the shocking twists and cliffhangers. When dance sequences were played, which were too many, my sisters would lift me up on their hands for me to have a quick look. A few minutes later Amma and Bhargavi *Maamma* joined us in pitched darkness. During interval as many men had hurriedly exited to relieve themselves, we got a foothold in the front from where the screen was partially visible. In those days there would be three intermissions as time was needed for reel switchovers by the projectionists and in those moments people would howl noisily. When the 3-hour long film was finally over I saw just half the cinema, the other half I imagined based on the dialogues and the story I heard earlier from my classmates. In those days the hangover of the movie would last for a week and during that time we would discuss the story, songs and dialogues many times where people gathered as we rejoiced each time.

Acting in those days was characterized by exaggerated expressions of emotion. We laughed at Aalummoodan's comical expressions and enjoyed the humorous idiosyncrasies of Sankaradi and S. P. Pillai. The comedy of that era was a far cry from what we enjoy today. Overacting, exaggerated expressions, monotonous dialogue, and unnecessary gestures were the hallmarks of comedy during that period. It was challenging to distinguish between wit and humour, as the dialogue delivery was often adapted from Tamil films, blending the two. Adoor Bhasi's and Bahadur's hilarious jokes had us bursting into laughter, and we would later retell them at school, laughing all over again as we remembered them. During interval in the school, many of my classmates reenacted the violent scenes of fisticuffs involving MGR and M N Nambiar from popular Tamil films which enjoyed a huge fandom.

Back then the show would be preceded by a news reel, the Indian News Review, which would last 10-15 minutes. The reels were exhibited between 1949 and 1974. Produced by the Films Division, Ministry of Broadcasting, the reels featured the programmes and stories of the central government. The newsreels covered politics, people, sports, science, agriculture, and everything related to national development. Almost all Newsreels, however, would be dominated by Indira Gandhi, the Prime Minister of the day. Newsreels were a popular source of information and entertainment for movie fans in a pre-television era as they enjoyed them as much as the films. It was through such reels that people came to know about the awesomeness of the wars. I had a faded memory of Indira Gandhi inaugurating a dam and then sharing some joyful moments with the villagers. We liked the reels as well as the monotonous narration in Malayalam, a filmic paean. People would come to the theatre well before the show so as not to miss the news reels which they revelled in immensely. However, the riff-raff in the audience showed utter disdain for the reels, and they spent time outside the theatre smoking cigarettes till the reels were over. As the show ended National Anthem would be played, a mandatory ritual which the uneducated villagers honoured by standing up in attention. By 1975 when Doordarhsan started airing news, the importance of newsreels paled into insignificance.

During the film, a couple of vendors would approach the audience in the middle of the movie selling hot tea, *masala kappalandi* and *paattu pusthakam,* small booklets containing the songs and a brief of the film. I always demanded a song book whenever we had gone for a movie and over the years those tiny books have accumulated making a collection. Munching on roasted peanuts, we sat completely engrossed as we enjoyed the film gleefully. The little urchins and unruly youths flew paper airplanes towards the screen and celebrated their joyful moments, much to the inconvenience of the crowd. While the uncouth among the audience would howl and scream when scenes involving violence and romance came alive on the screen. The violence usually consisted of fisticuffs between the hero and the villain, often enacted by Prem Nazir and Satyan. Each punch thrown by the hero and villain was accompanied by the loud "*dishum dishum*" sound, which thrilled us. Pappy and Thyagarajan were the two well-known stunt masters of the time who orchestrated those stunt scenes that would seem comical to the present-day audience.

In those days tickets were not needed for children below the age of five. As we neared the theatre, one of my sisters would carry me. Securely perched around her waist I sat astride as she carried me. Even when I was eight Amma continued to declare me as a five-year-old to the gate keeper and he would let me in though with a sense of hesitation. Before cushioned seats were installed, the first class was furnished with a few wooden easy chairs where the people watched the movie in a relaxed mood. My eldest brother Siva Prasad remembers that while going for cinema, Achan used to carry his *visary,* the hand-held fan, along as fans were not available then. I amusingly pictured Achan enjoying his favourite movie, lying comfortably in an easy chair, fanning himself. In this modest village Talkies, I have seen many a Malayalam cinema with their storylines ranging from romance, mysteries, comedies, thrillers, and every genre one can imagine. Back then Malayalam cinemas were few and old generation cinephiles satisfied their passion by watching Tamil films which were common. As the movie began, the villagers would greet the story with laughter, applause, and a range of other emotions that suited the story, creating a sense of togetherness and belonging.

In front of the Jayalakshmi Talkies, there was a shackle selling *Paattu Pusthakam, masala kappalandi, attaani,* and 'Goli soda'. The soda bottles would be arranged in a raw with a lemon on top of each bottle. Goli soda was bottled in unusually thick glass bottles with Codd-neck with a small marble (Goli) stopper. The bottle would be opened with an unusual type of opener. After gulping down the soda, the bottle had to be returned failing which extra money would be charged towards the cost of the glass bottle.

Back then, changes in cinemas were invariably on Fridays. We eagerly awaited this momentous occasion, signalled by a man appearing on the village road, pulling a handcart. On either side of the cart, two large, slanted canvases joined together at the top would be fixed, displaying huge, colourful posters of the new cinema. Announcing their arrival, a man would walk ahead, beating a drum. The cart puller would distribute notices, which children would collect for adults to read. These notices provided a brief description of the storyline, keeping the climax a well-guarded secret, and ended with the standard statement: "Watch the rest on the silver screen." This often served to arouse the curiosity of the people to see the movie. All such cinema notices have one thing in common: a close-up picture of the superhero alongside the heroine in revealing attire, which would likely fuel the teenage imagination. For films featuring violence and erotic or sexual themes, the customary "A" certificate would be prominently displayed on the notice. Interestingly, a few of my friends had the unusual hobby of collecting cinema notices. For blockbuster movies, announcements were made from Ambassador cars fitted with horn speakers. As the man in the rear seat announced the film's features, he would throw notices through the window. We would run behind those cars until they disappeared into a cloud of dust and smoke. I would stand still for a few minutes, inhaling dust and diesel fumes, gasping for breath.

Back then cinema reels would be dispatched from Madras in huge, rectangular metal boxes. On the release day, the film operator would wait with bated breath for the arrival of the *petty* containing the film rolls. The sight of the metal trunks would send the waiting crowd into an ecstatic mood. A lot has changed since then in the celluloid world. Such metal boxes containing film rolls are no more seen, so are the euphoric crowd who waited for hours for the arrival of the film reels. Today, in this digital age, tiny pen drives are the norm instead.

My cinematic journey would not be complete without mentioning Patel Talkies in Thoppumpady and Zaina Theatre in Fort Kochi. Patel Theatre in Kochi was once a landmark of the ancient town that finds mention in *The God of Small Things*, the acclaimed novel by Arundhati Roy, the Booker Prize-winning writer. Built by Ibrahim Patel Sait in 1961, the magnificent structure stood out from other theatres in Kochi due to its unique and stunning architecture, which resembled the Taj Mahal, and the grandeur. Patel Sait was not only a wealthy business man, but a great philanthropist too. Through his lasting contributions he etched a space in the historical milieu of Kochi. This modern theatre created history at a time when most theatres in Kerala were housed in thatched sheds, where the audience sat on bare floors, wooden benches, and chairs under the dim glow of bulbs. Patel was the first theatre in Kerala that was lighted up with 'tube lights', which local people called '*Vazha Pindy*' lights as they closely resembled the slim, white, innermost core of the plantain stem. It is said that people even from faraway places thronged the theatre to have a look at this historic building and its many tube lights that left them spellbound, marvelling at the sight.

The beautiful auditorium stood out due to the absence of pillars, which surprised many. The folding chairs neatly lined up on either side of the aisle and the balcony were a new experience for the people, which they enjoyed. Soon, the theatre became the talk of the town, and people stood in long queues waiting for the ticket counters to open. The view from the rear of the theatre was equally breathtaking, with many boats, chugging trains and approaching small planes gladdened the viewers. How can one forget those serene evenings we spent there, caressed by the gentle breeze, as we patiently waited for tickets. In the front courtyard, there was a well-manicured lawn with a huge statue of a woman carrying a pot of water in her hands, which added to the elegance of the building. Both sides of the entrance were lined with well-trimmed thickets of *mylanchy* (the Henna plant), forming a fence. By late seventies, this historic theatre was closed down and later ownership changed hands a couple of times. We will always remember the old Patel Talkies in all its glory—the Cinema Café that stood in front of it, the line of waiting Ambassador cars, and the bustling traffic island where weary traffic police struggled to bring order. I was around six when we watched *Bhargavi Nilayam,* the first ever horror thriller in Malayalam at Patel Theatre. Written by Vaikom Muhammed Basheer, the master story teller of Malayalam literature, the black and white film was a spine-chilling experience for me which continued to haunt me even after several decades. Later, the term *Bhargavi Nilayam* became a byword in Malayalam to describe any unused, uninhabited, and deserted houses. There were evenings when we would arrive at the theatre, hearts brimming with excitement, only to find it already houseful. Turning back on those nights felt like leaving behind a little piece of joy- we were deeply disappointed and quite crestfallen, each time.

Established in 1969 by V.K.Pareekutty, Zaina Theatre has the rare distinction of being the first 70mm theatre in Kerala. In its early days the theatre was well known for screening world class English films. The wide screen offered an entirely new cinematic experience to the people. The theatre exhibited Hollywood classics such as *The Bible, Benhur* and *Ten Commandments.* After the death of Pareekutty, the theatre was taken over by Kokers group. Pareekutty was taken the land on lease from the Cochin Municipal Corporation and after expiry of the lease period and two extensions, there was a long legal battle between the owners and the Corporation leading to its closure in 2017. Today, the once famous, Kerala's first 70mm theatre is in ruins, with wild growth spreading branches all over the structure. *Pazhassi Raja,* a Mammootty starrer, was the last film I watched in Kokers more than a decade ago.

Sometime in early seventies, Achan took us to a new theatre in Ernakulam which was recently opened. It was the famous Shenoy Theatre, Asia's second theatre having Vistarama Projection. We were amazed by the humongous screen that curved inward and was much larger than the ones we were familiar with. Achan explained that this was the vistarama screen, a rarity. I was equally amazed by the winding ramp that led to the balcony. What attracted me most, however, was the glittering red curtain fitted with lights all along its bottom margin. As the curtain was gently lifted to the accompaniment of the tune of a famous Hindi film song, the beautiful lights on the ceiling dimmed gradually turning off creating a dark interior. The film occupied just the centre part of the huge screen that had disappointed me. By interval, we started shivering, as we were not used to the cool comforts of an air-conditioned auditorium. However, we thoroughly enjoyed the cinematic marvel.

I loved watching movies at Menaka Theatre for the sheer pleasure of watching the curtain raise. There used to be two curtains, as one moves up, another one- a split curtain, that would separate sideways. Both the curtains parted simultaneously which delighted my cinematic experience. In those days, most movie theatres had beautiful, pleated curtains decorated with attractive frills. Jayalakshmi Talkies was conspicuous by the absence of a curtain. Later, theatres one after another, stopped using curtains for unknown reasons.

During the past decade, we started witnessing the emergence of multiplexes in huge shopping malls that slowly replaced the ubiquitous stand-alone theatres. With multiple screens, the multiplexes opened up a new cinematic experience for the new generation viewers. All of them have mindboggling sight and sound technologies with plush interiors and luxurious reclining seats. The mushrooming multiplexes began to make inroads into the clientele of the traditional theatres. With multiplexes offering opportunities for entertainment along with shopping and dining, the old generation single-screen theatres are fast disappearing. During a show in a multiplex as my son placed order on his smartphone for popcorn and soft drinks, soon a youth in uniform served them in our seats. As I slowly munched the corn, my thoughts drifted to a bygone era when Amma would buy roasted peanuts wrapped in paper cones from a middle-aged vendor, while we sat, immersed in the movie, drenched in sweat. Cramped inside the tin-roofed, ill-ventilated auditorium, we sat cheek by jowl, inhaling air thick with cigarette smoke. Yet as we watched the film, we were transcended to another world of boundless joy and happiness. Our minds were completely enthralled, as the celluloid world cast a magical spell on our imagination, making us oblivious of the physical discomforts we endured. I thought to myself, 'Mom, you may not have had the comforts, conveniences, and prosperity that we enjoy today, but you still managed to live life to the fullest'.

From The Annals Of History.

The Shenoy family of Kochi has a very special place in the hearts of film lovers. The family owned many modern cinema theatres in Kochi including Lakshman, Padma, and Sridhar. While almost all theatres exhibited Tamil, Malayalam and Hindi cinema, Sridhar stood out as an exception with its tradition of exhibiting English films. In the 1950s, a group of foreigners visiting to watch an English film introduced the Shenoy family to the innovative concept of Vistarama screens. This chance encounter inspired the family to build Shenoy's Theatre, a groundbreaking cinema that would become India's first and Asia's second Vistarama theatre.

The massive movie house boasted an impressive 80-foot-long, 30-foot-wide, inwardly curved screen, leaving audiences in awe. Renowned architect Govinda Rao from Chennai skilfully designed the landmark building, harmoniously shaping it to complement the curved screen. The theatre was inaugurated by none other than the President of India, Varaha Giri Venkata Giri in 1969 and the first film was *Winning*, an American movie that combined the excitement of racing with the complexities of personal relationships. However, to keep in tune with the changing times, the theatre has undergone extensive renovation lasting 5 years and was transformed into a multiplex with 5 screens in 2021. But the old generation of Kerala still has vivid memories of the circular theatre and its gigantic screen.

In fact, Malayalam film has many firsts to its credit: in 1982 *Padayottam* became the first 70 mm Indian film, in 1984 *My Dear Kuttichathan*, the first 3D film in India, in 1993 *O' Fabby* became the first animation film in India, and in 2006 *Moonnamathoral* the first digital film in India.

14.

White Washing and Painting in Bygone Decades: Nostalgic Memories.

Recently a fresh coat of paint was given to my eighty plus year old ancestral home which had been through several rounds of renovation over the years. Despite those renovations and restoration efforts the central portion, the vital part of the building still remains intact, with brick walls, wooden ceilings and a roof of tiles. The white washing works were carried out after a long period as against the annual exercise that used to be several years ago. Modern day paints and other materials are long lasting though expensive. This negates the need for frequent white washing and painting, a process which was a very laborious and difficult process. For a couple of weeks during which white washing and painting were done the life would be thrown out of gear. With mountains of household items including heavy cupboards, cots, boxes, and furniture littered everywhere, the most arduous task was to clear them for the painters to do their jobs. They would be shifted to safety and covered with bed sheets to protect them from dust and garbage. Several framed photos and wall clocks would be removed meticulously.

Several years ago, white washing and painting used to be an annual ritual which was often performed by December/January when the sky would be bright and clear after a long spell of rain. Achan would entrust the task to Viswambharan better known by his nickname Vichu. One day he would come, making a quick survey of the entire building, followed by the calculation of estimated expenses.

In the coming days Vichu would come with a couple of sacks containing the lime shells that would be precariously placed on the carrier of his bicycle. In those days no vehicle other than bicycles would be able to take to our house as the alleys were so narrow and winding. A day before the commencement of his work, Vichu would empty the shells from the sack into large drums and water would be added. As I watched with enthusiasm, the shells would start boiling with bubbles and heat emanating from the drums with a sound. This extraordinary process had surprised me as I could not believe that adding cold water to the shells would result in such intense heat. Later the surprise gave way to understanding when in my class we came to learn about exothermic reactions.

After some time, the still hot mass of lime paste would be transferred onto a tin sheet forming a small mound. The work would begin in the coming days which would begin with scraping off the peels of old white washed surfaces with a chisel like object. This would be followed by washing with a copious amount of water, filling the gaps and holes on the walls and ceiling with a thick paste of putty.

The actual process of white washing would begin when Vichu would transfer the thick lime paste into a large drum, to be diluted with water and then mix thoroughly to make a viscous solution. To this he would add a few drops of *Neelam*, the fabric whitener, to impart the liquid a light attractive blue shade. The solution would be then poured into small containers and his assistants would do the job. The lime solution would be applied using coir brushes with long bamboo handles. As a rule, the ceiling would be painted white while we preferred an array of colours for rooms, a different colour for each room. For this Vichu would add a few drops of the stainer of the choicest colour with meticulous care. It was a common practice to change the colour of the interior every few years to alleviate the monotony. When such colour changes were needed two coats of white washing would be given to mask the old colour beneath the fresh coat. The entrance to our house featured a charming veranda, flanked by half walls (*charupady/aramathil)* and two imposing pillars on either side. These sturdy brick pillars, accompanied by smaller ones at each end, were painted a vibrant yellow and adorned with colourful mosaic spots, creating a striking visual effect that added to the house's beauty.

Varnish on the wooden ceiling would be carefully applied using small cotton puffs, a painstaking and labour-intensive process that required great attention to detail. This tedious task demanded patience and precision, as each puff was meticulously used to coat the surface with a thin, even layer of varnish. Paint works would start after finishing the white washing. Windows and doors would be painted white while the grills would be painted with a combination of white, black and grey shades imparting a beautiful finish. Paints would come in different colours and shades in tins. At the bottom of the tin the colour of the paint inside would be indicated by small dots. During those days the workers would continue their job till late into the night. In their eager to finish the work in time, they were least bothered about winding up their work in time.

The bottom part of the foundation would be painted black with "Black Japan" which would guard against the constant attack by termites. Once completed, the newly white washed building would adorn with a new majestic look, a sight that enthralled me.

After the whitewashing and painting were complete, it would take several days to meticulously clean the floors, removing stray droplets of paint and varnish. This painstaking task fell to Amma and my two elder sisters, who would diligently scrub and wipe away every last speck. For a few days after painting, the air inside would be thick with the peculiar pungent smell of varnish, paint and turpentine mixture that I loved immensely. With my nostrils wide open I would deeply breath in the unique scent disregarding Amma's warnings of my breathing trouble getting aggravated.

Later new technologies were introduced in paint and the old procedures of mixing lime with water and staining the lime solution, all became part of memories. The two-meter-long coir brush was replaced with small hand-held rollers. Cleaning has been taken over by high-pressure jet pumps. A dozen or so workers clad in jeans and colourful T shirts come in the morning in their sleek bikes. At the strike of five in the evening, they wind up the day's work and return. Nowadays the plastic emulsion paints come in a universal basic colour of white into which infinite shades of varying colours can be added using computers. Contemporary painting techniques have significantly reduced labour requirements while enhancing colour quality, resulting in unique and captivating environments. However, this increased aesthetic appeal comes at a higher cost.

15.

Kochi-A City By The Sea And Lagoons.

Today, Kochi, the *"Queen of the Arabian Sea"* is known globally as an important port city in the west coast which lies in the centre of an important maritime trade route. Kochi backwaters, a part of lake Vembanad which flows through the territory, is the life line of the city, the pulsating artery, that divides the landscape into two unequal geographical halves. (Vembanad Lake is the third-largest brackish water lake in India, after Chilika Lake in Odisha and Pulicat Lake that is straddling the borders of Andhra and Tamil Nadu. It connects to the Arabian Sea at three points along its 96.5 KM long journey—Azhikode in the north, Kochi in the centre, and Thottappally in the south. Once a thriving habitat for a diverse array of fish, the lake has suffered greatly due to man-made catastrophes such as encroachment, landfilling, and pollution, pushing many species to the brink of extinction.) The terrain on the east is the East Kochi, while its poor cousin lying across the *kaayal,* the West Kochi. In between these two strikingly different landmasses lies the famed Willingdon Island, the largest man-made island in the country. Here the lake branches into several small lakes and streams and finally ends up as narrow canals. Once the banks of the lake were thick with lush green mangroves which stretched out along the shore. Sadly barring a few small patches, the rest have been wantonly destroyed for construction activities both legal and otherwise. Together they form an entangled waterscape that embraces our land as firmly as a mother does her newborn. The lush greenery and picturesque landscape made Kochi one of the most wonderful places in the country. Today East Kochi is a throbbing metropolitan city whereas West Kochi still retains its identity as a heritage city with idyllic streets, picturesque buildings and tantalising promenades.

Years ago, when the land was still a small town, erstwhile Cochin, what we call West Kochi today, was a vibrant business hub while East Kochi known as Ernakulam was a small but growing city. Those were the decades when Cochin famed itself as a vibrant business hub abound with several factories and manufacturing facilities dotted across the town. The town earned its reputation as a thriving industrial area, a vibrant entrepreneurial ecosystem for trades in spices and marine products. The spice route of India has attracted many alien visitors with their eye on the inexhaustible spices, coir and seafoods. Many established their businesses in the narrow coastal strip extending from Mattancherry in the north to Edakochi in the south engaging in diverse businesses like ship building, export of spices, coir, coconut oil and seafoods. Mattancherry bazaar was agog with activities where numerous mammoth godowns called *Paandika Saalas* existed, engaged in the trade of spices and coir. Cochin has transformed into a citadel of seafood trade with several canning companies and units engaged in the production of prawn pulp came up with their businesses concentrated mainly in Mattancherry area. Madhura Company, Cochin Company, Brunton Shipyard, Giovanola Binny Company, Tessy Company, Lakshmi Starch Factory, Choice Canning Company, Indo-Marine Agencies, Abad Fisheries, United Industries of Cochin, Excel Seafoods, Karthika Fisheries, India Seafoods, Philson Fisheries, Caico,

Crystal Chemicals, KMP Oil Mills, Anand Water Meter Manufacturing Company, Pankaj Soaps and a couple of coconut oil companies and a silicate company were a few among those companies that had transformed the village into a small town.

Once Palluruthy, my birthplace, was a small, quiet hamlet inhabited by the poor belonging to different cultures and faiths where we celebrated our quirky childhood. Yet they cohabited in peace and harmony. The life of the villagers was quiet, idyllic and slow paced where people cared about each other. My Amma, Achan, uncles and aunts, they all belonged to another era, an era marked by human bonding, love, mutual affection and benevolence. One's problem was everyone's. When in need of help they would gather together around the person who needs help and extended their support, warmth and care. The health and wellbeing of every one was important enough for everyone else. We tend to be cocooned in our own world with slightest concern for the world beyond. Together they shared their small pleasures and pains in their lives. Occasionally, they would bicker over trivial matters, and the atmosphere would momentarily become strained. However, their petty squabbles never lasted long, as they would soon put aside their differences and resume their carefree conversations, a testament to their innocence.

In the mid-1960s, when I was just five years old, a vivid memory remains etched in my mind. A devastating fire ravaged the thatched home of my dear friend and neighbour, Robert, leaving the family of Palackal Xavier, his wife, and their six children homeless. Xavier eked out a living by rolling beedis. I used to watch with amazement the way he rolled beedis using his nicotine tainted fingers with long nails. The inferno reduced their tiny home along with their modest belongings and dreams to ashes in a split second. The entire neighbourhood swiftly rallied around the family, providing unwavering support to rebuild their home and lives. For several weeks, Robert's elder brothers, George and Josy, found refuge in our home. Amma welcomed them and selflessly offered a small room alongside the veranda with a wooden cot for their exclusive use. She also provided them food, and clothing during those trying times. Whenever a tragedy struck, the neighbourhood became a beacon of hope for the victims. Years later through hard work and dedication Josy was catapulted to the position of the Manager of a seafood export company in Vizag where he permanently settled. Later, during his brief stay in Palluruthy, Josy used to visit Amma and recollect those wonderful memories of her admirable benevolence. He once told me that the news of Amma's passing pained him too much.

Chory *Pulayan* and Thevan *Pulayan* were the two individuals responsible for preparing the land twice a year to make the soil fertile. Chory was tall and lean, with jet-black skin, while Thevan was short and stout. Chory had a prominent Adam's apple that protruded from his throat and moved rhythmically when he spoke. In contrast to Thevan's reserved nature, Chory was quite talkative and would often share his thoughts with Amma about the evolving political situation after the war. Though lacking formal education, he possessed a keen understanding of the prevailing political climate in the country. Chory always kept a half-smoked beedi, known as a *muribeedi,* tucked behind his earlobe, saving it to finish later at his leisure. (*Dinesh beedi* was quite popular among the working class and earned a reputation as poor man's cigarette. Manufactured by Kerala Dinesh Beedi (KDB) Workers' Cooperative Society, this tiny Ciggy finds a place in the workers' movement in Kerala.) He belonged to a downtrodden caste that had converted to Christianity several decades earlier, during his childhood years. Just before the onset of the monsoon, the duo would create small earthen mounds around the compound. This allowed rainwater to collect in the surrounding furrows, preventing it from escaping. Once the rainy season ended, they would level the mounds using their *thoomba*, a triangular-shaped spade with unusually long and thin handles made from betelnut stems.

The ploughing process brought fertile soil from deep down to the surface, and repeated ploughing enhanced the soil's fertility. Amma would then sow seeds of long beans, spinach, pumpkins, and other vegetables, striving to create a modest kitchen garden. In those days, she would serve simple yet delicious meals to the labourers, who would reciprocate by working long hours beyond their regular schedule. I would watch with envy as they ate their lunch, mixing rice with fish curry and buttermilk, shaping it into balls, and devouring them. They would sit on the floor of the sit-out, enjoying their hearty lunch from plantain leaves.

Although the nearest beach at Mundamveli was barely 3 miles from my home, I didn't see the ocean until I was 16. The sight of the sun-drenched beach, where tiny crabs scurried into small pits in the sand, and the blue sea with its endless waves leaving trails of frothy surf was captivating. We scribbled '*Kadalamma Kalli*', (The mischievous Mother Ocean), in the soft, wet sand, only for the ferocious waves to wash it away. This reinforced our childhood notion that the sea could read our language and would erase the derogatory phrase.

The small lake that flowed along our village was unnamed. At Chirackal, its free flow was halted by a barrage (*chira*), across which was a large sluice gate in the middle that allowed water to flow to the lower reaches. The bund, *pandarachira,* connected the mainland to the lush paddy fields that stretched across a vast area. Beyond this point, the lake narrowed into a small canal. I have vivid memories of a stone slab at the beginning of the embankment, engraved with "BRITISH KOCHI" with a few other vital information in small letters. Later, when the old bund was replaced with a new bridge, the stone slab was removed, and due to carelessness of the officials an artifact of historical significance was lost forever.

Bordered by a quietly flowing stream on the western edge, the village boasts of a couple of schools, an old cinema hall, a small library, a fish and grocery market, a small radio kiosk where people gathered in the evenings to listen to music and news, a few clinics and pharmacies, a post office, village temples and churches and a small mosque, a graveyard, a couple of arrack shops and a police station. The menfolk thronged the small village tea shops where they sipped 'light', 'medium' and 'strong' hot, frothy tea, some with sugar while others 'without' depending on their tastes and preferences. Some others preferred black tea, the *kattan chaya.* Village liquor shops and barber shops were beehives of activity where people hotly debated politics and freely exchanged opinions on everything. As night descended, villagers rarely ventured out, fearful of ghosts and supernatural creatures. However, a few prostitutes in the area capitalized on these deep-seated fears. Under the veil of darkness, their clients would secretly visit and then disappear before dawn, exploiting the shadows for their immoral activities.

In those simpler times a small cake of '501' bar soap was sufficient for a family to wash clothes and it would be stuck firmly on the edge of the washing stone and when worn-out a fresh piece of cake would be stuck onto the surface of the old one. Some even used '501' for bathing as well. A cake of 'Rekha' or 'Chandrika' soap, two popular and desi brands, was enough for an entire family of seven or eight to bath which they used for many days till the soap was reduced to the size of a molecule. With bathrooms a luxury, people would often bathe in nearby ponds and streams. Interestingly, women bathing in the open were treated with respect and dignity, their privacy implicitly protected by societal norms. A single piece of cloth, the ubiquitous *thorthu,* was enough for a family that they used as common towel. Personal bathing towel and bath soaps were a rarity which only a few could afford. They had few things of their own and they shared everything perhaps except the undergarments.

Most of my neighbours lacked toilets and instead used the vast, overgrown grounds as open defecation areas. In pre-dawn darkness, under the cover of trees, in the middle of wild bushes they found privacy to answer the nature's call and after the early morning ritual they cleaned themselves in nearby unused ponds. In some families, simple toilets with tin drums, known as '*paatta kakkoose*' or 'dry latrines,' were used to collect human waste. These basic sanitation facilities consisted of a tin drum placed under an open commode, allowing for manual removal and disposal of waste at regular intervals. However, this practice of manual scavenging, which was quite unhygienic and inhuman, was later stopped completely. Residents living near the river and small canals would build simple, makeshift toilets by positioning two long wooden logs parallel to each other and covering the structure with coconut thatch. On my early morning bus commute with Amma, often to visit hospitals, Willingdon Island often presented a familiar yet stark scene: men smoking beedis, women and children using the railway tracks for defecation, and people chatting as if it were a communal activity. To clean the teeth *umikkari* (burnt rice husks) mixed with salt was the norm while some used mango leaves which was separated along the mid-rib and then rolled to make an improvised brush. To clean tongue, people used *eerkkil,* the dried midrib of coconut leaflets, as tongue cleaners. In those days young women of the family depended on home-made sanitary napkins fashioned out of old clothes during their bleeding days and secretly and safely disposed of them. In those painful days women would be isolated and allowed to take rest in separate menstrual period rooms where they spent their unhappy days in exile. We used newspaper bags and paper bits to wrap groceries, while meat and fish were swaddled with *chembila,* the unusually large leaf of Colocasia. On festive occasions we decorated our homes and places of worship with *kuruthola,* the neatly cut and split coconut leaves which imparted an ethereal beauty. Food parcels and *pothychoru* were neatly wrapped in pre-heated plantain leaves.

The boys would roam freely around every nook and cranny of the village, unbridled and carefree. However, the hygiene and health conditions of these children from impoverished backgrounds were far from ideal. Many of them had persistent nasal discharge, with long streams of thick, yellowish mucus dripping down from their nostrils, glistening in the sunlight like tiny elephant tusks. As they forcefully breathed in, the mucus would momentarily disappear into their nasal cavities, only to reappear again. Scabies was also prevalent, with round, thickened skin lesions emitting a foul odour. Their parents would occasionally attempt to clean the wounds using a paste made from coconut cakes (*Thenga pinnakku*), that was believed to alleviate the skin disease. In our school, it was a common sight to see these children silently enduring their struggles. Some children also suffered from ear infections, which led to discharge from their ears. Although they cleverly managed to plug the leaking ears, the underlying infection caused a foul and unpleasant odour. Girls often had long hair infested with lice, leading to frequent scratching. Many parents turned to DDT powder to eliminate the lice. Although this treatment proved effective, parents were unaware of its detrimental impact on their children's health, as well as their own. It was indeed a hilarious sight that occasionally, middle-aged women would sit leisurely in a circle, each meticulously picking lice from the hair of the woman sitting in front of her.

I belonged to the fortunate few as we have Pears and Mysore Sandalwood soaps for bath. Nevertheless, occasionally we had to undergo the odium of the customary *thechu kuli;* an elaborate bath process when Amma would scrub my well-oiled body with a scrubber made of *incha,* (the dried bark of a tree, *Acasia caesia,* that is cut, beaten and dried to get fine fibres that is used as scrub for Ayurvedic oil bath). To remove the oil the body would be smeared with *vellila thaali,* the viscous paste made of the mucilaginous sap of *vellila, Mussaenda frondosa,* a distant cousin of colourful Mussaenda plant. She would scrub till the body pains, but at the end the whole body would be rendered clean and shiny, getting rid of the accumulated dirt. During those days, it was common to cleanse one's stomach by taking a few drops of castor oil, a health practice known as *Virechana kriya/Vayarilakkal*. This routine purging was typically carried out during holidays. By evening, we would have visited the toilet numerous times, each visit marked by the noisy, gassy, and forceful expulsion of watery stool, along with accumulated toxic waste from the intestine. The whole day, we would be confined indoors with only a *thorthu* wrapped around the waist for ease. (The *thorthu,* a ubiquitous three-foot-long piece of coarse cloth, was a quintessential part of a Malayalee's daily life. Although primarily used as a bath towel, it served as an essential accessory for various activities, ranging from cooking to religious rituals). The day-long ordeal would have left us utterly drained by evening, despite the brief respites to grab some light food whenever we weren't confined to the toilet. While talking about this ritual of purging, Suvarna, my wife, said that apart from castor oil, this cleansing process can be induced by *Triphala,* a wonderful combination of three medicinal fruits: *kadukka* (ink nut), *nellikka* (gooseberry), and *thaannikka* (beleric myrobalan). She then added as an afterthought that the loose motion can be arrested anytime by consuming buttermilk or *kanjivellom* sprinkled with a pinch of salt. Being the daughter of Dr K.K. Hypatia, a renowned Ayurvedic physician of yesteryears, Suvarna possesses many secrets of Ayurveda.

In my childhood, elderly people often passed away peacefully at home, surrounded by loved ones. As they neared their final moments, family members would bid them an emotional farewell, chanting prayers from the Ramayan and other scriptures. Among Christians, a traditional ritual involved whispering prayers in the ears of the dying or gravely ill, known as '*chevittorma,*' often followed by the last sacrament administered by a priest. (In contrast, modern times have seen a shift away from natural deaths. Instead, we often prolong the suffering of the elderly by keeping them on life-support machines, denying them a peaceful end. This can be cruel, and paradoxically, our ICUs can become torture chambers where the dying are subjected to painful medical procedures despite their impending passing).

I have a deep attachment to my birthplace and this is one of the reasons for my decision to spend my entire life here in the beautiful countryside. The lure of the mega cities was irresistible but I resisted those temptations of migrating to one of them and making a living better than what I have now. By the end of sixties, the village was on the threshold of an evolution into a small town. Cochin Municipality has been elevated to a corporation along with Kozhikode and Thiruvananthapuram. It was in mid-sixties that the export-oriented seafood industry began to transform itself into a major business and to cater to the needs of such companies, a number of shrimps peeling factories came up in every nook and cranny of the small village. A number of state-of-the-art seafood processing companies dotted the road stretching from Mattancherry to end of Jew Town Road. Companies like Abad Fisheries, K E Kesavan & Sons, Chemmeens, Indo Marine Agencies and the huge factory of Kerala Fisheries Corporation are a few among them that have completely transformed the village landscape. Youngsters who passed out from schools got employed in these companies. Prawn pulp (*chemmeen parippu*) was a toothsome and delicious seafood item made from small shrimps. The placid waters of the lake teemed with small sized *thelly chemmen*. Prawn pulp was made in a unique process where whole shrimp would be cooked in saline water, then sundried, and finally the shells would be removed by thrashing the shrimps enclosed in gunny bags. When fried in coconut oil, the prawn pulp would yield a highly delectable item of seafood. Back then it was a major item of export that was exported to countries like Burma, Cylon and Singapore. Later technologically superior preservation methods like canning and freezing were employed to preserve peeled shrimp. It provided livelihoods to hundreds of women in the locality which played a vital role in improving their socio-economic conditions. However, the pre-processing work that was a backbreaking job, was done in peeling sheds that was not a part of the factories where under inhuman conditions the women were forced to work and had taken a heavy toll on their health. Squatting on the floors of the dirty and stinky peeling sheds for long hours, they peeled and cleaned shrimp under less-than-ideal conditions, far from hygienic. The gentle summer breeze carried the smell of rotting shrimp, filling our nostrils. Sitting on their haunches their heads gently moved back and forth in rhythm as they shelled shrimp. Continued exposure to ice cold water made their palms and fingers appear wrinkled and their skin peeled off. Huge ice blocks packed in sawdust would be stacked in a corner that would be crushed into small chunks to keep shrimp cool. Once we begged for an ice piece and the supervisor, a sympathetic soul gave us a couple of pieces. We ran through the village paths in gleeful abandon, keeping the ice pieces on our heads. In the sweltering heat the ice melted away in seconds bathing us in cold water which provided instant relief. However, my joy was short lived as I was down with high fever the next day and bedridden for the following few days. To escape Amma's scolds I told an innocent lie. Those poor, illiterate women shrimp peelers were exploited by their rich bosses not only economically but even sexually harassed. The abject poverty forced them to endure all such abuses and hardships silently for the sake of their family.

Gradually labourers began rallying behind trade unions helmed by political parties. Toward the end of the seventies, many of these manufacturing companies started downing their shutters due to a variety of factors, the hegemonic attitude of the trade unions being the major reason. The working class were overly conscious of their rights and privileges that often led to strikes and agitations against the oppressive tendencies of the "bourgeoisie" management. Intimidated by the highhandedness of the labour unions and the unhealthy practice of *attimari* had their impacts on the industry. Most of the seafood companies shifted operations to nearby Aroor where cheap labour was aplenty. Labour unrest and prolonged violent protests spearheaded by trade unions forced the owners of Giovanola Binny, Madhura Company, K M P Oil Mills and Crystal Chemicals to completely wound up their operations and opted disengage themselves from continuing their businesses. All these undesirable after effects of trade unionism has discredited the once glorious position of Kochi as a thriving business hub of Kerala and has brought much ignominy to the region. A steady progress in the socio-economic conditions of the people has made them to search for better career opportunities abandoning the traditional sectors which have led to the shortage of skilled workers.

With the businesses disappearing from this area, West Kochi is slowly becoming a much sought after residential area with several high-rise apartments and individual homes scattered throughout the region. Population keeps swelling day by day. Perhaps Indian Navy is the largest holder of the residential complexes with several skyscrapers located along Fort Kochi, Mundamveli and Palluruthy. Till a few decades ago all these places were paddy fields which have been converted to residential areas. Then we had what is known as raw houses or line buildings, that brick walled, tile-roofed, unusually long buildings with several doors in the front. These doors opened to an inner world of a few small rooms. Many who did not have a house of their own dwelled in such line houses in peace and harmony. During hot summer evenings they spent their time in the spacious front courtyard basked in the golden glow of setting sun. A fine example of community living. Those line buildings with common courtyards reminded one of the *agrahaara* of Palakkad Brahmins.

The unemployed youths, who made a living by doing unskilled jobs, would often huddle under the pavement trees and embankments where they would exchange gossips and exaggerated stories. As young girls from affluent families walked by, those uncouth rural youths would often make derogatory remarks and unsolicited comments, which, surprisingly, a few of the girls seemed to relish. The village urchins were a motley crew of solipsistic slackers who enjoyed making unwarranted remarks about locals. They often displayed their machismo through vulgar behaviours. However, whenever accidents or calamities occurred in the vicinity, these same youths would incarnate as saviours and would be the first to respond and initiate rescue efforts.

Years ago, the pristine waters of Kochi's backwaters (*Kaayal*) swarmed with valuable food fish, living in abundance and feeding on small fish and waterweed. The waters were home to a variety of fish, including *Karimeen* (Pearl spot), *Pallathy* (Orange Chromid), (a miniature version of *Karimeen), Poomeen* (Milkfish), *Kanambu* (Mullet), its larger cousin *Thirutha* (Grey Mullet), as well as crabs and clams in abundance. Many people relied on subsistence fishing to make a living. However, over time, pollution, unchecked reclamation, and overfishing have brought these prized fish to the brink of extinction. The iconic Chinese fishing nets of Fort Kochi, a cultural symbol of the city, have seen dwindling catches despite a steady increase in demand.

Back then we had only three brands of cars; Ambassador, Premier Padmini, a version of Fiat, and Standard Harold, the latter being rare. However, the former reigned the streets. Taxis, as rule, were all Ambassadors painted black with their roof-tops painted yellow. Later, tourist taxis arrived, lining the streets with their sleek, single-coloured fleets, predominantly white. During this time, a few air-conditioned taxis also appeared on the roads. They had prominently written warnings: "Air-conditioned Car; No hand signal" painted in red in the rear on the boot. In the past, vehicles lacked turn signal lights. Drivers relied on hand gestures to indicate left and right turns as well as slowing down. However, air-conditioned cars with their windows kept closed denied this liberty of hand signalling. This was the need for the warning. The villagers looked at Narayan's car, the only taxi in our neighbourhood, enviously. Later Korankodath Viswanathan bought one, raising the number of Taxi cars to two. In the latter's car, I rode a couple of times, when I was taken to hospital. Though exhausted and struggling for breath, I still enjoyed the ride. In those days up to ten people comfortably travelled in an Ambassador car meant for five, each enjoying the ride through narrow, dusty, and zigzagging streets. With three passengers in the driver seat, the driver would be pushed to the edge as he struggled to shift the steering-mounted gears. The bench-type rear seat would be happily shared by five to six people. In occasions like marriage, more passengers would be accommodated by a sort of sardine-packing. Those sitting by the window, a space usually reserved for the men, would proudly rest their elbows on the open window frames, their arms folded in comfort. As the journey progressed, the car's engine would heat up, spewing hot steam from the radiator, signalling that it needed cooling. For the water-cooled engines of yesteryear, such temporary halts were the norm. During these stops, the driver would pour cold water into the radiator and leave the hood of the engine compartment open for a few minutes to allow the engine to cool down. After a brief wait, the driver would confirm that the engine had cooled sufficiently, and the journey would resume, much to the passengers' delight. This ordeal, however, did not dampen their spirits. In those days, fuel stations were scarce and far between, so taxi drivers would often carry full cans of petrol and diesel as a reserve that would be available in all fuel stations. Most cars were outdated and had either faulty or non-functioning fuel level indicators. This often resulted in the vehicle coming to an abrupt stop in the middle of the journey, frequently at busy intersections, causing inconvenience to both the driver and passengers. The driver would then emerge from the car and retrieve the fuel can from the trunk (dicky) to pour fuel into the tank and the journey would continue after the refuelling halt. Such sights were not unusual in those days. During long drives, they would keep sufficient number of such cans containing either Petrol or Diesel. I vividly remember the tall, rectangular tin cans painted green, with "Castrol", the brand of Burmah Oil Company, prominently displayed on the sides. (Back then the supply of petrol and diesel were the monopoly of foreign oil companies like Burmah Shell, Caltex, and Esso. During the Ido-Pak War of 1971, foreign owned private oil companies had refused to supply fuel to the Indian Navy and Indian Air Force at the behest of the US. This unexpected move at a critical moment has precipitated an energy crisis in India that had the potential to tilt the outcome of the war in favour of Pakistan. In retaliation, immediately after the war Mrs Indira Gandhi, the then Prime Minister, nationalised all private oil companies by forming Indian Oil Corporation (IOC), the Hindustan Petroleum Corporation (HPCL), and the Bharat Petroleum Corporation (BPCL). These companies are required to keep a minimum stock for the supply to the military as and when the need arises). Back then a car was a car. Its model, age or features hardly mattered. Ambassador, the iconic brand, was the first Indian-made car that conquered Indian streets in 1957. During its five and a half decades of existence, the car had incarnated in many versions beginning with Mark I, through Mark II, Mark III, Mark IV, Ambassador Nova and finally Ambassador Classic, each with cosmetic changes over the previous one. However, major changes like replacing steering mounted gear shift to platform gear, power-steering, power-window and air conditioning were made only in Nova. The interesting fact is that all through these six avatars, the signature round head lamps and the conspicuous tail lamps survived. The ad slogan "Cars will come, cars will go, but Ambassador is for ever" is a captivating tagline that highlighted the enduring popularity, reliability and timeless appeal of Ambassador. It implied that while other models may rise and fall, the Ambassador will remain for ever as a heritage. Until the turn of the century, no one could ever imagine that a day will come soon when Ambassador, the King of Roads, would become a part of our cherished memory. Even after the manufacture of the legendary car was ceased in 2014, many passionate customers, who had unwavering trust in the car, vainly hoped to own one. The iconic car represents an era when owning a car was considered a symbol of family pride and prestige.

Prabhat Studio of Thoppumpady was one of the oldest studios in Kochi where villagers used to take photos of the living and dead. Started in 1942, Purushothama Shenoy Brothers was a family business with a legacy of several decades and it excelled in textiles business. The fourth generation is currently running the business with the same ethics and values that their founders had established.

Nevertheless, Kochi, like other parts of the country, has its own sordid story of communal tensions. The 1960s witnessed a surge in communal tensions in Kochi, marked by a violent flare-up that left a lasting impact on the city. Communal clashes between two groups led to police firing, resulting in the loss of lives. This tragic incident tarnished Kochi's and Kerala's reputation as a citadel of communal harmony and peace. The elderly still recall those disturbing memories. Meanwhile, the Naxalite movement of the time had a significant impact in Kochi too as many youngsters joined the movement taking inspiration from the Pulpally police station attack and the subsequent events leading to the shooting of Varghese, a young Naxalite, that form part of the state's turbulent political history.

The *chappa* (token) system that was in force until mid-fifties were an inhuman way of recruiting labourers to work in the Cochin Port. The chief labour contractor called *Mooppan* would throw copper *chappa* into the middle of a waiting crowd early in the morning. The hundreds of impoverished workers would vie with each other to get hold of one, desperate for a day's work. The labourers who fought against this barbaric system of labour recruitment led to the Mattancherry police firing in mid-1950s, leading to the tragic death of three labourers.

By mid-eighties our village ceased to be a quaint village as it transformed into a small town. Since then, the transmogrification into a vibrant city was at an unimaginable pace. A demographic shift has been underway driven largely by the rapid urbanization. The situation no different from any other Indian city, the inevitable growth pains. Attracting migrant workers from across the country, this demographic change is worrisome.

Quite interestingly, West Kochi has evolved into a microcosm of India, populated by people from almost every Indian state. Resourceful people from Gujarat have made Kochi their second home long back and today the strong Gujarati community of Kochi constitutes a sizeable number. They have their own school and a college and majority are engaged in business contributing to the development of their adopted home. *Katchi Memans* are Muslims from Kutch in Gujarat who migrated to Kochi many generations ago and engaged in the business of spices and seafood. Kashmiris have carved a space for them in the landscape of Kochi and embraced the cultural heritage as many are into the trade of spices and herbs and also the famed Kashmiri shawl and other textiles. One can also see people from other states like

Tamil Nadu, Andhra, Karnataka, Maharashtra and Goa. And Jews, Parsis and Konkani Brahmins from Goa and Mangalore. They brought along not only their businesses, but also their festivals, traditions and culture. Festivals like Diwali, Pooja, Holi, Raksha Bandhan, *Akshaya Thritheeya* and their likes which are not popular celebrations in Kochi are celebrated with all their sanctity and religious fervour thanks to the influence of the north Indian population. During my childhood days *Deepavali,* as *Diwali* is known in this part of the country, was celebrated in a subdued atmosphere. The celebrations included Amma ladling coconut oil into our hairs, followed by a lavish bath early in the morning. *Aval vilayichathu,* the rice flakes mixed with molten jaggery syrup and grated coconut, formed the most important item which we ate gleefully as our *Deepavali* sweets. A few lighted *chiraat* would be kept in front of the home, that marked the culmination of the celebration of the festival of lights. However, at present *Diwali* is celebrated with the same enthusiasm and fervour as we celebrate the native festivals like Onam and Vishu, a testament to the diversity of the city. The ever-growing numbers of migrant workers from Assam, West Bengal, Bihar and the north east have brought about a vast demographic shift in the composition and dynamics of Kochi. Apart from these denizens who migrated from other Indian states, Kochi also boasts of a small Jewish community. The contributions of the tiny Jewish community are no less significant. S Samuel Koder was an illustrious Jewish businessman who owned the Cochin Electric Company, which once distributed electricity in western parts of Kochi. While the majority of the Jews have already moved to their "promised land" in Israel, only very few are actually living here. The Pardesi Synagogue, along with the Jew Street in Kochi are much sought-after tourist attractions. West Kochi is indeed a fine example of communal harmony where people belonging to different cultures, faiths, traditions and nationalities live together happily in peace and harmony. Once subjugated by foreign powers, Kochi has shed its colonial past long back, yet retaining the many architectural marvels which are part of history and the old-world charms.

Today Kochi has evolved into a thriving metropolitan city bussing with activities. Its skyscape is dotted with countless towering high-rises, crowded streets, congested traffic, clogged drains, and carelessly discarded garbage piles, typical of modern cities. The sprawling residential apartments of the Indian Navy christened Jal-Vayu Nagar has transformed the once quaint Mundamveli into a bustling urban suburb, a beehive of activities. The once familiar path that zig-zagged through the lush paddy fields are now tarred roads, surrounded by wet lands, with isolated patches of mangroves. The busy New Forty Foot Road, that connects Palluruthy with Thoppumpady, is an important arterial road today. Though planned in the early seventies, the road, that cuts through the western perimeter of our family property, became a reality only by 2000. Achan has sacrificed a considerable part of our prime land to the Cochin Corporation for the construction of the road that has significantly altered the area's social dynamics.

Around the same time, East Kochi too had undergone a great amount of transmogrification. The most notable development was the ambitious creation of Marine Drive through land reclamation extending from Rajendra Maidan in the south to the High Court in the north. The groundbreaking feat paved the way for the city's rapid transformation into a modern metropolis. Today, many high-rises along the promenade—such as the Taj Gateway Hotel, Federal Towers, numerous shopping complexes, the Water Metro jetty, and several smaller ferry stations—stand majestically on land that was once the placid waters of a lagoon teeming with aquatic life.

In my earliest memories, the road median in front of Penta Menaka used to brush shoulders with the backwaters. *Anubhavangal Paalichakal,* the classic Malayalam film starring Satyan, vividly captured the old Shanmugham Road—flanked on one side by the backwaters and on the other by landmarks like Menaka Theatre, Sridhar Theatre, Hotel Sea Lord, the Police Commissioner's Office, and Queen Mary Buildings.

Many buildings that once stood as iconic landmarks of Ernakulam city have vanished over time. Madras Café, Jos Brothers, Cochin Bakery, Menaka Theatre, Lakshman Theatre, and Hotel Terminus are just a few of the names that live on in memory.

Half a century ago, the city's main Post Office stood near the Penta Menaka shopping complex, while another functioned near MG Road close to where Alappat Jewellery now stands.

The canal running along the northern edge of Broadway was once a bustling waterway. Massive *kettuvalloms*, laden with vegetables, fruits, and groceries, would dock there, unloading their goods directly into the Ernakulam market. This market had thriving waterway links with distant towns such as Kollam, Kottappuram, Kodungalloor, and Alappuzha.

16.

Marvellous Dinnertime Talks: When Meals Were A Celebration.

Dinner time was once a rare and special occasion for the whole family to gather, relaxed and content, around the dining table. Unlike hurried breakfasts and quick lunches, dinner was a time for lively conversations, strengthening family bonds, values, and relationships. Breakfast in many families would be a lonely ritual often driven by the work time of the elders and school time of the children. Many would be hurriedly breakfasted with just a coffee or tea with some snacks. In olden days menfolk in the family would leave early after a modest breakfast to reach far off work places.

Lunch would be normally consumed either in the office or canteens by the working members while women members of the family had no particular time as they would gulp down something in between their unending household chores. During our school days we would leave to school in the morning after a quick breakfast. While my elder sister, who was in college, typically rushed through breakfast, standing on one leg while the other was bent backward, her foot resting against the wall behind her, a habitual pose that Amma would discourage. A plate in her hand with some hot *kanji* and curry, she had her breakfast quickly, dumping the half-finished food in the waste bucket. Now it's time for her bus to the college.

In those days, dinner time was a wonderful occasion when the whole family would assemble around the dining table marking the end of another arduous and eventful day. Long conversations made the dinner time quite lively and pleasant which played a crucial role in strengthening family ties, values and relationships. With no TV or mobile screens to distract us, meals provided an opportunity for face-to-face interaction, storytelling, gossips, exaggerated realities, political debates and cracking some jokes, those times were really marvellous. With no rush to finish, we talked endlessly and noisily and the relaxed conversations continued late into the night. I marvel at those fascinating occasions which reinforced family bonding, love and tenderness with a cheerful clamour.

The noisy pack of children in the family, who romped around in the forecourt would be served first. We sat around on wooden stools around an old wooden desk, what we called the dining table.

Achan, however, followed strict dining etiquette, a quality attribute which he inherited from his long service in Air Force. Even after retirement, he not only followed those table manners diligently, but enforced on us also. According to that etiquette, we were not allowed to talk while eating which robbed the pleasures of dinner talks. Talking while eating was considered bad etiquette and we were compelled to follow his rule. While we dined, only the sound of nibbling foods and the clattering of cutlery broke an otherwise silent dinner. Nevertheless, we used to have a pre-dinner chat session which was as lively and interesting as the dinner time talks, often complemented with a game of carroms in which all grown up family members took part. By late evening everyone would gather in the front courtyard. Achan, along with two elder brothers would sit on steel chairs, while Amma, my two elder sisters and myself would sit on the steps leading to the veranda. The long chats of Achan and two brothers would be related to Air Force and as Achan would share his many personal experiences with his two junior service personnel, they would listen in rapt attention. The beeps of Akasha Vani for the 9 O'clock English news bulletin signalled the end of chats and games, as Achan and my two elder brothers would sit around the transistor radio, their ears glued to the set. After the headlines, dinner would be served.

In the early nineties, following our marriage, dinner at my wife's family home was always a grand occasion. Extended family members, about a dozen in total, would gather around the large dining table, enjoying delicious meals and engaging in lively conversations that lasted long into the night. We shared gossips, half-truths, and exaggerated realities. Those were the rare occasions to share myths and realities. As the family later grew with the arrival of the next generation, this was replaced with a larger, glass-topped one. Every event, whether significant or trivial had resonated continually through our talks. Dr Hypatia, my mother-in-law, who was a renowned Ayurvedic doctor and a retired District Medical Officer (DMO), would lovingly prepare sumptuous dinners that we savoured slowly, relishing every bite and the warm company. After finishing dinner, we would continue our conversations and laughter. Once, when I suggested to my father-in-law, a soft-spoken gentleman, that he fix a lazy Susan on the dining table to ease the task of serving atop that gigantic table, he smiled approvingly.

The charm of the dinnertime conversations of the past is a memory today. We used to discuss everything ranging from food to football, spirituality to sexuality, cricket to crime stories. In those moments the family members unburdened their personal issues and emotions. Problems were discussed and solutions were found. When in trouble, the elders in the family gave wise advices and illuminated our path in life. Those casual moments enriched our life with latest news and local stories.

COVID-19 pandemic has significantly changed our lives in unimaginable ways, including the way we work. Post-COVID, many companies in the IT sector embraced the idea of work-from-home which has its positive sides and negative as well. The positive impact is that one need not rush to the office anymore in the morning, instead she can work in the security and comforts of the home. The negatives are the long work hours and too much work pressure she is forced to endure. In my family, my daughter and daughter-in-law, both work for two US based companies their work hours stretching beyond midnight, son full time engaged with his businesses, wife, a home maker, always busy with her endless household works. While we are physically close, psychologically we are miles apart, straddling different time zones and geographies.

The charm of those dinner time chats now evokes nostalgia and warmth, a memory to cherish. In such joyful dinner times where we share the pangs and pleasures of everyday life, my advice to all is to keep every electronic gadget away, switch off TV, engross in the hilarious conversation while having a hearty dinner. Take care to avoid talks about deaths, and that kind of shocking incidents, violence and accidents, talk instead about a book you love or a movie you like, plan for your child's future and find time to share some interesting incidents. This will make your nights enjoyable and carefree, particularly if you are a homebody.

The dinnertime chats of bygone days evoke a sense of nostalgia and warmth which we cannot afford anymore.

The Essem Institute and Rajan Master's Contribution.

In our youth, village youngsters aspired to gain typing skills after completing higher secondary, with some aiming for shorthand to pursue higher professions. Several typewriting institutes were available, including the renowned Essem Institute, located on the first floor of the Sree Dharma Paripalana Yogam's impressive double-storey office building. It was out of respect for his mother's wishes that he founded the institute at Palluruthy in April 1971, when he was just 21. The name of the institute, ESSEM, is derived from the initials of his father, Sankunni Menon.

A steep wooden staircase from the rear led to the institute, adjacent to a tiny tile-roofed building that functioned as Natesan Bhagavathar's music class. Rajan Master, a charismatic young principal, oversaw the institute, where students learned typing skills that were in high demand before the computer era. Many friends took typing seriously, attending classes without affecting their studies. Although I was interested in joining, my parents didn't favour it due to my asthma. Interestingly, Rajan Master later typed and bound my MSc thesis remarkably well. Since its inception in April 1971, the institute has trained hundreds of youths, equipping them for jobs in government and private sectors. Rajan Master was an exceptional teacher who dedicatedly taught typing and shorthand creating many skilled typists and stenographers. In those days, stenographers were an integral part of many offices and institutions, always ready to take down lengthy dictations verbatim. In this age of voice typing and Google translations, it is difficult to fathom the immense challenges they once endured.

In those days, most typewriters were foreign brands like *Remington, Hermes, Olivetti,* and *Underwood. Brother* and a few other brands too had their presence in Indian market. Later, other brands like *Godrej, Halda* and *Facit* entered the market. *Godrej* was the pioneer Indian company to manufacture typewriter with their iconic brand *Godrej Prima.*

Typing required a lot of patience, skill, and concentration, as correcting typos was challenging. Typing legal documents was particularly demanding, as they needed to be error-free. With the advent of electronic typewriters, editing became easier, but photocopy machines were still rare. Students relied on Rajan Master for typing copies of certificates, which he would attest with "TRUE COPY" in capital letters. Those "True Copies" were important testimonials that formed part of the documents for admission to higher classes. I enjoyed his careful diction in chaste English, delivered to students pursuing shorthand courses. His speech was marked by clarity, with well-placed pauses and stresses. The gentle touch on the keyboard produced a cacophony of clacking sounds, interspersed with the 'margin bell' signalling the end of a line, audible from a distance. Master maintained a friendly relationship with my father that was built on mutual respect and love.

During the heyday of typewriting, Rajan Master enjoyed tremendous respect and popularity in the locality. There was a gold rush of young aspirants, passionate about typewriting and shorthand. At one time, his modest institute housed as many as 80 typewriters, yet they still fell short of meeting the needs of his growing student body.

By mid-eighties when computers slowly conquered the place once monopolised by typewriters, students opted for computer courses. Naturally, the aspirants for typing started dwindling. However, Rajan Master still continues his long tradition of imparting the know-how of typewriting to the new generation with a few typewriters in his modest institute on the first floor of his residence.

During our recent chat, Master recounted all those hilarious experiences. The once familiar clack of a typewriter still be heard as one pass by his institute.

17.

Rejuvenation Baths by the River: Mother's Timeless Tales

When in a vivacious and cheerful mood, Amma would often fondly recollect her magnificent childhood years almost a century ago. During such joyful moments on many occasions, she would share stories about an eclectic childhood from the past that both fascinated and astounded me. Those lived experiences of her as a young girl in the company of *Appuppan, Ammumma* and her siblings at Pullyadath Tharavadu, her ancestral home. Amidst her hilarious storytelling, she would pause briefly to spit out a red-tinted stream of betel-stained saliva with remarkable force. With her middle and index fingers forked over her lips, she would create a small opening through which she would skilfully aim and deposit the saliva into a waiting brass spittoon (*kolamby*). Here I am telling one such story told by Amma many years ago that resonates the life and times of a halcyon period.

In the distant past, when life was modest and needs were few, my maternal grandfather, *Appuppan,* would organize a weeklong pleasure trip to Aluva each year as an annual rejuvenation exercise to escape the monotony of rustic life, especially during the unbearable heat of the hottest summer days. Amma has repeated many times her infinitely enjoyable excursion to the lap of mother nature on many occasions. With each retelling, the narrative ignited my imagination and I envisioned and envied those marvellous occasions.

Amma thus told: for the tour he (*Appuppan*) would select the wonderful landscape of Aluva along the banks of River Periyar where he would arrange a temporary accommodation for the joint family to stay and enjoy a life entirely different from the routine. For the much-anticipated journey, *Appuppan* would engage a huge *Kettu Vallom* (gigantic wooden boat). On the day of the journey, the boat would be stocked with groceries and drinking water in pots, clothes and mattresses. The picnic team numbering a dozen or more comprising the family and a servant would embark on the joyous journey in the morning.

The lengthy space in the middle of the boat would be sheltered with an arched roof made of braided bamboo mat (*panambu*) and this space was the living area where they cooked their meagre food, ate and slept undisturbed by the everyday trials. Amma told that the view from the slow-moving boat was simply captivating and was beyond explanation. The entourage included *Appuppan, Ammumma,* four uncles along with their spouses and children, *Vallyamma* and her family, Amma, and a cook—altogether numbering approximately twenty people.

The cruise that started in the morning from a non-descript ferry at Chirackal, near Amma's *tharavadu,* would slowly move forward, being caressed by the gentle breeze, through the nameless river that flowed indifferently towards the south, to Kumbalangi *kaayal,* Kaithapuzha *kaayal,* Kochi *kaayal* and finally to Periyar, the life-line of central Kerala. From there the boat would move unhurriedly through Periyar, and the journey would culminate by evening at Aluva *manappuram*. The life on the floating house, enjoying the cool and calm sea breeze being cradled by the gentle waves was a wonderful experience. The sight of palm fringed, paradisiacal river banks was simply captivating. The salubrious climate in the village along the banks of Periyar was ideal for a refreshing break from an otherwise boring village life. Living along the banks of the calm and placid Periyar was a completely rejuvenating experience. The watery ride was indeed a significant event in an otherwise unremarkable life of Amma and her extended family. They would spend their brief but enchanting days laughing, chatting, singing, and dancing in wild abandon. The huge family shrunk to itself, quite oblivious of the world outside. They lived in a cocoon, insulated from the external world. The self-guided tour proved to be a smorgasbord of experience for the family. At the end of the trip both the body and mind would be unwound and rejuvenated. As Amma concluded her story-telling, we would be transported to another world, a journey on the wings of imagination.

Each retelling by Amma seemingly added a new element to the narrative. Her explicit description reminded me of the storyline of *Nadi,* the famous Malayalam film that told the story of three Christian families spending a few days in a similar *kettu vallom* and finally and unexpectedly meeting with a tragedy. A classic movie of yester years with an emotional story line, the film is also remembered for its melodious songs scripted by Vayalar Rama Verma and composed by Devarajan Master. The middle-class opulence of Amma's family offered them the luxury.

18.

The Great Flood Of 99-
A Century of Remembrance.

A few decades ago, on a rainy afternoon, my Amma first told me the story of the Great Flood of 1924 while I was making paper boats to float in the rainwater. It was a real-life story that she and her generation had experienced and endured several decades ago.

"Long ago, during a monsoon season like this," she began, "Kerala was hit by a great flood that transformed the entire state into a water world." Amma continued her story, and I listened with rapt attention, my eyes wide open with the curiosity of a seven-year-old.

According to Amma's recollection, it was the Malayalam Era 1099, and the month was mid-*Edavam.* The rains had been heavy for days, but she still went to her school, S D P Y School, at Palluruthy in Kochi, a mile away from her home. By noon, the rain intensified, and the downpour continued relentlessly. By evening, the school ground and surrounding areas were submerged in deep water, resembling a swollen river. Amma's father, *Appuppan,* came to take her home in a small wooden canoe, and she was enthralled by the cruise through the submerged village paths. When they reached their ancestral home, an old double story building, it looked like a tiny island in the vast expanse of water.

Amma remembered that she and many neighbours took refuge in the *maalika,* the loft of their home, where they spent three days and two nights without food or water. When the rain finally subsided and the floodwaters receded, they emerged to find their village devastated, with animal carcasses, damaged buildings, and destroyed crops. The flood took a heavy toll on the village as many had lost their lives and livelihoods and faced unimaginable hardship.

My Achan shared similar experiences from his childhood years. Though we experienced a similar flood in 2018, modern technologies like advance weather warning and timely relief and rescue operations on an unprecedented scale helped us avoid a catastrophe. 2018 flood witnessed one of the largest ever rescue operations employing 40 helicopters, 31 aircraft, 182 rescue teams and 18 medical teams. In 1924, the ordeal was unimaginable, with no electricity, cooking gas, or modern amenities.

The flood, known as "*thonootty onpathile vellappokkam*" (the great flood of 1099), occurred on July 4th, 1924 and continued incessantly for two weeks, with Kerala receiving an unprecedented 3368 mm rainfall, equal to 64% of the total monsoon rainfall. The flood even affected Munnar, a hill station 1500 m above sea level, which received 4850 mm rainfall during this period. The flood destroyed the Kundala Valley Railways, the first monorail system in India, which was later converted to 2feet narrow gauge railway. It had a length of 35 Km. The flood in its rage erased Kerala's history by destroying all government records and documents available till then. Karinthirimala, a huge mountain in Munnar had vanished in the flood water without leaving a trace.

Mahatma Gandhi spearheaded relief efforts by appealing to the public to donate generously, ultimately collecting Rs. 6,000 to support those affected by the flood

Renowned Malayalam litterateur Thakazhi Sivasankara Pillai was inspired by his childhood experience of the great flood and went on to write '*Vellapokkathil*', widely regarded as one of his finest short stories

As I write this, the rain outside shows no signs of relenting. This July in 2024 marks the centennial anniversary of the Great Flood of 1924, which devastated the entire state of Kerala and brought life to a standstill for several days, leaving a trail of destruction in its wake. The flood's impact was so profound that it remains etched in the collective memory of Keralites to this day.

19.

Kaavus of Kerala: Unique Ecosystems of Their Own.

The once ubiquitous *Kaavus*, Kerala's sacred groves, are now rare sanctuaries and unlikely places of worship. These *Kaavus* stand out as unique ecosystems, rich in biodiversity and ecological balance. Unlike other temples, *Kaavus* are nestled within forest patches of varying sizes—from a few cents to several acres, as seen in the expansive Iringole *Kaavu* in Perumbavoor, near Aluva. The idols of deities are typically placed on cement platforms without roofs, leaving them exposed to the natural elements, with only a few protected within temple structures. Thus, the deities exist in harmony with Mother Nature. Dedicated primarily to various incarnations of *Nagaraja,* the serpent deity like *Ananthan, Seshan, Kambakan, Thakshakan, Kaaliyan, Sankapalan, Dhritarashtra,* and *Naga Yakshy* such as *Vaasuki*, these *Kaavus* are serene abodes where gods, plants, trees, reptiles, birds, and other creatures coexist peacefully alongside perennial water bodies. Ancient *Kaavus* symbolize the symbiosis of divinity and nature, pulsating with life. They are profound reflections of cultural ethos, traditions, beliefs, and environmental guardianship, where the natural and supernatural realms intertwine.

Kerala was once dotted with thousands of *Kaavus*. Myths and legends have been woven around them with the prime aim of protecting the forest wealth by bestowing a sacred image to them. Regrettably, many have been wantonly destroyed in recent decades to make way for development.

The fact that most *Kaavus* are privately owned and maintained without government support has left them vulnerable. Encroachment of public lands and the breakdown of the joint families in Kerala spelled doom for many sacred groves bringing their number to less than one thousand. The ecosystem of a *Kaavu,* complete with ponds and streams inhabited by frogs, fish, snakes, and other aquatic life, is supported by an array of medicinal plants, herbs, shrubs, and towering trees. The water, filtered through this rich vegetation, is believed to possess remarkable healing properties, particularly for rare skin ailments. Our ancestors revered the *Kaavus,* recognizing the ancient forests as evolved sanctuaries that have endured for centuries, and understood the imperative to preserve these ecosystems for future generations.

Kaavus of Kerala are home to hundreds of rare plants which are of tremendous ecological and religious importance. A few among them are *Nagachempakam* (Nagakesar*); Vella Pine* (White dammar); *Vella Oak* (Indian white oak*); Paala* (Indian devil Tree); *Mullilam* (Spanish Cherry); *Marotti* (Chaulmoogra tree); *Aanjili* (Wild Jack fruit*); Nagalinga Pushpam* (Cannon ball tree); *Nenmeni Vaaka* (Siris tree); *Punna* (Alexandrian Laurel); *Koovalam* (Bael tree); *Karingotta* (Niepa bark tree); *Karinochi* (Chinese Chaste tree); and plants such as *Changalam peranda* (Veldt grape) and *Sathavari* (Wild Asperagus). The entire *Kaavu* is shaded by a thick canopy, allowing beams of sunlight to gently filter through and create irregular spots on the ground.

Kaavus are associated with several festivals and rituals all of which have environmental focus and the community take care in the maintenance and conservation of the sacred groves. The usual rituals involve *Kalamezhuthu, Pulluvan pattu/sarppam pattu, Sarppabali, Ayillyam pooja* and offering of *noorum paalum* to the *Nagaraja* and *Nagayakshy.* In essence, the rituals associated with the sacred groves are rooted in spirituality, cultural expression and protection of natural habitat. We are living in an era where nature faces the ever-present threat of reckless destruction, the surviving sacred groves are reminders for the need to protect and maintain these vital components of the ecosystem from disintegration. When we destroy them, we are destroying our own cultural heritage and rich biodiversity for ever. Of late the Kerala Forest Department is extending financial assistance to temples and individual owners for the protection of the sacred groves. It is high time the government undertake a mapping exercise to document and protect the indigenous flora and fauna of our sacred groves. School students should be encouraged to embark on a bioblitz by inviting environmentalists as observers to document the biodiversity of our sacred groves.

20.

The Rich Legacy Of Malayalam Drama.

Theatre has long been a powerful tool for social transformation and spreading political messages in Kerala. The state's unique cultural diversity, shaped by its complex history and high levels of political awareness have fostered a vibrant tradition of folk and classical performing arts

Malayalam drama in fact had a unique tradition and a celebrated theatrical period. Renowned thespians like NN Pillai, V T Bhattathiripad, O Madhavan, K T Muhammed, Thoppil Bhasi, Jagathy N K Achary, Ayyappa Paniker, and their followers, all of them contributed profoundly to the evolution and development of Malayalam drama. Kerala's rich cultural landscape has witnessed the profound impact of drama on societal transformation. The play "*Ningalenne Communistaakki*" ("You Made Me a Communist") is a notable example, influencing a whole generation and contributing to the formation of the world's first democratically elected Communist government. It is about the popular uprising against oppression and caste discrimination when the majority of the downtrodden population rallied behind the Communist. The credit for this drama rests entirely with Kerala People's Arts Club, better known by its acronym KAPC which has gifted many talented actors to Malayalam cinema. At the heart of the troupe was a motley crew of creative minds. In due course KPAC has carved out a unique space for itself in the cultural milieu of Kerala. The troupe cleverly used drama as a powerful tool to take the deeply political narratives to the masses. KPAC is indeed the cultural wing of the Communist Party of India (CPI). The split in the party in 1964 led to the formation of Communist Party of India (Marxist), CPI(M). The split had its repercussions in the cultural and political landscape of Kerala. In the aftermath of the split, KPAC remained with CPI, while a few theatre personalities under O. Madhavan, who were sympathetic to the newly formed party, left KPAC and formed a new troupe, Kalidasa Kalakendram. The style of Kalidasa Kalakendram was different and it adopted a story telling method that was less overly political but socially relevant. The dramas of that era captured the harsh political realities as vividly as they did the social truths. Melodious music was an inseparable part of those dramas that were more than ornamental. Even decades later the evergreen, popular songs of KPAC dramas are still hummed by the .older generations. *'Paambukalkku maalamundu, paravakalkkaakaasamundu, manushya puthranu thalachaykan mannilidamilla'* (the snakes have their holes, the birds have the sky, but the son of man has no place to lay his head) was a favourite among beggars, who sang it in mournful tones aboard crowded town buses and at bustling street corners, keeping rhythm with their wooden *chappla katta* (castanets).

A number of professional drama troupes of the day ruled the theatre and the most famous among them apart from KPAC and Kalidasa Kalakendram were Surya Soma, Alleppey Theatres, Viswa Kerala Kala Samiti, Sangamam Theatres, Changanasserry Geedha Theatres, Vaikom Malavika Theatres, and Naataka Kalri established by Ayyappa Panikkar. The temple festivals across the state provided the best opportunities for the professional theatre groups and most of them survived on their benevolences. Several decades ago, during the fifties and sixties people in our village waited eagerly for the arrival of *Naataka Vandi,* the minibus carrying the troupe and their paraphernalia needed for lighting and stage setting. The temple festivals provided them the chance to watch dramas.

However, the dramas of Kalanilayam Drama Scope differed from the traditional dramas as they blended modern light and sound techniques together with their trademark stage setting with vanishing scenes to create the illusion of magical experience for the audience. The massive 10,000-square-foot stage dwarfed the auditorium, where around 200 talented artists and technicians poured their hearts out to create an unforgettable audio-visual experience for the audience.

I had long harboured a deep desire to watch Kalanilayam's much-acclaimed, world-famous horror drama *Raktha Rakshas,* but I was too afraid to tell my father. The play had been drawing packed audiences for the past couple of months in the city. At Kaloor—where the Reserve Bank of India building now stands—Kalanilayam maintained a permanent stage, marking their constant presence in the cultural scene.

Several of my friends had already seen the drama and shared the spine-chilling story, embellished with their own exaggerated twists and turns. Their accounts only deepened my curiosity. Further fuelling my fascination were a few articles about the play that appeared in *Mathrubhumi* and *Manorama* newspapers.

Then one day, quite unexpectedly, Achan called me over and announced his decision to take Amma and me to watch the Kalanilayam drama. I was dumbstruck—I could hardly believe my ears. I jumped with irrepressible joy. It was, as the Malayalam adage goes, "*Vaidyan kalpichathum, rogi ichichathum paalu*": what the doctor ordered and what the patient wished for were one and the same—milk. I danced with uncontained excitement.

Thus, after many months of waiting at last the most anticipated moment has come: to see *Raktha Rakshas*. It was a December evening and the sky was clear and glowing. As we entered the ground I was really surprised by the sheer size of the temporary auditorium. With its walls and sloping roofs made of thatched coconut leaves, the makeshift structure was given a magnificent makeover which was so perfect that it barely appeared as a temporary building. As we patiently waited in front of the ticket booth in a line, the queue behind us lengthened suddenly reaching up to the gate. When we entered the auditorium, my surprise was escalated by the gigantic stage which was quite larger and spacious than the auditorium. Despite the hot and humid atmosphere inside the auditorium, the ambience remained remarkably cool and comfortable. My friends warned me to be cautious as the horrendous scenes synchronised with the high-pitched sound system and matching lights would shock anyone. An eerie silence filled the air, as all sounds vanished. Finally putting an end to my anxious wait, an announcement in a sonorous and melodious voice came live. It was a brief account about Kalanilayam Drama Scope. In his magnificent and powerful voice, the narrator tracing the history of the trope was evocative about the beginning and evolution of Kalanilayam as Asia's largest drama troupe. This was followed by a brief introduction about what *Raktha Rakshas* with the spine-chilling explanation of the existence of vampires as real creatures, creating a sense of fear and wonder among the audience. As the most feared monster appeared quite unexpectedly, we shivered with fear and wonder. The story has a happy beginning but soon takes a fascinating twist and the rest of the story is in flashback mode. It is interesting to see that unlike in traditional dramas, where the music teams would be in the background, the music troupes numbering a dozen or so sat in the foreground just in front of the audience, before the stage separated from the audience by a screened partition.

The curtain-raiser of the Kalanilayam dramas was an experience that simultaneously thrilled and captivated the audience. As I watched with excitement, the much famous, invocational signature song "SALKALA DEVATHE" was played in the background. It was not just a signature song, but an inexplicable experience accompanied by dramatic lighting, smoke effects, and the slow parting of the curtain towards the sides creating an atmosphere of awe and curiosity. When the two-piece curtain, separated by two massive pillars in the middle, parted sideways along with the pillars, another huge curtain painted exquisitely came into view as the auditorium was filled with fragrance and fear. In harmony with the music the lights dimmed one by one finally plunging the hall into pitch darkness. The audience listened in rapt silence as the curtain slowly raised revealing a plane landing. People thoroughly enjoyed the customary curtain raising along with the signature song as much as or even more than the drama itself. The change of stage setting in the flash of a second is a mystery even today. As the audience winked their eyes the scenes would be changed from the palace to jungle to airport with astonishing speed. It was beyond one's imagination that too at a time when light and sound technologies were in their infancy. In those days all these stage effects, which needed concentration, perfect timing and precision, were not computer generated but done by backstage hands. Spectators were amazed by the spectacular visual treat that were beyond their imagination- moving cars, flying beds, life-size elephant standing majestically, and aeroplanes landing on the stage. As we engrossed ourselves in the drama, we were quite oblivious of the world around. When the 3-hour long drama ended we had been through many hues of emotion, horror being the dominant one, spiced up with humour and romance in the right amount. Kalanilayam dramas earned a reputation for precision, perfection and professionalism. The vampire serves as a constant presence, a recurring leitmotif that drives the narrative and underscores the entire story. After watching the play, back in school our discussion for the next several days was about the play and the amazing stage arrangement that indeed put cinema to shame. We waxed eloquently about an experience that was so unique and exciting.

Later, three times I watched the visual spectacle in three different locations and in three different decades. Each time I enjoyed the drama with the enthusiasm of a first-time viewer. It was indeed a hilarious experience.

Tail Piece.

Founded in 1963 by Kalanilayam Krishnan Nair, Kalanilayam Stage Craft scripted history as the largest permanent theatre group in Asia. Its dramas were known for their grand stage setting, technical brilliance and emotionally rich storytelling.

The passing of Krishnan Nair in 1980 dealt a significant blow to the troupe, leading to its closure, much to the dismay of drama lovers. At that time, no one could have imagined that Kalanilayam would experience a resurrection. However, this is exactly what happened when, years later in 2003, Anantha Padmanabhan, Nair's son, teamed up with Jagathy Sreekumar, the legendary actor and son of Jagathy N. K. Achary, to revive Kalanilayam. Recently the troupe is reincarnated as Aries Kalanilayam Arts & Theatre Pvt. Ltd, teaming up with Aries Group.

21.

Mending Fences: An Emotional Resonance of an Annual Tradition.

It was an annual ritual of recurring nature that mending fences all around our vast homestead. Those were the days when brick walls and iron gates were uncommon. Only very few families in the locality that belonged to the affluent had compound walls and gates to protect their homes and land. A few aristocratic families in the locality had boundary walls and roofed gateway called *Padippura*.

Every year it was a stupendous and expensive affair to mend fences which circumvented the family property. It was usually a fortnight long exercise to complete the fences that surrounded our compound.

The enviable task was carefully carried out by Krishnan Velan and his two assistants Eesy and Ousepunni. Krishnan was dark and short in stature with a muscular body. He had a large lump in his throat, that moved rhythmically when he spoke. I was concerned that the moving lump might be painful and once asked him to alleviate my doubts. He simply smiled. Krishnan spoke in a deep baritone voice that resonated in the silence. His attire consisted of a worn-out towel (*thorthu)* that fell just above his knees, secured by a wide belt crafted from betel nut spathe (*paala*). The belt's pouch contained his meagre possessions: bits of betel nut, betel leaves, and dried tobacco (*pokala*), the ingredients for betel chewing. His ankle joints had developed thick calluses due to the continuous abrasion from the wood-climber's rope, locally known as *thalappu,* which resulted from his repeated climbs up coconut palms to pluck the nuts. Ousepunni stood tall, sporting a majestic handlebar moustache with ends curved elegantly upwards. His facial feature, however, was overshadowed by an oversized *komban meesa* (a traditional Indian moustache style), which seemed out of place on his small face. He often gently caressed his gigantic whiskers. Meanwhile Eesy struggled with painful foot corns on his leg, forcing him to walk with a noticeable limp. As a prelude to the construction of fences, Amma would keep ready the thatched coconut fronds. Every month when Krishnan Velan came to pluck coconuts, he would also cut the ripe fronds. He would then separate the fronds into two equal pieces along the middle by cutting with his razor-sharp machete, the *vaakathy*.

Those cut coconut fronds would be submerged in a nearby pond for a few days to cure the leaf. The dirty pond had deep blue water which was used by many in the neighbourhood to clean their bottoms after peacefully relieving themselves among the shrubs in the pre-dawn darkness.

Two women, a mother-daughter duo, who lived a little away from our home, would come and braid the still wet fronds. Mariam and her daughter Anna were highly experienced people in thatching the fronds which they used to do with extraordinary skills.

And the coming few days the braided fronds would be dried in the sun and would be then bundled in groups of 50 and would be stacked inside the makeshift shed. This stock was hardly sufficient for mending fence and the additional fronds would be sourced from the market along with arecanut stem. The banks of the *Pattini thodu* which literally means the canal of starvation, was the place where *Ola, kavungu* and other materials for making fence were brought in huge *kettu vallom* and sold. Back then this place, near Aquinas College at Edakochi is now located, a God-forsaken place and the helmsmen of the boat which brought *Ola* had to starve in the absence of hotels and tea shop. They sarcastically named the place as *Pattini thodu* which later became *Pashni thodu.* (Many such priceless stories have been shared by my eldest brother Siva Prasad, who has a photographic memory.)

On the appointed day Krishnan accompanied by his two assistants would come by early morning. Their first task is to discard disintegrating and termite eaten old fences. This would be followed by cutting the branches of the many *pooparuthy* and *murikku* trees that line up the boundary reinforcing the fence. The thin logs would be planted in the ground along the boundary where the old fence existed. The actual job of making fence commences by making a preliminary single layer of thatching which provides the base upon which the final layer is laid. To fasten this structure, the thick outer layer of the midrib of coconut fronds called *vazhuka* would be used. The thick layer of skin when passed through fire would become flexible enough to allow them to fasten. Mending fences is an art that Krishnan had mastered and performed well.

The arecanut stem would be split longitudinally into several thin, elongated sections that would be used for reinforcing the fence. Coconut leaves would be interwoven in horizontal layers throughout, reinforced by split arecanut logs (*adakkamara vaari*) laid across and tightly bound with coir ropes. I thoroughly enjoyed the construction of the fence and I would roam around the team silently relishing the work.

It was customary for the team to have the lunch served in our home. Amma would lovingly prepare and serve rice complete with a fish curry, fish fry, a *thoran* and either *pulisserry* or *sambar* to pour over the rice. A piece of *pappadam* and *naranga achaar* would make the meal a fantastic one. As Krishnan, Eesy and Ousepunni sat in the front veranda on the floor, hot, steaming rice would be served on spread plantain leaves. I would watch with childish delight the way Krishnan ate his meal by mixing it lavishly with the gravy (*meen chaar*) and *pulisserry*, made my mouth water with saliva. (In those days Amma used to serve such simple yet delicious meals to one and all who would come for doing unskilled work as they prized the food much more than the wages they earned. For them three square meals a day was a distant dream). After lunch Krishnan had an elaborate ritual of chewing paan with all the ingredients such as betel leaves, arecanut cut into small pieces, a piece of *pokala* and *chunnambu*. Amma would share those ingredients from her prized stock well-kept inside her brass *vettila thambaalam*. While his two assistants would leisurely sit underneath the huge mango tree smoking beedis.

Ousepunni would spin army tales during the rest time after meals, stories about his brief stint as the cook in an army camp. Part real and part imagined, I would roam around them to hear his thrilling tales. When it was time to resume their work, an elated Ousepunni would wind up his half an hour chronicle of his adventurous past, the endlessly dragging tales to be continued later.

During special occasions like marriages in our family, Krishnan would make special fences using unthatched coconut leaf tips called *thunjola* in Malayalam. Constructing the *thunjuvely* required meticulous skill and patience. The *thunjola* would be carefully positioned upright and intricately interlaced to form a seamless fence in intricate pattern. This labour-intensive process was time-consuming, but the end result was breathtaking. Upon completion, the *thunjuvely* would transform the entire structure, lending it a stunning appearance. Due to its demanding nature, this beautiful and intricate lattice work was typically reserved for the front facade alone.

He continued to work until he realised, he couldn't no longer. Age and years of hard labour had taken a heavy toll on him. He worked hard in his life to eke out a living for his family.

Till late seventies such fences made of braided coconut fronds were quite common in Kerala villages and symbolised the middle-class opulence. While the wealthy had sturdy partitions, the poor often made simple separators fashioned from thin poles of *murikku* or *paruthy/poovarasu*, called *pathal* and *vaary* fence. These stakes (*pathal*) with sharpened end at the bottom were the vertically placed along the perimeter by driving into the ground at regular intervals. They formed the upright structure of the fence. The horizontal elements, usually split arecant or bamboo stems are the *vaari* that are tied horizontally in three or four rows, fastened firmly with coir ropes to create a trellis-like barrier. In some places, the thorny branches of bamboo are used to make, *mulluveli*, the thorny fence. Although this crude lattice structure offered scant privacy, it clearly marked the boundary. They also served as trellis for vines of long beans and other legumes. In a bygone period, they stood as quiet sentinels around homes, farms and gardens.

When robust brick walls and iron gates slowly replaced fences, the time consuming and expensive mending of fences became a thing of the past. When Krishnan Velan died a few decades ago, with him, his stunning craftsmanship too eclipsed forever with no one else to continue his legacy of the dying traditional craft. And same is the case with Mariam and Anna as after them there are hardly anyone to continue with the ancient legacy. They were indeed the last practitioners of their vanishing traditions.

22.

Jain Light & Sound: The Forgotten Village Sound Engineers.

Dasan and his son Jain were the only people who owned and knew the subtle nuances of light and sound systems in our village in the period of fifties to late seventies. The father-son duo was an integral part of the village life and were well appreciated for their invaluable services. No celebrations were possible without their presence and involvement. All events ranging from temple festivals to religious ceremonies and marriages were made memorable by their selfless service.

In those days, the night before a wedding ceremony would be the most celebrated time. By evening, Dasan, accompanied by Jain would reach the house where the wedding ceremony would take place. They would tie two funnel shaped horn type loudspeakers atop the nearby coconut tree in the courtyard. The grey-coloured speaker was called *Kolamby* in local language (spittoon) reminiscing its close semblance to one. In the inner side of the horn the brand name "Ahuja" would be painted prominently. The loud speaker would be then connected to an Ahuja amplifier that would be kept safely on a table in a corner of the makeshift *Pandhal*. The record player, meticulously kept inside a leather box, a couple of microphones, its stainless-steel stand and other accessories would be placed near the table.

While Jain assiduously connected the record player, loud speakers and microphones, Dasan would watch with elation, taking pride in his skilled son. While the elders would surround him in their eagerness to watch the skilled job, he never allowed children to cluster around as he feared that electric shocks might strike the clamouring kids. However, we would watch the entire arcane procedures from a safe distance. Back then electricity has not yet come in our locality and Dasan put a generator set to use as a source of electricity. A couple of tube lights and bulbs would be installed in the *Pandhal.*

Once his cautious work was complete, he would start playing records from his repository of old, melodious songs one by one. Dasan would carefully remove the vinyl record from its sturdy paper sleeve and place it on the turntable. With great care, he'd position the needle on the outer edge of the record. However, repeated use had taken its toll, leaving scratches on the surface. Occasionally, the needle would skip or get stuck, causing the same line to repeat several times much to his consternation. To the delight of the children, this quirk turned listening into a playful experience. The sound quality would be periodically interrupted by the whistling from the amplifier. He had a fascinating collection of old drama songs from the famous plays of KPAC and other popular troupes. This would be followed by popular songs from old Malayalam and Tamil films which would entertain the guests.

By 10'O clock the stock of Dasan would have exhausted. This was the occasion for the family and guests to perform their musicality. The menfolk in alcoholic stupor would continue to irritate the audience and the neighbourhood with their lacklustre and dreary songs. Their musicality would continue late into midnight much to the dismay of everyone. The loud music from the party would keep the entire neighbourhood wakerife.

During the famous temple festival of Sree Bhavaneeswara Temple, Palluruthy, Jain Light and Sounds would descend on the temple grounds a couple of days before the festival began. This time they would have a well-stocked set of loud speakers numbering a dozen or so and other accessories to cater to the requirements. The eleven-day long festivities called for more elaborate than usual requirements for the light and sound facilities which Dasan would fulfil with panache. Apart from the commonplace tube lights, the festival demanded the installation of a number of high voltage lights provided with huge aluminium shades. The three stages where many cultural events would be staged would be decorated with such lights. Gigantic mercury lamps would hang over in the *aanapanthal,* the make-shift shelter where elephants would be paraded during the Pooram. The entire path that extended from the temple to the *aanapanthal* would be illuminated with lights. He never shied away from doing his responsibilities even when he was not sure about the remuneration for his skilled work.

For the meeting of political parties too the services of Jain Light and Sound were indispensable where he would play revolutionary songs from old Malayalam drama as a prelude to the high-octane political speeches. Dasan, a pioneer in light and sound technology, had a passion for creating nuanced audio experiences and wonderful visual displays. He earned deep understanding of the complex sound amplification which he created using his archaic instruments. Dasan and his Jane Light and Sound, however, paled into insignificance with the arrival of modern-day hi-tech light and sound systems. Nevertheless, he was once the indisputable 'sound engineer' of the village and his contributions failed to find mention in the history of Palluruthy.

23.

Raghavan Vaidyar: A Traditional Ayurvedic Alchemist.

In the quaint village where once lived an ayurvedic practitioner who etched a place for himself and his name was Raghavan *Vaidyar.* His *Vydyasala* was housed in a small, unassuming tiled building attached to his home. In those days he used to prepare all the unadulterated medicines in accordance with the elaborate procedures as mentioned in the ancient texts. He never compromised in the quality of the several ingredients that were used in the preparation of his traditional *lehyam, arishtam, choornam, kashaayam* and *kuzhambu.* The unmatched quality of his medicines and his excellent diagnostic skills, both contributed to the magical healing effects of his medicines. As a young boy I loved his sweet and mildly intoxicating *Dasamoolaarishtam* though I had a strong sense of dislike for his sour and pungent kashaayam which I used to take along with *induppu* (rock salt) as *membodi.*

Back then preparations of Ayurvedic medicines were a laborious job that needed a lot of patience and attention. Extraction of the drugs from the dried bark, roots, stem and leaves called for dedication and commitment which he possessed in good measure. Sourcing the innumerable ingredients from reliable suppliers was another gruelling challenge. Yet he made his several unique products in a way that made them extremely extraordinary. He was indeed a people's doctor who believed that the physician is nothing but a tool in the hands of the Almighty and the actual healer is the God himself.

A part of his modest house was used as the laboratory cum factory where he prepared many unique products and experimented with them.

He would sit on a wooden chair with armrests and a backrest behind a wooden table. The patient would sit on a stool kept nearby at arm's reach. The patients would patiently wait on a few chairs kept along the side of the room. In his modest consulting room privacy was always a victim as the patient narrated his/her symptoms, the description would be audible to the waiting patients much to the discomfort of the narrator. More over *Vaidyar* had a habit of loudly repeating the words of his patients as if to reassure himself. This has added to the embarrassment of the patients especially women. But *Vaidyar* always remained nonchalant. My friend Obby once shared an amusing anecdote about *Vaidyar.* One day, while waiting for his turn at *Vaidyasala,* a young woman hesitantly described her symptoms to *Vaidyar.* With his signature simplicity, he naively asked, '*Edo, enthupatti*?' (What brought you here?) She whispered her response, her voice barely audible. *Vaidyar*'s eyes widened in surprise as he loudly repeated, (*thooralanalle?*),'Oh, you have a case of loose motion?' The woman's face turned pale with embarrassment, while the waiting patients struggled to stifle their giggles. *Vaidyar*'s innocent inquiry only added to the humour. 'Had you eaten anything unusual today?' he asked. The woman leaned in closer, her voice even softer, and shared her secret. *Vaidyar*'s thunderous response once again echoed in the room: 'Oh, you had jackfruit yesterday?' (*tthan innale ckakka thinnalle*?) The woman stood motionless momentarily forgetting her loose motion; her head bowed in mortification. *Vaidyar*'s artless and whimsical nature only amplified the comedic effect, leaving a lasting impression on Obby.

Ammumma, my paternal grandmother, had deep faith in the diagnostic skills and healing power Raghavan *Vaidyar.* During her sunset days when she was plagued by age related illnesses, it was *Vaidyar* who came in our home on a few occasions, examined her and prescribed medication. Draped in white spotless *mundu* and shirt, a smiling *Vaidyar* would come, always with a black handbag in his armpit and an umbrella in the other hand. *"Vallyamme enthupatti?"* (Big Amma, what's troubling you?) a beaming *Vaidyar* would ask her? As if waiting for his question, *Ammumma* would unburden her health issues, most of which were psychological. His medicine however, had a magical effect on her ailments, both real and imagined. He would suggest someone to follow him to his pharmacy, half a mile away from our home to buy medicines. Usually, it was the duty of my two elder brothers to get medicines from his pharmacy.

Remuneration was never an issue for him and for many poor people he used to provide free treatment. He never depended on modern gadgets like stethoscope, BP apparatus or thermometer. He, instead, relied on the traditional system of diagnosis involving *darsanam,* (a close observation of the patient) *sparsanam* (a gentle touch on vital body parts like forehead, stomach and wrist to feel pulse) and *chodyavali* (a volley of questions). And at the end of the lengthy process, he would diagnose the disease with astonishing accuracy. Only rarely he would prescribe the patient to prepare Ayurvedic potions like *kashaayam* at home and for which he would give detailed instructions with the various ingredients needed along with their respective quantities, the way it has to be prepared and the way it had to be consumed. Those simple, old-fashioned remedies of *Vaidyar* worked wonders and often proved more effective than modern medicines. A God-fearing soul, he firmly believed in the healing powers of Lord Dhanwanthari, the God of health and wellness. He would start his day only after paying obeisance to the deity in the nearby Dhanwanthari temple.

He was a strong film fan and never missed an opportunity to see films in the nearest Jayalaksmi Talkies amid his busy schedule.

A life dedicated to Ayurveda, he explored as much as he experimented with the traditional system and finally enriched the age-old system of health care in his own modest manner. With his passing in the early 2000s, Raghavan *Vaidyar* left an enduring legacy that his son Ambujan diligently carried forward. This legacy later evolved into a modern Ayurveda hospital renowned for its expertise in *Marma Chikitsa,* Kerala's traditional Ayurvedic massage therapy.

24.

My Re Birth: The Tale I Had to Tell.

In the early 1990s, I was midway through my career, focusing on quality assurance for seafood products destined for export. By the end of 1992, I had returned to India from Kenya, marking the end of a brief and unsuccessful stint with the Alpha Group in Nairobi. The life in the East African nation was more of an adventure where one's future depended a lot on his luck. It was an African nightmare indeed. There was no security for life and property. The Indian diaspora, who constituted a major chunk of the emigrants working in varied fields, lived under constant fear and insecurity. We were confronted by ever present threat of looting and shooting which was quite common in Nairobi of nineties. I decided to cut short my highly dissatisfying stint and come back.

On return though I joined Poyilakada Fisheries, a reputed company based in Kollam, I could not continue for long there as my failing health and recurrent asthmatic attacks forced me to leave the job.

Back in Kochi I joined the new factory of Tri Tee Seafoods, which was coming up at Palluruthy. When joined the renovation of the building was still under progress. Construction works were going on in full swing.

During these days I had contracted severe cold and chest congestion which in due course aggravated. On those days I was under the treatment of Dr Baby J Pattom, affectionately addressed as BJP, a retired government doctor with three-decade long experience in health care. A few months after its establishment, the factory was commissioned. Since it was new, I found myself shouldering a multitude of responsibilities, many of which were beyond my designated role. In my routine lab-related tasks, I was assisted by two female colleagues. My workday began promptly at nine and typically stretched until seven or seven-thirty. On certain days, it extended as late as ten.

On November 18, 1994 my chest congestion worsened and the previous night I could not sleep as I experienced shortness of breath accompanied by severe cough. Though Suvarna's father, my father-in-law brought medicine the evening before, it had little effect on me. By early morning around 5 am came Sudhan, a distant relative, in his car to take me to Jesus Hospital, Karuvelippady, near Mattancherry. He sped me to the hospital along with Suvarna and her father without wasting any time. When we reached the hospital, the day was yet to break and the OP wore a deserted look. The doctor on duty attended on me and she introduced herself as Dr Rosy and added that we were classmates in Cochin College for Pre-Degree. My condition was so bad that I was in no mood to identify an old classmate and renew an old friendship.

She administered some medicine and injections and assured me that I would be alright within a couple of hours and would be able to leave the hospital by morning. Predictably my condition improved quickly but the relief was short lived as I experienced a sudden shortness of breath. I was gasping for breath and sensing my condition Dr Rosy put me immediately on oxygen support and administered some medicines to relieve my condition. In that small and ill-equipped hospital anything beyond this was unimaginable and unprepared to handle medical emergencies. All on a sudden my condition worsened and by this time Dr Baby J Patton reached the hospital. Seeing my condition, he administered a few injections but I was not responding to those medications. Minute by minute my condition worsened which unnerved the seasoned doctor so much so that he stood still unable to think about the next course of action. It was at this critical moment that the anaesthesiologist Dr Radhakrishnan Nair came to the ICU as he had to attend on a Cecaerian operation scheduled for the day. Sensing the gravity of my condition he came to the help of Dr Pattom. From that moment onwards Dr Radhakrishnan took over the control of my critical care treatment under the guidance of Dr Pattom. I was struggling hard and Dr Pattom tried in vain to pacify me. Both the doctors and the nursing staff were dismayed by the sudden change in my condition. I asked the doctor to administer Kena Cort — a powerful corticosteroid known for its serious side effects but also its potential to provide immediate relief. It had been used on me before, during moments when conventional inhalers had failed. A visibly anxious Dr. Pattom leaned in and whispered, almost helplessly, that even Kena Cort had been given — and now, there was nothing more he could do. I turned to Dr. Radhakrishnan, searching his eyes for reassurance. His silence, and the quiet confirmation in his gaze, echoed what I already feared. As I began slipping into a coma, Dr. Pattom, his voice trembling with urgency, implored me to pray. I knew then — I was dying. The end felt near. Suddenly, as if from thin air, Bahuleyan, my eldest brother-in-law, appeared in the room. I gazed into his eyes, helpless, as he took my arms tenderly, trying to calm the storm within me.

In that fleeting moment, my mind filled with the faces I loved most: my three-year-old son, my wife, my aging Achan and Amma. My eyes slowly closed, and a thick darkness enveloped everything.

By that time, the message had gone out to our close relatives. No one – except me – realized that while one life was ending, another was being born. Like Lazarus of Bethany, I was brought back – reborn. A revenant.

What followed was nothing short of miraculous. At that critical hour, the doctors had done all they could. Modern medicine had reached its limits. Just before I lost consciousness, the last sound I heard was the trembling voice of a man of science asking me to place my faith in prayer.

Then, it felt as though I was being drawn into another realm.

The rest, as they say, is history – a story of the extraordinary, later recounted by my wife.

The horrific incident proved that prayer can perform the incredible, even reviving someone from the brink of death. My wife's heartfelt prayers had a profound impact.

In those critical moments when even the most experienced and talented doctors felt helpless, the power of prayer worked wonders. As Angus Buchan so aptly puts it, "There is power in prayer. When men work, they work. But when men pray, God works." After five critical minutes, my heart began beating again, much to the delight of the doctors and nurses surrounding me in the modest, ill-equipped ICU.

Soon, they shared the news with my wife, Suvarna, who was waiting anxiously, and our relatives. However, the doctor cautioned them that if my condition recurred, it would worsen. As a precaution, he mentioned that even if I survived, there was a risk of memory loss or paralysis, or both. This warning was meant to prepare them for the reality.

Miraculously, my wife's prayers were answered. Even 30 plus years after that shocking incident, I am still alive. During my hospital recuperation, someone asked me how I felt when I was hovering between life and death. I recalled that the last scene I saw before falling unconscious was total darkness, illuminated only by a golden Ganesh idol.

As I recounted the story of the Ganapati idol, my wife suddenly remembered a vow she had made several months earlier, during my struggle with asthma. A woman from our Kollam neighbourhood had advised Suvarna to offer Appam to Kottarakkara Ganapati, assuring her that it would bring relief from my ailment. Now, it felt as though Kottarakkara Ganapati had come to my aid, gently reminding us of the promise we had once made.

Since that miraculous day, we have visited the Kottarakkara Maha Ganapati Temple over a hundred times, offering our prayers in gratitude and devotion. Each visit feels like a reaffirmation of the boundless grace that has touched our lives—an undeniable testament to the infinite blessings of God. When science falters, faith triumphs.

25.

Brewing Memories: The Iconic Indian Coffee House Where Tradition Meets Taste.

As a young student during my days at SH College, I always looked forward to have an occasional hot frothing coffee and its signature Vegetable cutlet from the Indian Coffee House. I used to save the balance from my bus fares just to savour the flavourful coffee from Indian Coffee House, that was housed in a spacious building just across the Cochin Shipyard. When finances allowed, I indulged in the delightful cold coffee, a refreshing brew that invigorated me and provided a much-needed boost, an occasional luxury. As one enters the restaurant, a rich aroma of steaming coffee and hot masala dosa welcome you. We used to spend long hours in the serene atmosphere there over a cup of coffee as the café was not a crowded place. During our evening hangouts at ICH, the calm urban space, we would discuss a host of topics, as the turbaned waiters in white uniforms waited patiently with a smile for our orders. The waiters, resplendent in their distinctive attire, seemed from a distant era. Adorned with crown-shaped turbans and broad, crimson belts cinched around their brass-buttoned overcoats, they appeared as if they had descended from a distant planet, bringing an air of unique charm to the Indian Coffee House. The unique uniform which is both elegant and distinct dates back to the pre-independence era. It largely remained unchanged over the years and the headgear has become iconic. They set a new benchmark in treating the customers with warmth and cordiality. One of the waiters was particularly friendly to the students and a few years later I happened to meet him at the ICH inside the campus of Cochin University. With a friendly smile he approached me and renewed our friendship. He took orders only after exchanging pleasantries. To this day I greatly relish the steaming coffee, tasty parotta with egg curry and the delicious vegetable cutlet with their trademark beetroot sauce. Beetroot is a universal ingredient in the preparations of ICH, as the Cheffs lavishly use it whether in vegetable cutlet, masala dosa or vegetable curry. Renowned scholar and Malayalam critic Prof. M. Krishnan Nair sarcastically observed in his popular weekly column '*Saahithya Vaaraphalam'*, that a man's love is akin to beetroot in Indian Coffee House (ICH) cuisine - generously used in every dish without restraint. In contrast, a woman's love, he humorously noted, resembles the salt shaker at ICH: no matter how hard you shake, the salt refuses to budge, only to pour out abundantly when least expected. Prof. Krishnan Nair was a sharp-eyed linguist and sharp-tongued critic, whose literary criticism was so harsh and unforgiving that many budding writers, fearing his scathing reviews, abandoned their writing careers altogether. Even seasoned writers struggled to withstand his sharp critiques. He had a tendency to compare even the smallest aspects of literature to world classics. His skilful definitions of common Malayalam terms were often hilariously insightful. *Saahitya Vaaraphalam* of Prof. Nair was one of the most celebrated Malayalam criticisms. The weekly column introduced ordinary readers to the extraordinary world of modern literature.

It is a fact that the foods served by ICH are of the same taste, flavour, and quality irrespective of the locations thanks to a perfectly standardized recipe. During long journeys I always look out for my favourite ICH restaurant. During my brief stay away from family for a few months in Kollam, I always preferred the breakfast and dinner of ICH. Till a decade back almost all restaurants of ICH were housed in heritage buildings with tiled roofs, high wooden ceilings and thick brick walls with massive windows. Once upon a time the intellectuals, politicians and literary buffs used to throng the outlets of ICH where they engrossed in discussions munching their favoured foods, an oasis of tranquillity. Recently an ICH has come up at Kaanjiramittam, a small-town about 15 KM away from Kochi city centre. Though housed in a modern building with a contemporary architectural style, complete with a well-manicured garden and children's play area, the spacious dining hall has an endearing charm and serenity away from the din and bustle of city life.

The quality, taste and affordable pricing; these are the factors that made the foods of ICH quite popular. With a limited menu, the items are the traditional foods of India. It was March 8th, 1958 that the first ICH was opened in Kerala at Thrissur, which was the fourth in the country. It was under the leadership of renowned trade union leader A K Gopalan that the workers were united to form the India Coffee Board Worker's Co-operative Society. Today the restaurant chain has a strong presence across the nation with over 500 coffee houses, majority of them in Kerala and Bengal. The first coffee house was opened in Bombay in 1936. With simple wooden tables and matching chairs, the ICH provided an old-world charm to the guests as they enjoyed the wonderful ambience and quietude. How many know that the Yaan Martel's Booker Prize winning novel *Life of Pi* was inspired by the Indian Coffee House at Puducherry? Though ICH has a strong presence in Kerala, I often wonder the conspicuous absence of one in West Kochi, an ancient city, a thriving tourist destination.

Over the years, the ICH has evolved as a cultural landmark of Kerala. Housed in heritage buildings with capacious rooms, there is an old-world charm lingering there, the walls adorned with framed photos of its founder AKG along with legends like Mahatma Gandhi, Nehru and Indira Gandhi. There is always a nostalgic appeal. The vintage décor, the modest wooden chairs and tables and the cozy ambience are unique to ICH. The menu, apart from coffee, features a number of Soth Indian culinary delights and beverages. Sipping a marvellously flavourful cold coffee of ICH would be an incredible experience.

With an ever-changing preference of the youth, the ICHs witnessed a sharp decline in footfall in recent decades. Though the moneyed and educated yuppies experimented with expensive blends like Kopi luwak, the traditional foods served by ICH remained unchanged and stood the test of time and so are the smiling faces of waiters clad in their classic uniforms.

In bygone eras, Indian Coffee House was more than just a coffee shop. They served as vibrant platforms for intellectual discourse, fostering heated debates and discussions among academics, thinkers, and political pundits. Over steaming cups of coffee, they passionately deliberated on pressing social and political issues, shaping the narrative of our nation. Once upon a time, many revolutionary movements were born within the walls of Indian Coffee that shaped the destiny of our nation. Today as custodians of a rare culinary tradition Indian Coffee House is continuing its victory journey. ICH is more than a restaurant chain - it's a revolutionary movement with a rich history and a legacy of warmth. For Malayalees, the Indian Coffee House is more than just a café – it's an emotional experience.

26.

Dr Aboobacker Koya: The Village Doctor.

During my early childhood days in mid-sixties, the care-givers of the village were Anchal Master, a trusted Homeopath and Raghavan *Vaidyar,* the famed Ayurvedic practitioner in whom the villagers reposed immense faith and hope. Though a couple of allopathy clinics existed, people approached them only in case of medical emergencies and these clinics had very few footfalls.

It was in early seventies that a new allopathy clinic named Riyaz Clinic came into being at Palluruthy Nada, near Azhakiyakavu Bhagavathy Temple by the side of the highway. The spacious building was in fact a hotel that was repurposed into a clinic with a large waiting room, a roomy consulting area and an equally large medicine room. We came to know about the clinic from our neighbor Daakshayani and she certified that the young doctor was quite affable, accessible, and affordable too. Believing her, after a few days Amma took me to the clinic for consultation of asthma. His name was Aboobacker Koya, and the young and charming doctor was very supportive and patiently listened to my symptoms. During those days I was under the treatment of Dr Clement and only in emergency situation Amma consulted other doctors. He was one such replacement. After an elaborate examination he gave a few tablets and a violet colour tincture and advised a review after taking the initial dose for a few days. I had a semblance of relief, though the breathing trouble persisted. As advised by the doctor, Amma took me for a review on the appointed date and after a careful review he suggested to continue the same medicines for another week.

Around this time *Ammumma,* my octogenarian paternal grandmother, who stayed along with us, was almost bed-ridden and was troubled by a host of age-related ailments. When we visited for the second review, Amma explained the pathetic condition of *Ammumma* and she requested if he could pay a visit to our home to have her examined. Without second thoughts, much to the surprise of Amma, he agreed to visit and asked her to send someone to take him to our place the very next day early in the evening, before his clinic's usual consulting time.

Amma shared the incredible news to everyone in the vicinity and they received the news with a pinch of salt. Once she heard the news *Ammumma* was on cloud nine. The next day, Bahuleyan, my eldest brother-in-law arrived at the clinic at the appointed time. A waiting Dr Koya accompanied by brother-in-law, drove his black Fiat for over a Mile before parking and walking the remaining half-mile to our home. They navigated slowly through the winding village alley, my brother-in-law, carrying the Doctor's black medical toolkit- its contents included stethoscope, thermometer, BP apparatus, a tendon hammer, and other essential equipment-led the way. On the way they had to cross a couple of narrow canals that were bridged with makeshift bridges made of coconut palm stems. He crossed them carefully despite struggling and shivering. Yet he continued his journey with determination. By the time they reached, a few women from the neighbourhood had already gathered in our front courtyard to catch a glimpse of an "English" doctor.

He sat beside the bed of *Ammumma*, opened his medical case and took out his paraphernalia. He thoroughly examined *Ammuma* and gave a patient ear to the elaborate description of Amma. At the end he scribbled something in his pad and asked brother-in-law to follow him to his clinic to collect the medicine and then returned as quietly as he came. An hour later brother-in-law came back with medicines, which provided considerable relief to *Ammumma*. Amma continued to treat *Ammumma* with Dr Koya's medicine till she died a few months later. It was a blessing for her that a friendly doctor like Dr Koya volunteered to treat her and provide relief during her final days. This act of benevolence from Dr Koya became a talk of the locality and has contributed his popularity as a people's doctor, which he really was.

Later Dr Koya continued to treat me for the coming few decades. Valsala, my eldest sister had great faith in his treatment skills and she used to consult him quite often till the time he closed down Riyaz Clinic a few years ago. Whenever anyone from my family visited him, Dr Koya would curiously enquire about my well-being, such was his genuine concern for his long-time patient. Achan held Dr. Koya in high esteem, and it was he who would rush to the doctor's clinic whenever I suffered a sudden asthmatic attack or breathing difficulties. In fact, my entire family -Achan, Amma, three sisters, two brothers, my nephews and even close friends - would often visit Dr Koya on my behalf, seeking medication to alleviate my breathlessness. After a few years, he shifted his clinic to another small, nondescript building nearby, from where the clinic functioned for many decades, till the end.

Dr. Koya's treatment approach was characterized by simplicity and caution. His prescriptions typically consisted of a few essential tablets and his signature violet-coloured medicated tincture, which he confidently recommended to all. Injections were reserved for absolute necessities, and when administered, his facial expressions suggested as if he felt his patients' pain. An injection-free treatment regimen made him the favourite physician of the children and the grown-up who had trypanophobia- an extreme and irrational fear of needles and injections.

However, during my severe asthma attacks, Dr Koya wouldn't hesitate to administer corticosteroid injections for rapid relief. Patients' well-being was his first priority and he would promptly refer complex cases requiring special care to other well-equipped hospitals.

He continued to extend his selfless services to the people of Palluruthy till the pandemic forced him to close down the clinic in 2020. After a year he died, leaving precious memories about a simple doctor of a small-time town who served the people for more than five decades with unmatched dedication and compassion. Upon his passing, the community came together to pay tribute to the beloved doctor and his humble Riyaz Clinic. Heartfelt reminiscences flooded newspapers and social media, celebrating a life dedicated to serving others. Dr. Koya's legacy was incomparable: he was, indeed, the people's physician. With his compassion, deep commitment and selflessness, he belonged to a rare breed of physicians and it's unlikely we will see his likes again.

27.

Remembering Indira Gandhi: A Legend in Her Own Time.

On October 31st, 2024, the nation paid rich tributes to Indira Gandhi, one of the greatest leaders that India has ever seen, on her 40th year of assassination.

31st October,1984 was just like any other day. It was a bright sunny morning in Panaji, the capital city of Goa. Panaji is indeed a city of paradoxes where centuries old ancient churches, heritage buildings, and other structures stand side by side with modern hotels and shopping centres, a place where antiquity and modernity coexist. The atmosphere was vibrant and the sky bright and clear after several months of rains. The ambience was quiet and cosy; our mood upbeat. We were in high spirits. The girls in our group squealed with delight. We were in Goa as part of our excursion arranged for the final semester Industrial Fisheries students of the University of Cochin, where we reached a couple of days back from Bombay. The previous night we celebrated with a sumptuous dinner in a Hotel in Panaji and then we watched the Hindi Movie Coolie, the Amitab Bachan starrer in a nearby movie house. (As we sat enjoying the film, I recalled that it was during the shoot of this film, that Bachan was critically injured in a fight scene in the sets in 1982. Coincidentally, it was on the same day that S K Pottekkat, the master story teller, wanderlust writer of Malayalam literature and Jnanpith awardee, was died. Sadly, all the vernacular newspapers in Malayalam gave undue importance to the accident of Bachan, and the news of S K's passing failed to get the attention it deserved. The newspaper barons might have realised that Bachan, being a Pan-Indian actor with an international appeal, has more news value.) A few of my friends had bought Feni – the native cashew-apple brew of Goa – and secretly stashed the bottles in the girls' baggage to evade the watchful eyes of inspectors at the Goa–Karnataka border check post, as it was illegal to carry the mildly alcoholic drink outside Goa. After visiting Goa's historic Dauna Paula beach, now we were at the Head Quarters of National Institute of Oceanography (NIO). As we reached the top of the tower we had a spectacular view of the palm fringed beach below. The girls in our group giggled with excitement, while the boys stood captivated, as our guiding teacher, Dr. Kuruvilla Mathew, waited patiently in a corner. Saira, Sabita, Suhara, and Preeti were absolutely on cloud nine. Suddenly, breaking the quietude, the news reached NIO, that Prime Minister Indira Gandhi had been shot dead at her residence in New Delhi. The shocking news left us dumfound. It took some time for us to regain composure. It was as if hell broke loose. A holiday was suddenly declared for the Institute and we were urged to leave the premises at once. The city that was buzzing with life till a few minutes ago had soon been transformed into a ghost town. Shops, restaurants, and bars hurriedly downed their shutters anticipating trouble. As we walked towards the waiting van, we saw people crowding the streets, many women wailing. The soulful tintinnabulation of the nearby church bell pierced the doleful silence. We spent a day filled with shock and fear in our hotel.

By evening we boarded the government bus Kadamba Travels aiming our next destination, Mangalore. By evening the whole town wore a deserted look. Except police in every few yards the climate was one of fear and anxiety. Before the bus started, the crew were instructed not to stop unless they have to and to be cautious. They were instructed not to take any deviations or side roads to avoid road blocks.

By seven in the evening, we began our anxiously awaited journey from Panaji to Mangalore, that marked the last lap of our three-stage excursion. A few minutes after exiting the ancient city, we were waylaid by an angry mob and a few persons forcibly got into the bus. They asked the conductor whether any one of Sikh origin was among the passengers and the frightened man said no. To allay their doubt, they caught hold of the passenger list and scanned it. Finally, being satisfied themselves, they exited our bus, much to our relief, and stopped another one which was closely behind ours. But our joy was short-lived as the road ahead had many such gangs on the lookout for people of Sikh origin. The fact that the charismatic and cheerful Prime Minister was killed by her own Sikh security men made the community a soft target of the attackers. It was evident from the evening AIR bulletin that arson and violence was spreading in different parts of the country. The national capital was on the fire as several hundreds of Sikhs had been killed and their homes and shops torched in an anti-Sikh riot. On the way we were waylaid in half a dozen locations, but everywhere we escaped the wrath of the arsonists by a whisker. By mid-night as we were into Karnataka, we were woken up by the sudden braking of the bus. As we gazed out through the wind-shield, we found the road ahead of us was burning with truck tyres. The angry mob holding flambeaux disappeared into the darkness. We were gripped by panic and as we waited patiently, a few local youths cleared the burnt debris and made way for us to proceed. By the time we reached Mangalore next morning, the entire town looked like a battle field with burnt shops, vehicles with smashed window panes. Except for the hurriedly moving police vehicles the town wore a deserted appearance. Soon we checked into a modest hostel in the Mangalore town where we spent a day and a night without food. As we became hungry, we moved out searching for some food and finally had a frugal lunch from the canteen of the nearby government hospital. Next morning Dr. Kuruvilla looked helpless and spent the day with his friend, Dr. Noble – a scientist working with a central government organization – leaving us to fend for ourselves in the hostel. As hunger and frustration launched a joint assault on us, we wandered out like chickens let loose in the moonlight, searching for food.

Winding up our week-long study tour, we came back on 3rd November and as we disembarked from the train which was late by a couple of hours, the usually crowded Ernakulam South railway station wore a deserted look. A waiting police team gave us a lift in their van to the Marine Science hostel of University of Cochin located hardly a mile and a half. Huddled in the hostel, we spent one more night, still trying to recover from the shock of the gruesome murder of the one of the most illustrious and charismatic Prime Ministers of India. In the evening, there was an all-party condolence meeting at the Rajendra Maidan, in which prominent citizens and leaders representing various political parties paid rich and glowing tributes to the departed leader. It indeed, is an irony that the best protected citizen, who had been provided with foolproof security after Operation Bluestar, was assassinated by her own security guards. Indira Gandhi's security cover was often regarded as impenetrable, yet her brutal assassination starkly illustrated the adage 'the fence eating the crop,' where those entrusted with protection ultimately proved to be her deadliest betrayers. It was after her assassination that the Special Protection Group (SPG), the elite commando force responsible for the security of Prime Ministers of India and their family members, was formed in 1984 and they provide an impenetrable security shield, Suraksha *kavach* around them.

****

The year was 1979 and it was a quiet, sunny morning in May. Obby and I, we were busily revising our lessons for the impending examinations. Then suddenly Obby reminded me that by noon Indira Gandhi was coming to our home town for electioneering. We have noticed that a few days ago a stage with a high-rise platform was constructed toward the northern end of the sprawling school playground, close to the Veterinary hospital. At once we decided to have a quick visit to the meeting venue. Changed our clothes and in a few minutes, we reached the venue. By the time we arrived, a huge crowd had already gathered there braving scorching summer shine. Crowd poured in from distant places such as Kumbalangi, Panangad, Fort Kochi and Mattancherry to listen to the charismatic speech of the leader they adored. A few had already occupied the stage and in a few minutes the meeting began. Some senior leaders of the congress and its alliance partners were among the leaders seated on the podium. We were least impressed by the speeches as we were waiting to have a glimpse of our heroine. Suddenly interrupting the speech, an announcement was made that Mrs Gandhi had arrived the nearby Naval airport and in a while she would be at the meeting site. The news thrilled the waiting crowd and they started shouting slogans praising Mrs Gandhi. The police had a tough time in controlling the crowd as everyone waited for her. In a few minutes, Mrs Gandhi arrived in a heavily guarded convoy and she alighted from her car surrounded by leaders, top aides and her security personnel. She wore a light-yellow cotton saree and an oversize framed sun glasses, Mrs Gandhi had a beautiful, quiet smile. She stood out from the rest with her genteel behaviour and impressive public appearance. Though I have seen her a thousand times on newspaper pages and News Reels, the sight of her in flesh and blood enthralled me. She walked briskly to the stage accompanied by many leaders and police personnel. She outpaced them as they struggled to keep pace with her and someone ran behind her with a huge, unfurled umbrella shielding her from the scorching heat. Getting on to the stage, she welcomed the waiting crowd with folded hands and a practised smile in her characteristic style as the people burst into slogan shouting praising her. She gestured to the euphoric, slogan-shouting crowd to keep quiet, and soon a pin-drop silence descended upon the venue. This was followed by her high-octane speech in her melodious sound that electrified the mammoth gathering. She spoke quickly yet clearly, delivering a stream of words with a fast rhythm and brief pauses between points. The audience listened in rapt silence to her rapid-fire patter. The euphoria of the crowd was evident as they enthusiastically watched their favourite leader with passion and patience. As she was on a whirlwind tour, she had no time to waste. K M Chandy, a senior Congress leader, translated the English speech into Malayalam without losing the spirit of her words, carefully retaining its essence. Eapen Verghese, the Kerala Congress candidate for the Assembly election stood beside her, basked in reflected glory. Her imposing presence made him seem dwarfed. She spoke in a euphonious voice and the speech was focussed. Her voice was sweet, soft, and soothing. I still carry that image of her deeply engraved in my memory. Quite interestingly, the opposing candidate was T P Peethambaran Master of the Congress (A), her long-time colleague and close associate in the party for many decades. She said, without naming him, that the opposition candidate was a senior leader of good standing, and an honest politician. However, due to misunderstanding he is in the opposition camp. She optimistically added that let us hope that soon he would realise his mistake and come back to the parent organisation. It was the duty of everyone to defeat him and to give a huge majority to the party candidate. Throughout her brief yet thoughtful speech, she never talked ill of the opponent, not uttered a single impolite word against her political foe, a rare quality indeed. Our present leaders can learn from her. The last Parliament election in 2024 has witnessed domineering by opponents and spreading manufactured hatred, engineered gossips, and unfounded accusations. At the end, once again bidding goodbye with folded hands, she left as quickly as she came. This was my first and last glimpse of Mrs Indira Gandhi, the strong-willed, determined, stubborn and iron-fisted Prime Minister of India, who lived, fought, and died for her country.

As Prime Minister she was a remarkable woman who left her indelible footprint in the political history of India. She was indeed the strongest and most influential woman of the 20th century who played a vital role in shaping the destiny of modern India. It was her leadership that led the country to scale new heights of economic growth through economic reforms and nationalization of banks, it was she who played a key role in scripting India's foreign policy including the Non-Aligned Movement. The 1971 Bangladesh Liberation War and the Indo-Pakistan War of 1971 and the Indian emergency of 1975-1977 proved challenging periods in her political life. Many of her ideas were often considered Avant-grade. She faced complex problems of political importance with same courage and fortitude as she surmounted everyday issues in her life. For millions, she was *Amma*, and for many, *Kaali*. In her heyday, the Congress slogan was "Indira is India and India is Indira" - a phrase that epitomized the sycophancy surrounding her. However, she eventually became a victim of the very coterie that had enveloped her, led by her trusted lieutenants, including R.K. Dhawan. Later in her life, the Prime Minister's Office had been reduced to a menagerie, with advisers, sycophants, and admirers huddled around her, exploiting her influence for their own gain.

The declaration of Emergency has, beyond doubt, tarnished her image as a world leader with good reputation, a drastic measure that had taken her friends, fans and foes by surprise. The Emergency was a pusillanimous political decision, a knee-jerk reaction to the Allahabad High Court's decision to declare her election void on the grounds of electoral malpractice and to declare her opposing candidate, Raj Narain, the winner. On 25th June, 1975 after a hurriedly summoned Cabinet meeting, she advised the President to proclaim an emergency saying that "a grave emergency exists whereby the security of India is threatened by internal disturbances". In the absence of effective restraints, she unleashed a rule of terror, imprisoning leaders from all major opposition parties. Like a huntress, she hunted her opponents mercilessly, driven by an unbridled demonic fervour. Almost all opposition leaders were arrested and incarcerated under the infamous Maintenance of Internal Security Act (MISA). MISA, a much-misused weapon against political opponents, gave unbridled power to both Central and state governments to detain any person up to one year without assigning any grounds for the detention. She later ruled the nation with the arrogance of a ruthless dictator, disregarding time-tested democratic principles. Her decision, which had far-reaching implications, caught even her senior party colleagues and mentors, including Vijaya Lakshmi Pundit, off guard. She was hell-bent on retaining power and pursued it with a fiendish attitude. In declaring the Emergency, Mrs. Gandhi rode roughshod over her party colleagues with arrogant disregard. The adage coined by Lord Acton, 'Power tends to corrupt, and absolute power corrupts absolutely,' proved particularly apt in describing her authoritarian rule. The politically compelled Emergency declaration exposed the weaknesses in our Constitution, which failed to safeguard the country's democratic foundations with adequate checks and balances. The days that followed were the most turbulent in her career and in the history of independent India. Having fallen out of favour, she was ousted through the ballot in the election that immediately followed the emergency. The Janata Party government, which came to power after Indira Gandhi's crushing defeat, appointed the Justice Shah Commission in 1977 to investigate the Emergency excesses. The report revealed several human rights violations and abuse of power. The commission found that Gandhi had imposed the Emergency without consulting her cabinet colleagues, making her solely responsible for the excesses. However, it was the trials by an overzealous media that haunted her, sensationalizing the issue with exaggerated stories to unbelievable proportions. Nevertheless, the findings had no impact on her political fortune, as she returned to power in 1980 with a huge majority. The post-emergency electoral debacle made political observers believe that the Indira Gandhi era had eclipsed in Indian politics. But they proved wrong as she came back into Indian political landscape like a storm. Her resounding victory, following the downfall of the Janata Party government, was celebrated by a section of the Indian commentariat, who praised her unprecedented success. This vindicated the observation made by a political analyst who noted that Indira without power was more powerful than when she was in office. However, a minority was unkind to her, sticking to their charges of emergency excesses. To her supporters, she was a leader of incomparable prowess, while her critics viewed her victory as the return of authoritarianism. As the adage goes, "Even after the rain ceases, the trees will still keep falling" proved valid in her case. Although she was singled out for the Emergency and its many undesirable consequences, this period also witnessed an efficient government machinery in Kerala. The bureaucracy, through its dedication and hard work, provided the much-needed healing touch to the common man as it struggled to implement the 20-point programme.

At least in Kerala, the Emergency period would be remembered as one where there was no bribery, nepotism, red tape, strikes, or sloganeering, as the government machinery worked like a well-oiled machine. Government servants, who had previously acted like demigods, suddenly became servants of the people. I have never seen, either before or after the Emergency, such a people-centric system of governance.

Perhaps this was the reason why the people of Kerala voted differently and once again gave their mandate to Indira Gandhi's Congress-led alliance with a landslide victory, while the Janata Party won in the rest of the country. The Congress-led UDF won 111 out of 140 assembly seats in Kerala, making it the only state where Congress won all the seats it contested. It was Henry Kissinger, the former United States Secretary of State, who described Indira Gandhi as the "Iron Lady" a nick name that reflected her tough personality. She loved music and arts. She had an adorable friend in Shehnai maestro Ustad Bismillah Khan who shared a wonderful relationship, admiring each other.

On that cold November night, while lying sleepless in the hostel room of my friends at the University of Cochin Lake Side Campus, I once again visualized her speech and inimitable body language, truly befitting a great leader. Indeed, she was one of the greatest political leaders of our time. Today, on 31st October 2024, as we remember her on the 40th anniversary of her martyrdom, I feel a sense of loss. I relive that fateful day again and again. Had she lived, she would have changed the destiny of the nation she led and the destiny of the people she worked so hard for. She faced her biggest challenges, lowest moments and toughest fights in her life with equal courage and determination. In hindsight, I can testify that she was one of the architects of modern India who played a pivotal role in shaping the fortunes of post-colonial India and transforming it into a strong nation that what India is today. She was in fact one among the most inspirational and influential political leaders of our time, a wellspring of courage and determination. A charismatic leader who left a lasting impact on her country's history. A leader like her comes only once in a great while, like an incarnation.

I would like to conclude my tribute to the Iron Lady of India with a couple of her famous quotes:

"Even if I die in the service of the nation, I would be proud of it. Every drop of my blood will contribute to the growth of this nation and to make it strong and dynamic."

"Whenever you take a step forward, you are bound to disturb something."

(Written on the 40th death anniversary of Indira Gandhi.)

28.

The Haunted House of Old Goa.

In the seventies and eighties, most seafood export companies were located in Kochi and Kollam, offering abundant career opportunities for young professionals. However, when I received an offer from a company in Goa immediately after completing my M.Sc. in Industrial Fisheries in 1985, I was thrilled at the rare pleasure of relocating there liberating myself from the stringent rules of my disciplinarian father. My decision was also influenced by a brief study tour to Goa a few months prior, during which we visited numerous tourist attractions, sparking my interest in the location. Thus, I started my career in 1985 as a Seafood Professional at Rahul Foods (Goa), a company located a couple of miles away from Old Goa, much against the will of my ageing parents. As a raw post graduate, I was a novice in the factory. Though I had only a brief stint there it was quite interesting.

Old Goa was then a small town shrouded in colonial glory, situated about 10 miles from Panaji. The journey through the zigzagging, narrow road took us through a picturesque landscape. The road passed along the banks of River Mandovi, the life line of Goa, crucial for the state's economy and tourism, lined with many ancient buildings that stood as mute witnesses to a turbulent past.

I was new to the place having joined the new company only a few days ago. The first few days, I was put up in Hotel Sunrise, a tourism class hotel at Panaji, provided by the company, and as promised, a week later, the company arranged accommodation at Old Goa. The two-storey building was located atop a small hillock a stone's throw away from the famed church at Old Goa. The unkempt building, its ill kept surroundings and the doleful silence that enveloped the landscape created a fearsome atmosphere. The building housed four single bedroom apartments, two in each floor. The interior of the modest apartment was, however, freshly whitewashed, it had a small living room, one bedroom, kitchen and a common washroom and bath. The bedroom had a large glass-paned window that offered an unhindered view of the street below. The factory manager Daniel was quite impressed and waxed eloquently about the difficulty in getting a decent accommodation in Goa, a tourist paradise. He then added that it's my sheer luck that I could live in such a comfortable apartment.

Next day I moved into my new abode with bag and baggage. My colleagues, Dinesh and Sunny, two mischievous youngsters, accompanied me. As they were both from Kerala, I had a special kind of friendship with them, even though their posts were far below mine. The duo took great interest in my well-being. Since I was away from home for the first time, I was gripped by intense depression and haunted by nostalgia. The whole building had an awe-inspiring atmosphere, and a frightening silence descended on it. However, I liked the new house as my part of the building was freshly painted, giving it a new look. The small corridor led to the doors of the two flats on opposite sides, with a staircase at the farther end leading to the upper floor.

The house was furnished with a few fresh pieces of furniture that included a wooden cot, a bed, a small steel table with wooden top, a couple of chairs and other minimal items that were needed for a bachelor to sustain himself. On my first day in the newly arranged apartment Dinesh kept company till late in the night and left after boosting my level of courage. Since I was the lone occupant in a huge, dilapidated building with no one around he was seemingly worried though I was not. That night turned out to be my first night alone, that too in an unknown, faraway place.

The first few days were spent organizing myself stoically in the new house and totally unfamiliar surroundings. I got up early the next morning, had a hurried breakfast, and left for the office on a rental bike (back then bike taxis were the only mode of transport available in Old Goa for commuting short distances. Those bikers would accommodate 3-4 passengers on a bike, women often sandwiched between the driver and the pillion rider in the rear. Since mine was a company-paid taxi, I enjoyed a royal ride as the lone rider). I returned in the evening, completely exhausted after a hectic day. This became my routine for the coming several days.

On my first morning in the new apartment, I was greeted by a dry faucet. Worried that I had to reach the office after a quick shower, I walked down to the house across the road and requested the middle-aged auntie for a bucket of water. The perplexed woman looked at me with wonder and awe, handed me a trough with an attached coir rope, and retreated to the interior of the house, as if I were a creature from another planet. A middle-aged, short, bare-chested, pot-bellied man in half pants, seems to be her husband, emerged from inside. Though I tried to strike a conversation with him, he too kept away from me for obscure reasons. In the nights that followed, I stood by the open window overlooking the main road and to alleviate loneliness and fear, I would loudly sing old Malayalam songs. It was by eight o clock in the night that the fear began to creep into my mind and that would soon peak. The calming quiet of the isolated building was awful enough to make me uneasy and anxious. The fading evening light cast a crepuscular sorrow—a quiet melancholy deepening with the encroaching shadows. The haunting twilight mood. At night, when I was alone, a strange sense of fear and alienation would settle over me. In an attempt to shake off my fears, I would loudly sing "*Ekanthathayude apaaratheeram,*" (the infinite seashore of solitude) a haunting song from *Bhargavi Nilayam,* the first Malayalam horror movie scripted by the legendary writer Vaikom Muhammed Basheer based on his story "Neela Velicham". Ironically, the song only intensified my fear, leaving me even more unsettled. Passersby, mostly labourers and staff from the nearby ICAR Ela farm, would glance curiously at the open window from which my voice echoed with a mixed expression of awe and surprise. Unfazed by their behaviour I would continue my late-night musical performance. Eventually, I would seek refuge under the blanket, wrapping myself tightly from head to toe, my eyes shut tight in an attempt to escape the frightening loneliness. But still I could not figure out why the neighbours were looking at me with the kind of bewilderment.

Since my food choices were limited and those were scarce in the locality I struggled to get homely meals. At last, I began my first ever culinary adventure. As part of my self-cooking journey, I picked up a kerosene stove, a classic wooden rolling board and pin, and just the bare essentials in utensils—minimalist, but just enough to cook something delicious. My first culinary attempts turned out to be messy disasters. Beena, my niece, who was staying at Panaji where she worked as an Engineer with Military Engineering Service, came one Sunday morning along with Teresa, her bosom friend and gave me a class on fundamentals of cooking like making chapati, dal, and simple cuisine. Thanks to her culinary classes, I learnt the basic skill of making chapati and dhal, wonderful combination.

A couple of days after shifting to the new home, one evening in the afterhours I went straight to the city with the intention of getting a copy of the English newspaper apart from meeting Beena. After a brief chat with Beena in her hostel, I had a cup of coffee and a plate of hot Masala Dosa from the famed Kamath Restaurant, that was located on the top floor of Panaji bus terminal. The restaurant offered a picturesque view of the ancient city and River Mondovi- the sight of huge barges laden with iron ore, moving lazily through the river was simply superb. The bus station was indeed a round double storied building and the waiting buses to different locations were parked all around the unique structure in order. The capital city of Goa was well connected with public transportation with rest of the state and neighbouring states of Maharashtra and Karnataka. I returned to Old Goa a couple of hour later. As I alighted from the bus at the Old Goa bus stop on a winter evening in 1985, the entire town looked desolate and lonely. The centuries-old Basilica of Bom Jesus stood basking in the glow from lamps hanging from posts. I took the right path where the road bifurcated and walked past the Muje Jesus provision shop and a few houses, whose visitor rooms had been repurposed into mini bars where middle aged Goan women clothed in western outfits served cheap liquor and love. Local youths and backpackers from distant locations frequented those "home bars," getting intoxicated. When I left in the early evening, the small town was bustling with visitors wandering through the streets of this ancient town. But quite strangely now the town was deserted and as I walked, I noticed that all the houses by the road were locked from inside with dim lights shedding a faint glow in their open veranda. Music could be heard flowing from inside. This was quite new to me as I was used to a life back in my hometown in Kochi where people would withdraw to their homes only at bedtime late in the night. My apartment looked like a ghost house in the darkness. A deadly silence enveloped the building and its surroundings. A sudden, inexplicable fear gripped me as I walked up. The crumbling sound of the dry leaves which formed a thick layer of carpet, heightened my fear. As I was entering my apartment trying to get over my fear, I noticed a huge black dog with a long tail, its eyes sparkling in the darkness, standing on the way. The beast looked like one that had come out of a Hollywood horror movie. Suddenly a strange fear overpowered me. Dumbfounded, I walked effortfully into the building, switched on the bulb in the corridor, unlocked the door, rushed into the room and hurriedly closed the door behind with a bang. I was breathless for a moment as I gasped for air.

A few days later on one night the dog appeared again as I was spreading wet laundry on the clothesline in the dilapidated work area, this time it came from the neighbouring vacant plot through the gaping hole in the boundary wall. She stood up there for some time like a sentinel and then disappeared. A few more times I spotted her in the yard. Once I offered her some food but she left without eating it and this has surprised me. She never tried to harm me, barked or howled unlike other dogs, instead gazed at me as if the creature wanted to convey something to me. However, I didn't give much attention to the animal.

A few weeks later, Chandra Sekhar Joshy, a young man from Ratnagiri, joined the factory as my assistant. I happily invited him to my apartment, and his presence provided some respite from the severe loneliness and homesickness I had been experiencing, though I couldn't get along well with him for long.

During those days I derived a peculiar pleasure from visiting abandoned churches with mysterious histories that were too many in the locality. Babu and Xavier joined me on these adventurous excursions through deserted villages and hillocks. One such journey took us to a church perched atop a steep hill, far from the Basilica, which was only opened for worship once a year. According to local lore, the adjacent monastery was once home to a saint who embarked on a long, arduous journey that took him through Karnataka and Kerala, ultimately ending in Sri Lanka. With no other soul around apart from us, the lonely atmosphere was really frightening. The church door was closed from outside, but the nearby dilapidated building was kept open. The sight of a historical structure in ruins pained me. Together we surveyed the building and its surroundings before we left. Our strange quirk took us to many such lesser-known and obscure locations. We experienced a kind of wild pleasure when we visited such old, lonely, and deserted churches. The pleasure of wandering through uncharted places as an unhurried observer exploring the unknown was inexplicable. During those silent peregrinations, I found rare joy in the mystery of the unknown.

Around this time, my skin infection due to an allergy worsened. Asthma and skin allergy proved to be a double whammy in my life: as one subsided, the other intensified. After discussing it with Achan, I decided to resign to continue my treatment back home by Dr Gopalakrishnan, the eminent skin specialist of Kochi. Thus, after seven months, I resigned from Rahul Foods, much to the dismay of Roland David, its proprietor.

As I packed my baggage, Dinesh arrived to help me to box my belongings. Before bidding a final farewell to what had been my home for the past few months, I took a walk around the apartment. Dinesh, who followed me, said with a mischievous smile, "Venu, since you're leaving here forever, shall I tell you something about this building?" I looked at him, bewildered, as he continued, "you know? the previous occupants of the four apartments were a group of girls from Kerala. In this house, in the very room where you slept, a 25-year-old girl named Padmini committed suicide by hanging from the fan a few years ago. Since then, no one was willing to occupy the building, and it remained unoccupied for a long time, like a haunted house. Manager Daniel instructed me not to reveal this story to you, so I kept it a secret until now."

I was shell-shocked, unable to speak for a while as my mouth went dry. Slowly regaining my composure, I stepped out and searched the courtyard for the huge black Alsatian dog that frequented the place, but she was nowhere to be seen.

As I stepped into the waiting car, my curiosity prompted me to ask Dinesh more about Padmini and the incidents that led to her suicide. According to Dinesh, Padmini worked in a shrimp processing factory with many other girls of her age under a Keralite labour contractor, and they were housed in the four apartments where I lived. Cheated by her loved one, she became pregnant. When he refused to accept her, the humiliation became too much to bear, leading to her tragic demise.

I suddenly realized why the auntie who stayed across the apartment looked at me with a mixed emotion of awe and astonishment and why the passersby gazed at me in bewilderment as I sang "*Eekanthathayude apaaratheeram*".

A mysterious gloom seemed to fill the building; a deadly silence enveloped the surroundings even in broad daylight. Though I was alone, I was often overcome with a rare sense of felicity. During my brief stay, I was never disturbed by the invisible spirit that the local people feared. Instead, the gigantic black dog served as a watchful companion. On those lonely nights, when I sang old Malayalam melodies, the spirit might have enjoyed them, perhaps even caressing me as a gentle breeze as a token of its appreciation.

As I sat in the car, immersed in thought, the vehicle sped past the Basilica of Old Goa, and many other ancient churches. Throughout the hour-long journey to the airport, I couldn't help but think about the black beast that haunted the premises of my home. Was the animal a personification of the wandering spirit of Padmini? Growing up, I was captivated by the ghost stories my brother Rajiv Chettan shared with me while he was pursuing his Pre-Degree studies in the early sixties. Our neighbour Sivan's paranormal experiences also added to the eerie tales. According to village lore, the spirits of those who met with accidental or self-inflicted deaths would roam restlessly. However, in a surprising departure from this belief, Padmini's spirit, despite its tragic history, left me unharmed. I remain grateful to her spirit for this kindness, just as I appreciate Dinesh's and Daniel's decision in keeping the secret from me. Memories galore.

Post Script.

With its lush greenery, clear blue skies, turquoise waters, charming, serene, and paradisiacal beaches, palm fringed canals and several fascinating historical monuments, Goa, the smallest Indian state is a remarkable landscape, a traveller's paradise. I have always been drawn to the rich culture and legacy of Goa, the tiny coastal state with a storied past. It's interesting to note that this tiny landscape, home to several famous beaches and centuries-old churches and monuments, was part of the Portuguese empire for a long time. Among them the Basilica of Bom Jesus has a special place, the centuries-old Basilica sported an ancient look on the exterior, but the interior was bright, and an unusual radiance exuded from the altar. The Basilica is famed as the place where the sacred relics of St Francis Xavier, considered as the Patron of Goa, is kept. People from different faiths and different geographies throng this ancient church to see the Sacred relics of "Goencho Saib". It was on 18th June,1946, that the first Goa Liberation Movement started by socialist leader Ram Manohar Lohia and Dr Julias Menezes and the day is observed every year as *Kranti Din*. The main arterial road of Panaji is named 18th June Road to commemorate Goa Revolution. Even after India gained independence in 1947, the Portuguese colonial rulers refused to leave the land they had built over centuries, (long 451 years, from 1510 to 1961). Finally, on December 19, 1961, the Indian Army forcibly took possession of the land, and Goa, along with Daman and Diu, was officially integrated into India. This historic day is celebrated annually as Goa Liberation Day on December 19. The Union Territory was elevated to statehood on May 30,

1987. Goa gained international recognition when it hosted the Commonwealth Heads of Government Meeting (CHOGM) in 1983. The event significantly boosted the tourism industry, catapulting the state to an enviable position as a major tourist destination. Since 2004, Goa has been the permanent venue of the prestigious International Film Festival of India (IFFI).

29.

On Books Read, Unread, And Everything In Between.

My study would always be cluttered with messy piles of unread books and unfinished writings. This has been my habit for decades. During my student days at school and college, Amma would clean the garbage once in a while. After marriage my wife has willingly taken over the thankless responsibility. In the evening, back from office, looking at the clean table I would seethe with anger and shout at my wife in frustration. Poor lady she doesn't know what is what and she made a mess of my messy desk. Recently my daughter had taken over the task.

Recently I developed the habit of buying books by getting myself attracted to the book reviews in *The Hindu* and *Frontline*, of course the appealing cover also influenced my purchasing decision. Online shopping has made the exercise easier and from the comfort of my home I select favourite books of my choice and place order. This has negated the need for me to travel to the bookstore, the nearest one a few miles away from my home. However, the online purchases can never substitute the thrilling experience of visiting a book store and browsing through the attractively and orderly stacked fragrant books.

On special occasions like my birthday, wedding anniversary and festivals like Onam, my wife, children and nephews and nieces used to gift me apparels, pens, leather wallets, and similar gifts for everyday use. Over the years this has added to my ever-increasing inventory of clothes so much that I struggle to keep up them in good stead. Occasionally I reduce the mounting pile of clothes by gifting them to orphanages.

A few days before my 60th birthday, anticipating a huge inflow of gifts, I appealed to my children and siblings not to bring any more clothes and if they genuinely wanted to give a gift, I suggested a book would be the perfect gift. Quite unexpectedly, for my birthday my niece Beena presented me with a copy of *Pride, Prejudice and Punditry* by Shashi Tharoor, a book I long desired to read and another relative too gifted me a book along with branded shirts. For my 63rd birth anniversary in November,2024, my niece Binu surprised me with a copy of *A Wonderland of Words* again by Shashi Tharoor, a book that delves deep into the wonderland of English language. My humble request has ended up as double trouble for them.

Now I have close to 500 books in my bookshelf that adorn my modest library, mostly English books comprising fiction and non-fiction. This is exclusive of a fairly good collection of journals and magazines like *National Geographic, Scientific American, Readers Digest* and *Frontline.* Trade journals on fisheries which I have been subscribing for the past few decades had accumulated to occupy a considerable portion of my study room. As a solution to this issue, a few years back I gifted a few cartons full of trade journals and magazines to the School of Industrial Fisheries library. This act of benevolence has a thinning effect on my ever-growing collection of books and periodicals.

Tsundoku is a Japanese term that is used to describe the growing pile of unread books. It also means the habit of buying books by book worms but never read them. The mere pleasure of owning books prompt them into buying new books and adding them to the growing collection.

During my adolescent years, when I had time to read, I was cash strapped, now I have enough money to spend but time to read has shrunk. This is one of the many paradoxes of life. I admit that I am a slow reader. Every now and then I would pause momentarily, reflect on what I have read, sometimes I would be transported to an imaginary world. Some sentences and paragraphs that I find interesting or touching, I would reread those portions and then continue reading. Recently I took more than 5 months to complete the 700 plus page captivating novel *Covenant of Water* by Abraham Varghese. The novelist might have taken less than this time to complete such a vast novel. Even at this ripe age I relish the mesmerizing scent of new books and in that sense, I have strong *Bibliosmia,* the pleasure derived from inhaling the aroma of books.

During my high school days, I devoured the novels of S.K. Pottekkatt, M.T. Vasudevan Nair, Uroob, Takazhi, Vaikom Muhammed Basheer, and M. Mukundan with great passion and unfathomable interest. It was during my 8th grade that I read *Oru Desathinte Katha,* the masterpiece of S.K. Pottekkatt, a renowned storyteller and travelogue writer in Malayalam literature. The novel took several days to finish, and as I slowly navigated through its impressive narrative, the rustic charm of Athiranippadom, the fictional landscape and its fascinating history came alive in my teenage imagination. Characters like Sreedharan, Basra Kunjappu, Njandu Govindan, Kittan Poojari, Thadichi Kungichi Amma, her brother Kanari, and Krishnan Master, along with the night travellers of the village (*supper sarkkeetu sangham*), left an indelible mark. Years later, when the novel won the

Jnanpith Award, I re-read it. However, the characters that had once captivated me seemed less impressive. Perhaps the hectic college life and its demanding syllabus had dulled my imaginative powers. It was with the same enthusiasm that I later read *Mayyazhipuzhayude Theerangalil*, the magnum opus of M. Mukundan, followed by *Smaraka Silakal* (*Memorial Stones*) by Punathil Kunjabdulla, and, a few years later, *Daivathinte Vikruthikal* (*God's Mischief*), another classic by Mukundan, which was serialized in *Kalakaumudi* weekly. In fact, *Kalakaumudi* had published several modern classics, including *Randamoozham* by M. T. Vasudevan Nair and *Parinaamam* (Evolution) by M. P. Narayana Pillai—his only novel, the rest of his works being short stories. When the English translation of *Randamoozham* was released as *The Lone Warrior*, I quickly got a copy. But it didn't evoke the same joy or emotional depth I had experienced in Malayalam. *Paleri Manikyam: Oru Pathira Kolapathakathinte Katha* by T. P. Rajeevan stood out for its unusual narrative style, cantering on a murder and the ensuing complexities. However, despite winning several awards, (Mammootty has won several awards, including the State Award for Best Actor, for his sterling performance portraying three entirely distinct characters—one of them being his memorable role as Murikkumkunnath Ahamed Haji.), the cinematic adaptation didn't quite live up to the layered storytelling of the novel.

Ettamathe Mothiram, the autobiography of veteran media reporter and influential media baron K.M. Mathew, was an engaging read that I savoured over the course of a week. With its many twists and turns, the narrative unfolds not just as the story of Mathew himself, but also as a compelling chronicle of Kerala's evolution. I later came across its English translation, *The Eighth Ring,* which proved to be just as captivating as the original Malayalam version, as it preserved the soul of the original. The book masterfully traces Kerala's socio-political and cultural evolution through the eyes of someone who didn't just witness history, but helped shape it.

A couple of years ago, Dr. P.X. Tomy—my closest friend and family physician for over two and a half decades—published *Pratyāsayude Padavukal,* his autobiography: a true rags-to-riches story. This remarkable book recounts the extraordinary journey of an orphaned village boy, born into the humblest of circumstances, who rose to become a doctor of modern medicine. I thoroughly enjoyed reading it—it's a wondrous voyage through memories, filled with resilience, inspiration, and quiet triumphs. Dr. Tomy, who treated his patients with a tender blend of medicine and compassion, passed away just a few months after the long-awaited launch of his book. The memories of this gentle, endearing, and soft-spoken doctor—and his humble Jeevan Clinic—remain deeply etched in my heart.

In college, a friend enthusiastically recommended a book he had read, *Vashalan* (The Spoiled Brat), a novel by Pamman, a Malayalam novelist known for his provocative narratives. He regaled his classmates with explicit details, embellished with his own fanciful additions. Soon, a long queue formed in the library, eager to find the novel that had by then gained notoriety. Sensing the mood, the librarian, a witty man, wisely withdrew the novel from circulation, disappointing many prospective readers.

Once, during my adolescent years, I accidently caught hold of a copy of Nancy Friday's *My Secret Garden,* a best seller that explores female sexuality through fantasies, from the public library. The exaggerated and explicit details of women's fantasies had a whimsical charm and I greedily read and greatly enjoyed the book. Later I secretly shared the book with my closest friend who devoured it in two days. Such was the influence of the book on our young minds that fired our teenage reveries to a new level.

Recent years have reignited my passion for literature and this has made me to keep my books on Fisheries and related topics, the subject in which I'm specialized, to the back burner. With hardly any space for new books, my bookshelves are already full, bursting at the seams. Despite this, the bibliophile in me never permits me to gift a few of them to libraries. Nevertheless, I recently donated a few books, though hesitantly to a library run by a cultural institution.

I have lost a few marvellous books from my prized collection as the close friends who borrowed them failed to return them. Among my lost possessions are *The Maximum City*, a stunning narrative on Mumbai by Suketu Mehta and *Lanthan Batheriyile Luthiyinakal*, (Litanies of Dutch Battery), a timeless masterpiece by N S Madhavan.

In bygone years, most books boasted unembellished and prosaic covers, yet they were rich in content, making for magnificent reads. However, these days, books often have marvellously designed covers, although in many cases, the contents are average, mediocre, or run-of-the-mill. As the idiom aptly puts it, "never judge a book by its cover," for an attractive cover may misrepresent the contents it holds.

Digital devices like e-books, Kindles, and audiobooks are poor substitutes for print books, as they cannot replicate the unique reading experience and pleasure offered by physical books. Furthermore, our growing reliance on digital reading has had a detrimental impact on the attention span of younger generations. In the past, attention spans were significantly longer, averaging around 40 minutes – a duration reflected in the traditional 40-minute school period. However, this duration has plummeted to just 12 seconds in 2000 and a mere 8.25 seconds in 2023. Interestingly, goldfish now surpass humans in attention span, with an average of 9 seconds – a sobering comparison.

"What on earth could be more luxurious than a sofa, a book, and a cup of coffee?"

-Anthony Trollope.

There is only one thing that could replace a book: the next book.

--Unknown.

There is no friend as loyal as a book.

-Earnest Hemingway.

To read without reflecting is like eating without digesting.

---Edmund Burke (1729-1797)

A reader lives a thousand lives before he dies. The man who never reads lives only one.

— George R.R. Martin

30.

Sabarimala Pilgrimage: A Pilgrimage to the Lap of Nature

It was in late seventies that I had the golden opportunity to visit and pray at the world-renowned Lord Ayyappa temple at Sabarimala. This once-in-a-lifetime experience was a fulfilment of a vow (*nercha*) Amma had made when I was troubled by asthma. When the persistent attacks became so frequent that I struggled to continue my studies, Amma vowed that when my asthma subsided and I could lead a healthy life, she would send me to Sabarimala.

It was to fulfil her "*nercha*", the votive, that on a winter morning in December, I embarked on my first-ever pilgrimage to the hilly shrine in the late seventies. My uncle Raman guided me through the arduous forest journey. As a prelude to the journey, I underwent mandala *vrutam* lasting 41 days, abstaining from non-vegetarian meals and subsisting on frugal vegetarian meals. It's to prepare the body and mind for the arduous trek that devotees undergo the 41-day-long pious observance, where they renounce beloved foods and other worldly comforts, observing strict celibacy.

On the day of our pilgrimage, I visited the Sree Bhavaneeswara temple in the morning, accompanied by Amma and Achan. We performed the ritualistic "*kettunira,*" filling small cloth bags with rice, *aval,* and *malar* amid chanting of "*saranam vili.*" The priest guided me through the nuances of the sacred practices. This was followed by "*mudra nirakkal,*" the custom of filling ghee inside a clean, de-husked coconut, tightly sealed with cork and sealing wax. The coconut was then stuffed into a large cloth bag with two equal parts, the "*irumudi.*"

In this wonderful journey we joined a large group of pilgrims from our locality and started the journey early in the morning. Along the way, we visited ancient temples, including the Vaikom Mahadevar temple and the Ettumanoor temple. I sat by the window, silently enjoying the scenic landscape while others in the group vocally and endlessly chanted "*Swamiye saram Ayyappo.*" By afternoon, we reached the famed Erumeli Sastha temple, where we were greeted by the "*Petta thullal,*" a customary dance in a frenzied mood. As a "*Kanni Ayyappan,* " *Ammavan* suggested I join the crowd, but I was too shy to participate. Instead, I politely declined his suggestion.

After offering prayers at the Erumeli temple and visiting the nearby Vaavar Mosque, dedicated to Vaavar, the bosom friend of Ayyappa, we continued our journey to Pamba, traveling through the narrow, zigzagging mountainous path. We reached Pamba after sunset and disembarked from the bus. A temporary wooden bridge connected the two sides of the river and beneath it, Pamba River was flowing quietly through the valley. My classmate Murali once told me about *Pamba Vilakku,* a ritual of floating innumerable lighted lamps in pieces of *vazha pola,* the outer sheath of plantain stem, which he witnessed during his visit. *Pamba Vilakku* is a once-a-year event that falls on the last day of the Malayalam month of *Dhanu*. Devotees celebrate the occasion by lighting handmade lamps that float on the River Pamba. These unique lamps resemble small towers, crafted from bamboo reeds and plantain stems. Those who have witnessed the spectacular display of floating lamps on the river describe it as a breathtakingly splendid and magnificent sight. Luck has eluded me as I could not witness this spectacular annual event, that formed a fantastic part of the traditional Sabarimala pilgrimage.

Following a brief holy dip in Pamba, we began our climb through the woods, navigating the stone-laden forest path. I was told that we had to trek for almost 3 to 3.5 hours to reach the "*sannidhanam,*" as this was the shortest route. This new knowledge unnerved me, as I worried whether my breathing problem would resurface.

During the long trek, while climbing sharp peaks, I struggled for breath. A few elderly women in the group had similar experiences. *Periyaswamy*, the group leader, suggested that the group take a rest for a few minutes after each climb. At one point, *Periyaswamy* announced that we had reached Appachimedu, a historically significant place related to the legend of Lord Ayyappa. Appachimedu is believed to be the abode of forest spirits or divine sentinels who protect the sacred path to Lord Ayyappa's shrine. Pilgrims often pause here to offer prayers, acknowledging these unseen guardians before proceeding. Periyaswamy instructed us to perform the ritual of throwing *Appam* into the gorge below. I had kept a few rice balls sweetened with jaggery, the *Avalosunda,* ready for the ritual and threw them one by one into the deep chasm. In the pitch darkness, I couldn't see anything beyond the edge of the precipice where we stood.

We continued our trek until we reached the *Saramkuthy Aaal,* a peepal tree. There, I was instructed by *Ammavan* to buy an arrow from a nearby shack run by the Devaswam Board and stick it onto the banyan tree. As I followed his instructions, I noticed innumerable such arrows already stuck in the tree. According to legend, every *Kanni Ayyappa* had to perform this ritual, and every day *Malikappurathamma,* the female deity and fiancée of Ayyappa, would visit the *Saramkuthy* to check if any arrows had been stuck. This symbolic gesture announces the arrival of *Kanni Ayyappas,* as Lord Ayyappa had promised *Malikappuram* that he would marry the day no *Kanni Ayyappa* climbed the hill. As a *Nitya Brahmachari,* he knew well that this day would never come in his life, and he could continue his celibacy undisturbed.

At the end of the arduous climb, we reached the courtyard of the temple, the *Sannidhhanam,* where there were several make-shift shelters made of thatched coconut leaves. The *Periyaswamy* informed us that we would have *darshan* the early next morning and would spend our night in the pilgrim's shelter. We slept on a *thazha paaya* on the bare grounds a ritual called "*virivekkal*". Back then the comforts were bare minimum, even a pillow was a luxury then, and I enjoyed sleeping in the lap of Mother Nature, surrounded by the woods. I cuddled next to *Ammavan* and slept serenely breathing in the unpolluted forest air. The temple as well as its surroundings merged perfectly with the landscape. No permanent structures were hardly visible in the vicinity. Huge mountains enveloped with thick mists, the cold air and the occasional whooshing of breeze through the trees together created an entirely different atmosphere and I thoroughly enjoyed it. Pointing to a distant mountain *Ammavan* said that it was the *Ponnambalamedu,* the sacred hillock where the divine *Makara Vilakku* would appear on the evening of *Makara Samkranti.* I looked at the mountain with awe and wonder.

Next morning after a quick shower, the crow's bath, we climbed the *pathinettampadi,* the holy 18 steps made of granite, prayerfully chanting *Swami Saranam Ayyappa Saranam*, seeking the blessings of Ayyappa. Before the steep climb, everyone broke a coconut on the steps. Being a first-time devotee (*Kanni Ayyappa*), I broke one on the first step as suggested by *Ammavan*. Later this practice of breaking coconuts on the holy steps was stopped completely as in the process, the steps were damaged. Many years later the holy steps were covered with golden sheets by a well-known business group.

As I climbed the steps, there was a crowd ahead of us. We patiently waited for a while, and then we were all led to the front of the *Sreekovil.* From an arm's length, I had a *Divya Darshana* of the golden idol of Lord Ayyappa – a sight that lasted hardly a few seconds, moments of quietude but left an indelible mark on me. The power of the Lord was such that I felt as if certain invisible rays emerged from the idol, passing through my body. Was this the blessing that Lord Ayyappa had bestowed upon a sick boy in return for the fulfilment of a votive of his loving mother? Or was it simply the product of my spiritually charged imagination? I would love to believe that this experience was indeed a divine blessing.

As we began our return journey from the Sabarimala Ayyappa temple in the afternoon, I felt an overwhelming sense of calm and peace. In that moment, I understood the true meaning of a pilgrim's delight – the profound fulfilment that comes from completing a sacred vow - the once-in -a-life time experience.

31.

Scent of the Past: How Smell Transport Us Back in Time.

A curious relationship exists between smell and memory. Certain scents have the power to evoke old memories, transporting us back to a forgotten time and rekindling nostalgia. Smell has an uncanny and inexplicable connection with memory. Certain scents can stimulate memories that are somehow associated with that particular smell. The scent of jasmine, for instance, instantly brings to mind the occasion of my marriage. The influence of olfaction on memory recall is truly astounding.

When I was in second grade, my five-year-old neighbor and classmate, Sheela, died of childhood illnesses. She was the eldest child of the Puthanpurackal Mathew-Baby couple. Her death deeply saddened us, her classmates.

On the day of her passing, our class teacher guided us to Sheela's home. As we circled the table where she lay still in a tiny wooden coffin adorned with decorative works, she seemed to be in eternal slumber, hardly conscious of the presence of her close friends and wailing parents. Dressed in a gleaming white frock and cap, she was adorned with two white fluffy wings on her shoulders. Looking heavenward, she lay in her small coffin, her tiny palms, clad in white gloves, tightly grasping a delicate cross. Inside the coffin, she appeared like an angel, with an unusual calm on her face as she gazed heavenward.

Behind the coffin stood a small cross with the inscription: "*Innu Njaan, Naale Nee*" (Today, its I. Tomorrow it will be You). On a nearby wooden stand, a few incense sticks burned, spreading their aroma around the body. The scent, whose name I don't know, filled the atmosphere with a doleful aroma.

Surprisingly, even after several decades, whenever I breathe in that particular scent, I am instantly transported back in time and space, standing near Sheela's coffin, surrounded by our classmates. The scent has a magical spell in recollecting memories with emotional resonance.

Scientific investigations have revealed the astonishing relationship between scent and memory, known as olfactory memory. Within the brain, smells are processed in the olfactory bulb, directly connected to the amygdala and hippocampus, responsible for emotion, memory, and learning.

This smell-memory connection has incredible power in vividly recollecting memories associated with specific scents. Even after five and a half decades, the scent of incense sticks burned on Sheela's funeral day brings back memories as vividly as if I were experiencing them in the present.

Is this a kind of time slip?

During his annual leave, whenever my father opened his huge steel trunk stuffed with numerous items, a rare and enjoyable smell would emanate. A mixed scent of biscuits, toffees, jams, Pear's soap, and Mysore Sandalwood soap, combined with the smell of his perfumed clothes and hair oil, created a wonderful feeling.

Years later, when I smelled a similar scent, my memory took me back to the past, and I became a little boy again, enjoying the warmth of the smell.

The mesmerising scent of Jasmine flowers always evoked evergreen memories of my marriage, the *kathirmandapam* embellished with jasmine and the flower bedecked *maniyara,* and my bride who came coyly into the small room with a glass of hot milk. The moment was heralding a new life together- Jasmine scented memories.

After the annual painting and whitewash of our house, a peculiar smell of drying paint and turpentine mixture would linger in the air the next morning. I greatly enjoyed the smell, and many years later, when I breathed it in again, I was reminded of my childhood days.

Aanachoohru is the Malayalam word used to describe the distinctive, pungent smell of an elephant, which foretells the presence of the majestic creature. Whenever I catch a whiff of it, I am reminded of the *Pakalpooram* at Sree Bhavaneeswara temple, our nearby village temple, where 11-15 elephants, adorned with *nettipattom* and parasols, would be paraded for the annual temple festival. The aroma instantly transports me to a bygone era. For me, this penetrating smell is synonymous with my early childhood, when I would eagerly demand toys during the temple festival. One particular memory stands out - I had insisted on a wooden elephant cutout, painted black with gleaming white tusks, mounted on a small wooden platform with wheels.

Bahuleyan, my eldest brother-in-law used to smoke *Panama* Cigarettes in his youth, and whenever I came across that cigarette smell, I thought of him.

Recently, I sensed a peculiar aroma that reminded me of the captivating smell Malayalam textbook in second grade, that was soon to be followed by a rush of joy associated with my childhood. Our transistor radio was encased in a leather jacket that produced a rare smell of leather and plastic. Later, whenever I sensed something similar, I would be reminded of that old transistor radio.

Gopalan Elayachan, a distant cousin of my father, who worked at TTK & Co., had a wonderful smell when he visited us. Though he passed away over forty years ago, I still think of him whenever the sweet smell of his perfume fills my nostrils.

The sharp smell of roasted cashews takes me to the evenings before Vishu, when Amma assisted by my two sisters would extricate the nuts from its burnt shells after roasting them atop a wood-fired hearth in an earthen pot with many holes in the bottom.

The scent of *Ashtagandhakam,* a sacred blend of eight Ayurvedic herbal powders, instantly transports me to a poignant time in my life. This fragrant mixture, typically burned in temples during puja, reminds me of my maternal grandmother's final days. As our elders read the Ramayana aloud, Amma would burn *Ashtagandhakam,* filling the air with its comforting aroma.

Ammuma lay in her deathbed, motionless, her eyes closed, as Rugmini Vallyamma, a distant relative of Achan, recited a prayer in devotion. Her harsh voice filled the air with the poignant words: "*Dehavum dehiyum verpedum kaalath, Devaki nandanan vannuthangename.*" (when the soul gets separated from the body, let the son of Devaki come and support).

The acrid smell of Dhanwanthram *Kuzhambu*, the Ayurvedic oil, evokes memories of Ammumma, my maternal grandmother who used to smear her body with the oil.

The smell of freshly cut grass and jackfruit leaves instantly transports me back to my teenage years, when we raised a few goats at our home. Similarly, the earthy aroma of dried mud evokes memories of my boyhood days, when our family pond would drain out.

Whenever I catch a whiff of the pungent smell of phenol and surgical spirit, my mind instantly transports me back to my childhood days when I spent nearly a month at Ernakulam General Hospital. The memories of those painful sufferings come alive in my mind, the grim reminder of countless injections, although I consciously try rather not to recall those harsh experiences.

There's a complex and powerful relationship between smell and memory that reconnects our senses, emotions, and experiences.

32.

Sacred Memories: My Days At Sacred Heart College.

Although I attended three different colleges during my higher education, my time at Sacred Heart College (SH) remains etched in my memory. I studied Pre-Degree at Cochin College, graduated from SH, and post-graduated from the University of Cochin, with a brief stint at Maharajas College in between. However, it was my salad days at SH that left an indelible mark.

The magnificent and well-maintained buildings of Sacred Heart College in Thevara, along with the beautiful gardens surrounding them, have recently become a hotspot in Kochi. Film production companies and social media platforms frequently flock to the campus for video shoots. The college's insignia, featured under its attractive coat of arms, reads "COR RECTUM INQUIRIT SCIENTIAM," which translates to "A righteous heart seeks after wisdom". The splendid and well-maintained basketball court in the front courtyard is one of the best in the region, and it proudly hosts the annual Batholomew Trophy. The sprawling play ground in the backside of the college, where sports events were held, is equally captivating. Located by the side of Vembanad lake, the picturesque view of Willingdon Island from there offered a breathtaking experience. Located in one corner of the ground was a shooting range with an enormous berm, where budding marksmen, honed their shooting skills.

My classmates were a sort of an *omnium gatherum*, coming from different backgrounds and cultures yet bound by a common thread, the sacred spirit of the college. The wonderful combination included adorable Rani who always preferred bell-bottom pants and slim-fit shirts, Ajitha the fashionista, Krishnan who was a well-known artist, Mariamma, the most mischievous of the lot, Remadevi, who seldom spoke, Sivadas, whose humours tickled our funny bones, Gregory, the politician cum actor who had a huge fan following, Rasheed, whose records were simply superb, Sandhya the *padippist* (studious one), Helen, the soft-spoken girl with large almond shaped eyes, that tilted at the corners, Rosamma, a gifted singer with a melodious voice that lingered in my memory and the list went on... During our college days, despite sharing strong personal bonding, a respectable distance was maintained between boys and girls and we set our own invisible boundary around us.

When I joined as a BSc Botany student in 1979, I was apprehensive about my academic progress. Some classmates had shared stories about the strictness of the priests-cum-teachers, and I was warned of being treated differently as a Hindu student. However, these fears dissipated during the introductory lecture by Father Principal Fr. Mathai Archengel.

The Principal's speech was followed by a prayer service at the nearby church, led by Fr. Daniel Thottakkara. Contrary to my expectations, his sermon was quite engaging and insightful. One advice that struck me was to never blame circumstances, but instead, strive to overcome them. Fr. Daniel's classes were always fascinating, and his expertise in English and psychology made him an exceptional professor.

The Botany department boasted an impressive faculty, including Prof. T.U. Joseph, an erudite Professor of unmatched pedagogical skills, who authored our Pre-Degree textbook. His knowledge and teaching style were unparalleled, and his lecture notes were highly sought after. Another notable teacher was Prof. Zakariah Mathews, whose exceptional teaching talents made complex topics seem simple. In simple terms using remarkably drawn sketches and diagrams Prof: Zakaria succinctly described the complex lessons of photosynthesis, anatomy, taxonomy, and embryology. A man of few words, his classes were a class apart. Even after four decades, I can recall the scientific names of common plants, thanks to his simple and pragmatic teaching methods that left an indelible impression in my mind.

The practical sessions in Zoology class were always daunting for me, as I struggled with dissecting frogs to display their anatomical features. Mounting the skeleton of frogs was particularly challenging. To overcome this, my friends Krishna Kumar, Xavier, and I visited Pappu Chettan's house. As the attender of the Zoology lab, he supplied frogs to the college and kept many in a concrete tank near his home. He generously gave each of us a frog from his collection, free of charge, which we used for mounting the skeleton. On the day designated for submitting the skeleton mounted on thick black mounting paper, that provided an attractive background, all of us, except Remadevi, presented our specimens to Prof. Reppayi. When he pressed for the reason behind her inability to submit as directed, to the amusement of the class and the fury of the teacher, she said that a crow had taken her specimen away, (*kaakka kondupoyi saar*). An innocent girl, she was right; she had kept the bones out to dry, and a cunning crow had taken the lot much to her surprise, leaving her no time to make a new one. My Sacred Heart (SH) days were filled with many such interesting stories.

In those days, animal dissections were a part of the course. This necessity forced many to opt for other subjects, despite their passion for Zoology. As my friends enthusiastically dissected their specimens, I approached mine with trepidation and fear. While some of us saw this as a necessary evil, our teacher, Prof. Reppayi, tried to reassure us that this experience would ultimately benefit those aspiring to pursue a career in medical science. With a hint of sarcasm, he'd add, "The only difference, of course, is that your future patients won't be frogs - they'll be human beings." Once while I was carefully dissecting the bundle of nerves that form the sciatic plexus of frog, and probing them from its origin, I broke a tiny nerve much to my shock and disappointment. Looking at the meticulously dissected specimens of Krishnan and Rani made me envious. However, in 2014, the UGC banned animal dissections in colleges, bowing to pressure from environmental and animal rights organizations like PETA. This move brought relief to many animal enthusiasts and students who dreaded the practice.

Creating an herbarium was another challenging task. We trekked through unknown village paths lined with herbs and shrubs, meticulously collecting and sharing them among friends. Once, to collect some rare species, Vikraman, Sivadas, and I wandered around Rasheed's homestead in Kanjiramattom. Alighting from the bus, Rasheed guided us along the village road, which branched off near the railway station. His quaint, thatched house stood atop a hill, nestled within a lush rubber plantation surrounded by dense thickets. Looking at the picturesque view from the top of the hill, it was Sivadas who commented that the landscape was a replica of the picture in the poem about a train (*koo koo kookum theevandee*) in our first standard Malayalam textbook. After a hearty meal lovingly served by his mother, he took us through the meandering alleys of the village. The village was then a captivating landscape full of lush vegetation. As we wandered through the village paths, Rasheed pointed to a large, old house nestled in the midst of a sprawling compound. "That's Suja K John's house," he said, referring to our quiet and reserved classmate. We craned our necks above the thatched fence and peered into the courtyard, hoping to catch a glimpse of her. However, there was no sign of anyone. We continued on our way. We collected *Pullani* (paper flower climber), *Vishamandari* (wild jasmine or Glory Bower), and *African malli* (Eryngium), along with a few other rare plants, near the famed mosque. (The quaint, calm, and slumberous town of Kanjiramattom, near Kochi, is famed for its Sheikh Fareeduddin mosque, where the mortal remains of the Sufi saint are entombed. Every year, thousands of pilgrims visit the Dargah, and the mosque is renowned as a pilgrim centre of communal harmony. The famous *Kodikuthu* festival and *Chandanakkudam Mahotsavam,* which falls on January 14th (1st *Makaram*), attracts hundreds of Ayyappa devotees. Hindu pilgrims pray and break coconuts at the shrine of Vavar Swamy, the companion and close friend of Ayyappa. Interestingly, the *Kodikuthu* ritual coincides with the *Makara vilakku* festival of Sabarimala temple, giving credence to the story about the friendship between Ayyappa and Vavar.)

My failing health prevented me from joining the week-long study tour to Ooty. However, my friends generously contributed some plant specimens from their collection. They shared a vivid account of their journey, and using their narrative as a foundation, I crafted a report enriched with my own imaginative additions. Ironically, I scored the highest marks for the report on a study tour I had never attended, much to the envy of my friends. The process involved drying the twigs by sandwiching them between paper layers and pressing them with wooden planks. I used to keep weights over them to hasten the process of drying. Improperly dried plants would attract fungal growth, impairing their colour. Identifying unfamiliar plant species was a stupendous task. The most unenviable job was pasting each plant piece onto thick drawing paper and penning detailed taxonomic notes, a crucial component of the herbarium. To pass the practical examination we needed to present an herbarium consisting of minimum of one hundred different plant species. Herbarium of rare plant species always scored high marks.

Prof. Seetharama Iyer's chemistry classes were an interesting experience. Prof. Joseph, affectionately known as 'London Sir,' having taught English in a London college, would often boast, "When I was in London..." to his students' amusement. A kind person, he authored an excellent English grammar book, prescribed as a textbook for our first-year BSc syllabus. London Sir diligently corrected our solecisms, which we committed all too often and to an excessive degree. Fr Austin has always been a source of help and cooperation who mingled with students without reservations. His fine manners were laced with both courtesy and civility. He was the Bursar and also a faculty who taught us Zoology. Prof. C

S Jayaram's English classes were a class apart as he spoke eloquently and always connected us to World English Literature. He was a well-known theatre person and an artist par excellence who guided Krishnan in his artistic journey. During one College annual day, under his direction Macbeth was enacted in the college auditorium by a hurriedly constituted troupe of teachers and students. The performance won wide appreciation. Malayalam classes of Prof. Mathew Ulakamthara, who has earned himself a reputation as a renowned writer, was equally captivating. His classes were so interesting and delightful that even students from Hindi classes used to attend his lectures on *Saakunthalam,* that was interspersed with sexually explicit narratives. He loved telling stories from epics, embellishing them with finest details. On those rare occasions, the spacious gallery of our classroom would be packed with students who waited anxiously for the celebrated teacher.

Other esteemed teachers, including Fr. Aquinas, who had a saintly appearance, Prof. Appachan, Lecturer Joseph Thayyil, and Jr. Lecturer Dominic, contributed to the department's excellence. Later Fr. Aquinas was promoted as the Principal on the retirement of Fr. Archangel much to our delight. Together, they created an environment where teachers and students collaborated, making the Botany department at SH a model for others.

As I settled into college life, I began to excel academically. Regular examinations helped me track my progress, and I gradually improved my grades. By the end of the first year, I secured the top spot, and eventually, I won the Eliamma Mathew Elamthuruthil memorial gold medal for achieving the highest score in the final examination.

Sacred Heart College played a pivotal role in shaping my destiny. The lush greenery, picturesque lake shore, beautiful auditorium, well-equipped laboratories, fantastic Zoology Museum full of wild wonders, and well-stocked library are etched in my memory. The Bhat's Book Store, a nondescript shop selling books and other stationaries owned by Bhat, an old man who on many occasions provided new books on credit, Readers' Delight, another modern bookstore nearby, Hotel Chandrika where we spent our time munching on frugal foods and the surrounding landscape remain vivid reminders of my time at SH. During my college days, I occasionally had lunch at Hotel De Paris, a nearby eatery. *Ikka,* the hotel's affable owner, would lovingly serve me my favourite Masala Dosa. His warm smile and hospitality made our meal breaks a delight.

The college anthem,

"We are one in the heart,

We are one in the spirit

And we pray that we are all the children of the heart

Sacred Heart we are of the children of the heart,"

which we chorused during every event, echoes the spirit of unity, evokes a great deal of nostalgia and the spirit of college days.

However, our daily commute was a different story. The 2-mile journey from Thevara junction to our college campus was exhausting, especially on rainy days. To make matters worse, public transportation was scarce, with only a couple of buses plying the route via Thevara Ferry. On rare occasions, senior students with political connections would commandeer a bus headed to Fort Kochi and divert it to our campus. We'd enjoy the free ride, but this tactic didn't always go unnoticed.

One memorable instance, the driver of the hijacked bus took us on an unexpected detour - straight to the nearby Town Police Station. The police intervened, leaving us with a stern warning. Deflated and disappointed, we returned to college, shouting slogans against the police and the bus operator for their perceived anti-student stance. This incident marked the end of our bus-hijacking escapades.

Having established by the Carmelites of Mary Immaculate (CMI) congregation in 1944, the Sacred Heart college has a glorious history. It was founded by Fr. John Berchmans and Fr Thomas Pynumkal was its first Principal. Over the past eight decades, the college has evolved itself into a premier educational institution in South India providing quality education. The college now prides itself on its rich legacy and gentility.

33.

The Days When Custard Apple Tree Blossomed.

Several decades ago, a custard apple tree stood tall in our northern yard. Although we had a couple of custard apple trees, this one was distinct from the others. Typically, custard apples are green and grow to a maximum size of a clenched fist. This common variety, known as *Seethapazham*, is ubiquitous and enjoyed wide distribution. It's a tasty fruit, though not very fleshy.

However, the tree that stood in front of our cow shed was a different one. Called *Raamapazham*, its fruit was considerably larger, more delicious, fleshy, nutritious, and succulent. The leaves are large and elongated compared to the smaller leaves of *Seethapazham*. A relative once pointed to the tree, laden with fruits, and mentioned that *Raamapazham* has several medicinal qualities.

The tree in our courtyard was a huge one, with enormous branches spreading all around, stretching into a canopy. During one vacation, the family of Elayachan (Achan's half-brother) visited us, and we spent wonderful days together. Mehar, Ullas, Anand, Sanjeev, and I celebrated those days with laughter and excitement. Under the shade of the custard apple tree, we built tiny huts from discarded palm leaves and twigs. We spent our days singing, accompanied by drum beats. Mehar and Ullas loved climbing the spreading branches. Since I was a reluctant adventurer, I kept myself away from this risky venture. Full of child-like energy and enthusiasm, Sajeev proved to be the most mischievous of the lot.

One day, Ullas lost his balance and fell, bruising his back. My mother applied Vicks to his wounds while Chellamma Auntie, his mother scolded him for his misadventure. When they left after a brief but splendid visit, I was overcome with emotion.

The custard apple tree eventually disintegrated due to old age. Among Elayachan's seven children, I remained in contact only with Ullas, an intellectual who occasionally surprised me with his deep knowledge and eloquent words via WhatsApp messages. Even his hurriedly scripted messages and WhatsApp chats served as proof of the profound depths and vastness of his knowledge. His language was breathtakingly beautiful, mesmerizing me with its crystalline clarity and effortless elegance. A chronic bachelor, after retiring from the Department of Statistics, he led a lonely life surrounded by books. His remarkable memory allowed him to recall our childhood days spent beneath the custard apple tree.

Recently, just a couple of days after New Year's Day in 2025, I was shocked to learn about Ullas's death in an automobile accident. The news suddenly brought back memories of the custard apple tree and our delightful days filled with laughter and enthusiasm. Though it turned out to be a pretty hectic day for me, I visited his home along with my eldest brother and bade him final farewell.

34.

A Generation at a Crossroads: Navigating Dilemmas and Paradoxes

I belong to a generation born in the early sixties, a time of great social and cultural change. Those of us born in the fifties and sixties find ourselves at a crossroads, perplexed by the rapid pace of transformation in the world around us. We are a unique breed, having spent our formative as well as youthful years in the twentieth century and now navigating the sunset years in threshold of the twenty-first century.

During this transitional period, spanning two centuries and two millennia, we witnessed profound changes that have reshaped the world beyond recognition. The pace of change was dizzying, leaving our generation struggling to adapt. Life has become pretty hectic.

Growing up in an era that was both human-centric and eco-centric, we were raised under the guidance of our parents, grandparents, and siblings. Our elders wielded authority, and we were taught to obey and respect them. Our childhood was a vibrant tapestry of friendships, social interactions, and community bonds.

However, the turn of the century and the millennium has upended our values and traditions. As our children left to pursue better lives in distant lands, we were left to face the challenges of aging alone. Our homes, once filled with laughter and warmth, now stand empty and deserted, an eerie silence reverberates.

The contrast between our modest upbringing and the opulent lifestyle of the younger generation is stark. We, who were accustomed to a minimalist lifestyle, watch with a mix of dismay and resignation as the millennials and Gen Z indulge in a life of unrestrained luxury. We refrain from offering advice, fearful of being met with indifference or even hostility.

Though our youthful years were spent in penury and hardship, we had a rich social life that endeared us to everyone in our village. During our student days, we had no electricity and learned our lessons under the faint glow of kerosene lamps. Few of us had more than two set of clothes, most of us travelled barefoot as footwear was then a luxury. Most of us began our schooling with a broken slate and stubs of pencils, which served as our prized writing tools. Despite these humble beginnings, we thoroughly enjoyed our school life. On rainy days, we waded through knee-deep waters together, sharing laughter, lessons, and quarrels. We learned the art of sharing while exchanging stubs of pencils and a few precious drops of ink with the friend sitting nearby. Through those precious drops of ink, we were truly sharing the simple joys and innocence of village life.

Many a child from poor families came to school, enticed by the free noon meal provided under the CARE (Cooperative for American Relief Everywhere) program. (The mid-day meals programme was introduced by the Government of India in 1961 with the economic burden shared by CARE.) As an accompaniment, they would buy a sachet of tongue-tingling *naaranga achaar* for 2 paise from *Aluvakkaran Muthalay's* shop. While they greedily gulped down the *kanji*—its flavour enhanced by the spicy tang of the pickle—I would find myself gazing enviously at their mouths, despite my own tiffin holding rice and a simple yet delicious curry. We were oblivious to our caste and class distinctions. Regardless of our religious backgrounds, we would pray at the nearby Sree Bhavaneeswara Temple before examinations. The annual temple festival in March was a time of celebration for us, and we would secretly peek through the open classroom windows to catch a glimpse of the elaborately decorated temple elephants paraded in the vast ground.

In contrast, our children today have access to all modern amenities, yet they often feel lonely, rarely socializing with friends and relatives. From a tender age, they were taught to view their classmates as competitors and potential rivals, rather than friends.

Petty squabbles over trivial matters were common. However, elders would intervene, suggesting solutions that the warring parties obeyed unquestioningly. An air of unadulterated love and affection prevailed. We followed a eudaimonic lifestyle, vastly different from today's, which often prioritizes immediate gratification of needs and desires. For many, life has become a self-imposed exile, isolating them from society and often leading to emotional distress. The unusually long and unearthly working times have taken a heavy toll on their emotional health and mental well-being. The unprecedented rise in suicide rates serves as a grim reminder of the growing disillusionment among educated youth.

In the past, despite deprivation, people enjoyed life, deriving pleasure from simple things. Modern life has been a cultural shock for past generations, who lived contentedly with meagre resources. They had aspirations, but set boundaries, even for their dreams.

The pandemic, which struck unexpectedly, led the government to confine seniors under the guise of protection, thereby curtailing their freedom of movement and livelihood. For many, the lack of adequate social security measures made this confinement more severe than the pandemic itself. The elderly faced untold hardships, struggling to survive in their twilight years. They were made to walk on eggshells. A generation that had toiled to build the nation we inhabit today was subjected to extreme cruelty. Meanwhile, the younger generation, beset by their own problems, lacks the time and patience to care for their ailing and aging parents and grandparents.

In today's world, where material wealth abounds, we often find ourselves devoid of life's true pleasures and happiness. Ironically, our ancestors, who possessed fewer worldly goods, lived more fulfilling lives. As our lives become increasingly luxurious, happiness seems to elude us. This paradox is starkly illustrated by the alarming rise in suicide rates in recent years, highlighting the disconnect between wealth and happiness.

The arrival of electricity transformed the villager's life in ways they never imagined. This paved the way for the evolution of a peaceful village into a vibrant and bustling city. The advent of modern amenities like cars, bikes, TVs, ACs, and others has transformed our lives in unimaginable ways. The smartphone is arguably the most significant 21st-century invention, revolutionizing and reshaping human existence. With a gentle touch on the mobile screen, you can communicate with the world, conduct banking transactions, learn, and do business from the comfort of your home. Life has never been simpler. Yet, ironically, we find ourselves starving for love, recognition, respect, support, and happiness – the very things we once enjoyed freely.

The social concepts of family, marriage and motherhood have undergone significant changes in recent years. As joint families disintegrated, nuclear families emerged. Today, the traditional notion of family has further fragmented, leaving homes that once buzzed with shared lives now reduced to isolated individuals living separate existences. They remain insensitive to the feelings of others. The emotional impact of this shift in family concept on people is enormous. Many men and women now prefer living-together relationships, and same-sex marriages and LGBTQ+ relationships are gaining societal acceptance and legal support. In Indian society, they argue, traditional marriages often confined women to domestic roles, limiting their intellectual and creative potential. Modern women tend to view marriage as a necessary compromise, where they shoulder responsibilities like childcare and unpaid domestic work. Some young couples even opt for pet parenting over having children. With access to education and modern amenities, women can now pursue their ambitions and lead independent lives. The 21st-century woman has made significant strides in terms of worldly comforts, enjoying greater control over their assets and lives. However, this progress has also led to a focus on material wealth and social status as measures of success. Unfortunately, this has resulted in a rise in debt, divorces, and increased use of alcohol and psychotropic substances like MDMA among educated youth.

In contrast, our forefathers and foremothers lived simpler lives, finding joy despite hardships. They maintained physical and mental health through physically demanding work and nurturing relationships. Their secret to happiness lay in hard work, sincere connections, and celebrating life surrounded by loved ones.

Until a few decades ago, I couldn't have imagined, even in my wildest dreams, that things would take such a drastic turn in such an unimaginable way. In this game of generational chaos spanning centuries, the survivors are those who can adapt and turn the tide to their advantage. My grandson Alekh and I belong to two generations separated by more than half a century, or rather two millennia. As generationally challenged human beings, we are destined to live together, sharing our time, space, and resources. In the distant past, mutual help and support enabled our ancestors to navigate life's complexities effectively and admirably. Compromises and sacrifices made their relationships meaningful. They shared their pangs and pleasures, delights and disappointments, peaks and pitfalls in their lives with equanimity. In those bygone decades, we had elders in our family who served as pillars of support, allowing us to unburden ourselves of life's stresses and struggles. Unfortunately, we no longer have such supportive figures in our lives, with whom we can share the severe trauma and suffering we experience.

Compared to previous generations, the younger generation tends to be more ambitious, materialistic, extravagant, and self-centered, yet less idealistic, spiritual, minimalistic, passionate, and benevolent. For them, life is a complex enigma. Most youngsters end up in IT professions that offer nothing apart from a fat pay packet. The educated youths are simply wasting their energy and time that they could have used more fruitfully for the betterment of themselves and the world. The older generations had remarkable abilities to live with the unacceptable, to cope with the imperfections in life. This quality prepared them to face the uncertainties and risks in life with fortitude while enjoying little joys of life.

I'm not unduly nostalgic about a bygone time and its old - world charm-just reliving those fine moments in my life, the changing landscapes, ephemerality of human life, transient nature of human relationship, its many insecurities and imperfections. It's not my intention to glorify bygone days or denigrate the present moment. Undoubtedly, we're on a wonderful journey in a world abundant with worldly comforts. What we miss, however, are the pleasures stemming from interpersonal relationships, mutual respect, and friendships that formed the foundation of a happy life. Slowly, I realize that this new century and the new millennium do not belong to us. We, the twentieth century denizens, are indeed destined to live the remainder our lives in borrowed time alongside Gen Z and millennials who are in a rat-race to eke out a living for themselves and their loved ones if they really have one.

35.

From Temple Priest to Seafood Professional: A Village Boy's Limitless Ambitions.

Every child dream of becoming someone they admire when they grow up. It's a universal truth that childhood ambitions are shaped by the environment and surroundings. Without ambitions, no one has ever achieved success in life, although whether those ambitions and dreams are realized as imagined is another matter. Childhood ambitions serve as the fuel that drives one's growth, motivates, and encourages risk-taking in life. Boys often look up to their fathers as their role models, while girls admire their mothers. For some inexplicable reason, I never aspired to follow in my father's footsteps and pursue a career in the Indian Defence Forces, unlike my two brothers. In my case, my earliest childhood ambition was to become a *Poojari,* a temple priest. This aspiration was sparked by the respect and awe with which devotees, especially women, treated the priests during our temple. The priests' charisma and kindness only strengthened my desire to follow in their footsteps. I have noticed that the devotees always treated them with immense respect and awe as if they were God incarnate. While giving the *prasadam* and blessing them the young women would glimpse the young and handsome priest with a mixed emotion of respect, love and adoration. The priests in turn would reciprocate such lovely gazing with their equally loving glances.

However, during subsequent visits, I was disillusioned by the priests' attire, which revealed more than it concealed.

The attire revealed the loincloths in silhouette as the priest prostrated every time as part of his ritualistic practices. This disappointment led me to abandon my ambition and explore alternative careers.

My next aspiration was to become a postman, inspired by the khaki-clad postman who brought letters and Money Orders from my father and brothers serving in distant places. His enthusiasm and kindness earned him Amma's respect and gratitude. Witnessing the appreciation he received, I too wanted to become a village postman.

But fate had other plans. One night, a theft occurred in our store where coconuts were kept, and Amma reported it to the local police. Their prompt investigation and heroic spirit left a lasting impression on me, and I decided to become a police officer. However, my elder sisters mocked my decision, leaving me disheartened.

During those days, I travelled in a taxi and was fascinated by the driver's skill in navigating narrow streets. In a split second, I decided to become a car driver. However, my elder sisters pointed out that driving was not a respectable profession, and many drivers had a reputation for being alcohol users. This information shattered my illusions, and I abandoned my ambition. They had scant respect for my choices.

My frequent visits to doctors with recurring childhood maladies inspired me to become a doctor. In my teenage daydreams, I envisioned myself as a doctor, seated behind a huge glass-topped table adorned with imposing medical books, a blood pressure monitor, and other professional equipment. A stethoscope hung around my neck, and a queue of patients waited patiently in the elegant waiting room of a grand hospital formed part of my dreams. But instead, I became a well-known patient of not-so-well-known doctors as my parents took me consulting qualified doctors seeking a solution to my ailment that was a constant concern for them. As I grew older and more educated, my ambitions changed. I aspired to become a professor like my Botany professors, T.U. Joseph and Zachariah Mathew, who commanded respect and admiration from their students.

During my master's programme, I was inspired by scientists from research institutes like Central Institute Fisheries Technology (CIFT) and Central Marine Fisheries Research Institute (CMFRI). Dr. T.S.G. Iyer's mesmerizing knowledge sparked my desire to become a scientist. I am grateful to Dr. Iyer for encouraging me to write about multiple aspects of fisheries and related topics.

In reality, I didn't become any of the professionals I aspired to be. Instead, I entered the business world, a career I least liked and expected. However, as the saying goes, "When you don't get what you like, like what you get." This is exactly what I did for the past four decades, and I became successful in my career.

In a twist of fate, the humble aspiration of a five-year-old to become a temple priest was fulfilled in a manner both unexpected and profound. These are stories I need to share, so the truth isn't lost forever.

36.

Aga Khan Palace of Pune: A Monument of Historical Importance.

I recently visited Pune with Suvarna, my wife to receive the prestigious Golden Book Award for my book, *Kerala Kaleidoscope*. Since we arrived a day before the event, we had ample time to explore the city and learn about its history. Our cab driver, Ramdas, was an affable and friendly person who took us on a tour of the town. He provided us with an itinerary that would last the whole day, and our first stop was the Aga Khan Palace, located in a corner of the bustling city.

Although I wasn't particularly interested in visiting the palace, I went along with Ramdas' plan. However, once inside, I was awestruck by the palace's significance in India's independence movement. We walked through the rooms leisurely, reading the detailed descriptions about the palace, which was deserted at the time. Soon, a group of school children joined us, rushing in and out, disregarding their teachers' requests.

The Aga Khan Palace played a crucial role in India's freedom struggle. In response to Gandhi's Quit India Movement, the British arrested Gandhiji, Kasturba Gandhi, Sarojini Naidu, Mahadev Desai, and several other front-line leaders on August 9, 1942. The arrests sparked widespread protests, and the British, fearing public backlash, secretly shifted the detainees to the Aga Khan Palace, where they were incarcerated until 1944.

Mahadev Desai, who served as the personal secretary of Mahatma Gandhi for 25 years, had spent his last days while under house arrest in Aga Khan palace. He obediently and quietly managed everything in Gandhi's life and stood up as a pillar of support during his difficult times. Raj Mohan Gandhi reminisced Mahadev Desai thus: "Waking up before Gandhi in pre-dawn darkness, and going to sleep long after his Master, Desai lived Gandhi's day thrice over – first in an attempt to anticipate it, next in spending it alongside Gandhi, and finally in recording it into his diary". On the morning of 15th August, 1942, hardly a week after shifting to Aga Khan Palace, Mahadev Desai passed away suddenly due to a heart attack. Gandhi called out to him as Desai ceased to breathe. Later when asked why Gandhiji called out Desai's name when he knew well that Desai was no more, Gandhiji replied: "I felt that if Mahadev opened his eyes and looked at me, I would tell him to get up. He had never disobeyed me in his life. I was confident that if had he heard those words, he would have defied even death and got up". With shaking hands, Gandhiji himself washed Desai's body for the last time, then wrapped it in coarse sheets available in the jail, and was later cremated in the courtyard of the palace. His samadhi stands on the spot where he was cremated.

Eminent historian and author Ramachandra Guha once remarked, "Gandhiji invented India, Mahadev invented Gandhiji." While powerful, Guha's statement arguably overstates Mahadev Desai's role in shaping Gandhiji's life. Mahadev had long aspired to write a comprehensive biography of Gandhiji, but this dream remained unfulfilled due to his untimely death. His son, Narayan Das Desai, however, later honoured his father's dream by penning a monumental four-volume biography of Gandhi, titled *My Life is My Message*. This work drew extensively from Mahadev's meticulously kept diaries, making it not just a tribute to Gandhi, but also to Mahadev himself.

It was during this period that Kasturba Gandhi too passed away on February 22, 1944 while undergoing arrest in the palace. The room where Kasturba Gandhi spent her final moments is preserved as a sacred space, closed off to visitors. Through the glass door, one can glimpse a few simple artefacts once used by the Gandhis, now revered as priceless relics. A few faded black-and-white photographs adorning the palace walls offer a haunting reminder of that tragic chapter. Among them, the image of Gandhi seated in quiet meditation beside the lifeless body of his beloved Kasturba is especially heartrending. As per Gandhi's wishes, Kasturba was cremated in the palace courtyard. The Samadhi of Kasturba Gandhi lies in the same courtyard where Mahadev Desai was cremated; the two memorials stand close to each other, their occupants resting in eternal peace.

As we visited the Samadhi, I experienced a deep sense of tranquillity and peace, despite the chaos caused by the school children playing in the nearby lawns. The atmosphere was serene, with even the birds and squirrels seeming to respect the silence. Later, when Mahatma Gandhi was assassinated, a portion of his ashes was brought back to Pune and interred near Kasturba's Samadhi.

As we left the palace, I noticed a foreigner engrossed in a book, quite oblivious of the external world, and I couldn't help but feel a sense of sadness and despair. I thanked Ramdas for taking us to the historic Aga Khan Palace, which had witnessed a tumultuous phase of India's freedom struggle.

Built in 1892, the Aga Khan palace is known for its unique architecture and lush greenery and its sprawling gardens surrounding 19 acres. Located in the heart of Pune city, the magnificent palace was built by Aga Khan III of Nizari Ismaili religion is today an important historical landmark and tourist attraction. A few personal belongings of Mahatma Gandhi and Kasturba Gandhi are exhibited in the museum along with their statues that are pulsating with life. In 2003 the Archaeological Survey of India has declared the palace as a National Monument. The 2.5 metre wide, wrap around corridor is one of the attractions of this beautiful building. The captivating structure has many turrets and pediments that add to the splendour of the palace. The palace boasts of five magnificent halls that have been converted into the museum. The Aga Khan Palace in Pune is not just a stunning architectural landmark—it's a deeply symbolic site woven into the fabric of India's freedom struggle.

37.

On Nick Names And Insulting Appellations.

The villagers had often found pleasure by bestowing nicknames, often unkind and cruel, on their fellow villagers. Those nicknames were usually a reflection of the physical disability of the person. Thus, *Manthan* Vakko earned the derogatory monicker as he had a huge swelling of filariasis on one of his legs but later when he amputated his ailing leg, he was soon rechristened as *Ottakkalan* (one legged) Vakko; the one who constantly complained of stomach pain became *Vayarukazhappan*, an extremely tall Jose became *Kaalan* Jose implying his unusually long legs. *Kokku* Antho was very tall with a forward leaning while he walked that resembled the slow movement of a stork (*kokku*). Sometimes one's profession was given as prefix as in the case of Driver Joseph, Cleaner Kuttappan or Joker Kakki, who played the role of a Joker in *chavittunatakam*. *Kallu* Damodaran earned his nickname from his unrestrained habit of drinking toddy, the native brew of Kerala. The tailor in the locality lost his original identity and in due course came to be known as just Tailor (*thayyalkkaran*). A similar fate awaited an old lady in our neighbourhood who earned the nickname *undakkari* from her small-time job of selling *unda* (rice balls) in the locality. The people of the village found strange pleasure in this act of giving monicker that could hurt the people. People liberally used disparaging sobriquets such as *pottan* (deaf), *kurudan* (blind), and *ooma* (dumb), and *ponnathadiyan* which refers to a giant person and back then body shaming was a favourite pass time of the village people. Karunan had a patch of black pigmentation on the side of his neck and he was accorded with the nick name *Paandan* Karunan. Krishnan had a feminine look with a bride-like appearance that earned him the nickname *Manavatti* Krishnan.

In school, students were notoriously rude in giving nicknames to their teachers who would not find favour with them. In our high school we had an erudite personality as our chemistry teacher. His theory classes were as interesting as his practical classes. However, for some obscure reasons he fell suddenly silent. The normally insightful classes gave way to his silent mode of study devoid of lectures. From the beginning to the end of the class he would keep on writing notes on the black board which we were supposed to copy down in silence. With the teacher as well as the taught falling into silence the Chemistry class became a silent congregation, lost its charm for ever. The sudden change in his teaching style and behaviour prompted a few of us to confer him with the monicker "*ezhuthachan*", the lord of writing. (We did not regret having unintentionally used the name of Thunjath Ramanujan Ezhuthachan, revered as the Father of the Malayalam language, as a nickname to describe a peculiar habit of our teacher. In hindsight, I recognize the need for greater reverence and sensitivity when referring to such eminent cultural figures.) Though we left the school a year later, the nickname continued to haunt him for the rest of his career and even after. When he died recently (in February 2025) I felt sorry for the teenage mischief of my friends.

In our high school, there was a stunningly beautiful, tall, and fair lady teacher who had a unique sense of style. She would often wear handsome and attractive saris, and her hair would be put-up elegantly, supported by large buns. Donut-buns were commonly used by urban women that would make it appear that they have a huge updo by inserting the bun shaped tool. Her statuesque physique and impeccable appearance, which was the envy of other lady teachers, reminded us of the beautifully dressed mannequins found in textile showrooms. Fittingly, she was nicknamed "Partha's Lady," after the renowned textile brand of the time.

Ramakrishnan Master, a teacher at my high school, stood out from the other male teachers with his distinctive attire. He always wore colourful starched pants and a shirt, in contrast to the usual dress code of white *mundu* and white shirt. Because of this, he was nicknamed '*Kavara,*' which means 'bifurcated garment'.

In our college we had a security guard who was jet black though his hair, thick moustache, ill maintained stubble beard and hairs were all Snow White. A friend with a fantastic sense of imagination baptised him with the nickname "photo negative", a name that was so amusing and so appropriate for his visual appearance. People who migrated to distant places for job in distant past were often addressed by adding the name of the places where they migrated as prefixes. Thus, came people like *Poona* Prabhakaran, *Dubai* Kuttan and *Persia* Karunakaran.

My maternal grandmother, *Ammumma*, was a fair-skinned woman from a respectable middle-class family. We affectionately called her '*Veluthammumma,*' meaning 'white-skinned grandma,' to distinguish her from '*Karuthammumma*', our dark-skinned paternal grandmother. However, the latter had a deep-seated disdain for *Veluthammumma*.

Individuals with peculiar physical features, such as a bald head, thick moustache, and pot belly, would often be given nicknames with prefixes like *Kashandy, Meesa,* and *Kudavayaran.* A middle-aged man from a middle-class family, who was comfortably well-off but notorious for his frugal ways, was aptly nicknamed with the prefix *Lubdhan,* a term that literally means "miser." Villagers derived a childish delight in naming and shaming people with nicknames and monickers.

38.

Chacko: The Master Shoemaker of Palluruthy.

Chacko was once a renowned and sought-after cobbler in Palluruthy. Despite having a few competitors in the small town, his reputation remained unrivalled. His tiny workshop-cum-showroom was nestled in a small room beside the highway. With vast experience and profound expertise in crafting leather shoes, Chacko stood out from his peers. His leather shoes were highly popular, earning a reputation for combining exceptional craftsmanship with durability. He was, without a doubt, a master shoemaker of the time.

People from distant places would visit him to commission handmade shoes. Interestingly, despite the presence of a well-stocked and elegantly designed *Bata* showroom just a mile and a half away, customers continued to prefer Chacko's slippers. I would often marvel at the diverse array of slippers and chappals displayed on a brightly lit white surface whenever I passed by his shop. My family and I had purchased footwear from his shop on multiple occasions. During that time, wearing footwear was a luxury reserved for the privileged few.

When I completed my Higher Secondary education, my brother Rajiv Chettan gifted me a pair of shoes. He suggested that I get a tailor-made pair from Chacko, but I insisted on a branded pair from a popular brand. I was sceptical about Chacko's expertise, as his humble appearance and modest shop didn't match with my expectations of a shoe factory. Eventually, Rajiv Chettan relented and gifted me a fashionable pair of shoes that reflected the latest trends in footwear design.

Apart from being an exceptional cobbler, Chacko was also a skilled badminton player. In the evenings, he would play with his team on a makeshift court in front of Jayalakshmi Talkies. The sight of Chacko, clad in khaki trousers and a white vest, intensely playing badminton while adjusting his thick spectacles in place every now and then, was a familiar one. A small crowd of onlookers would gather around the court, savouring the lively match and enjoying the old film songs from the Jayalakshmi Talkies being carried by the gentle breeze.

Chacko was one of the many unsung heroes of Palluruthy, who passed away a few decades ago. In a world where everyday essentials, from apparel to footwear, smartphones, and automobiles, are dominated by international brands, the humble services provided by individuals like Chacko in a rustic backdrop will remain an enigma to the current generation.

39.

Wellness Wisdom: Simple Tips For A Happier, Healthier You.

"Health is wealth", is indeed a timeless proverb that reminds us that health is the most valuable of all possessions we have. We are all living a fast-paced life in an ever-changing world. We are constantly on the run- running after opportunities, running after wealth and possessions, running after our dreams. In this digital age, we are the victims of pressure, stress, strains and anxiety which our previous generations have not been subjected to. Work pressure, emotional trauma, societal stress, all paly their own parts in shaping the nature of our lives.

Our lives are full of unexpected ups and downs, as if a roller coaster ride. Modern life-style is quite stressful; we often struggle to overcome problems that are seemingly insurmountable. Problems in life come one after another as if to test our strength and endurance. A calm sea without waves is unimaginable. So is human life, where we are caught in an endless labyrinth of problems. But the important thing in life is to overcome those challenges with determination and resilience. To face the problems head on, not to run away. A determined mind can overcome even the toughest challenge. Our mind plays a pivotal role in shaping our destiny, although circumstances also have a significant impact. It's often said that we're mere pawns at the mercy of circumstances. However, our mind is a dynamic entity, torn between two opposing forces that act upon it simultaneously: the optimistic and pessimistic forces.

While we focus on the positive part of a problem a solution will naturally emerge from nowhere. Similarly, when we overly concern about the negative side of an issue, even an opportunity turns up into a problem. Achievers in life are not extraordinary people doing extraordinary things, rather they are ordinary mortals who do ordinary things in extraordinary ways. The greatest thing in our life is to keep ourselves always happy even when circumstances are not in our favour or control. Our physical, mental and emotional well-being play a part in keeping us happy and healthy. The simple truth about our life is that we are our own friend, bosom buddy and our own foe too. No one knows our problems, weaknesses, concerns, worries, anxieties, hopes, strengths, trials and tribulations better than us. Naturally no one else can suggest the best and most pragmatic solutions to our problems. No one can make us happy in life except ourselves and it's not the responsibility of anyone else. Our duty in life is to encourage and inspire the intimate "friend" in us and defeat the formidable "foe" living within us. Stay away from unnecessary arguments, keep away from negative people, learn to enjoy solitude, speak only half as you hear, never give advices unasked, don't stay where your presence is either not valued or not required, spent time with the elders, give ear to their stories as it will please them as much as they enlighten us. Refrain from gossips, slanderous comments on people and canards, restrict your talks to subjects that would gladden the listener. Engage in self-talks that will improve your self-confidence. I often engage myself in self-talks that helps me in sharpening my thought process. You are living your own life and don't let anyone to set boundaries for your life.

Our mind is in fact a wonderful machine that produces results based on the raw material that we feed in the form of thoughts and imagination, both positive and negative. Positive thoughts will produce positive results in our body and mind. Body is capable of self-producing Happiness Hormones such as Dopamine, Oxytocin, endorphin, and Serotonin with positive thoughts that can be exacerbated by regular meditation and prayer. Today our younger generation is frantically searching for the elusive happiness in life and they often find refuge in drugs like Ganja and MDMA, those toxic chemicals that are capable of producing happiness albeit artificially. Tetrahydrocannabinol (THC) is the chemical present in Ganja that is the psychoactive ingredient that generates the ecstatic feeling when the drug is consumed in mild doses. Interestingly, Anandamide is a similar chemical that is produced by our system when we engross in meditation, yoga and such mind-stimulating activities. The name Anandamide has a meaningful and beautiful origin. Derived from the Sanskrit word "Ananda" which means extreme delight, bliss, this particular chemical produces the euphoric effects in the brain. This naturally occurring chemical compound and THC, both bind to the same receptors. The point I want to emphasise is that we are searching for that evasive happiness when it is entrenched in ourselves. We need only to give the right stimulus to enable their production.

In the current society many of us work as midnight professionals working for our overseas masters according to their time and convenience. This has taken a heavy toll on the health and emotional well-being of many young professionals, especially in IT sector. Our new work culture is reshaping the life style and raises serious ethical questions.

Sleep deprivation leads them to depression and trauma. In fact, our bodies naturally produce Melatonin, the sleep hormone, which peaks around 10 pm. Adequate sleep (6-8 hours) is crucial for maintaining psychosomatic balance. When forced to work in unearthly hours under the constant glow of computers, the production of melatonin gets affected. Our circadian rhythm is disrupted. Screen glow and artificial lights are affecting our normal sleep pattern and the biological clock within us.

Finally, food too has an impact on our thoughts and behaviour. It's said that 'you are what you eat'. It's also said that 'as the food so the mind, as the mind so the man'. These sayings overemphasise the role of food on one's physical and emotional health. Ancient people categorised foods into three broad groups such as *Satwick, Rajsik* and *Tamsik* foods. In order to have a healthy body and a healthy mind we should consume more *Satwick* foods like fruits and vegetables. *Rajsik* foods are mainly non vegetarian foods that have to be controlled while *Tamsik* foods such as pickled and salted foods should be avoided.

"NO LIFE IS PERFECT; WE ALL HAVE OUR PROBLEMS AND ISSUES, AND I BELIEVE IT'S GOOD TO BE TRUE TO WHO YOU ARE"

Liberty Ross. (British model and actress)

40.

From Pond to Plate: The Rise And Fall of Kochi's Frog Trade.

Half a century ago, frogs lived peacefully in the wetlands, ponds, and canals of rural villages. However, their tranquillity was disrupted when someone discovered that frogs were a valuable commodity, sought after as a delicacy on European dining tables. What followed was a dark chapter in history, a mad rush to catch, process and export frogs. Until then, entrepreneurs in India had exported shrimp and fish as seafood to Europe and the US. Soon, frogs found themselves added to the list of seafood exports. A few seafood companies in West Kochi began processing and exporting frog legs, which proved more lucrative than traditional seafood. Soon other exporters located elsewhere in the country followed suit. This led to a frenzied rush to harvest the innocent amphibians.

During the cold, dark hours of the night after a rain, the frog catchers would appear from nowhere with a lighted petromax lamp and gunnysacks in hand. As stunned by the blinding light the frogs would emerge from their safe burrows and this would make the task of catching them easier. The young men in lungi and banyan would catch them one by one and transfer them to their gunny sacks. Those hapless creatures would be sold for a fortune to the exporters in the vicinity. As the trade flourished, the village youths vied with one another to capture frogs and sell them to the greedy exporters. The village teenagers under the leadership of Michael soon became rich and they spent a considerable part of their ill-gotten money on gambling and boozing. My father vehemently objected their attempts to catch frogs from the ponds in our homestead as he believed the mass destruction of frogs would lead to proliferation of mosquitoes, a concern that was quite true indeed.

The unchecked exploitation of frogs brought them to the brink of extinction. The handling of these creatures was cruel and gruesome, with live frogs having their legs butchered, only to be discarded and left to die a painful death. The gruesome manner in which those hapless beings were killed brought ill-repute to India and tarnished our image. As frog legs were considered tasty and nutritious, locals also began consuming them. They soon gained a respected spot on the menu of local taverns (*Kallu Shappu*), where they became an indispensable accompaniment. It was believed that frog legs possessed medicinal properties. Someone even suggested frog legs as a remedy for my asthma, and my mother arranged for some frog legs to be force-fed to me. However, the experience was unpleasant, and she never tried that remedy again, despite my persistent asthma.

Several environmental organizations such as Beauty Without Cruelty, an Animal Rights organisation and Kerala Sastra Sahitya Parishad (KSSP) raised concerns about the ecological consequences of selectively removing frogs from the ecosystem. As the frog population dwindled, mosquitoes and other pests flourished at alarming rates. After prolonged efforts of such organisations, the government finally banned the export of frog legs in 1978 and classified the poor animals under wildlife, a conservation measure without which the species would have been completely extinct. The common frogs used for exports, *Hoplobatrachus tigerinus* and *Euphlyctis hexadactylus*, were included in Schedule II, Part 2 of the Wildlife (Protection) Act,1972 bestowing them with a new lease of life. Thanks to the government ban, today these little creatures joyfully leap around our courtyard, savouring on mosquitoes and promptly predicting us an impending rain- the rain forecasters of the nature.

41.

Onam- A Festival Like No Other.

Onam is a unique festival celebrated by Malayalees across the globe in an atmosphere of equality, harmony, and peace—transcending barriers of class, caste, and culture. Unlike many other festivals, Onam stands out as a truly secular celebration, embraced by people from all religious backgrounds. It evokes a sense of nostalgia for a bygone era—an era of joy and beauty—when the legendary Asura King Mahabali ruled a land where everyone was treated as equals, free from lies, deceit, and falsehood (*kallam, chathy* and *polivachanam*). In that sense, Onam continues to be a powerful symbol of unity in diversity, as vividly portrayed in the timeless *Onappattu,*

Maveli naaduvaaneedum kaalam

Maanusharellarum onnupole,

aamodathode vasikkum kaalam,

aapathangarkumottilla thanum.

translated thus:

When Maveli ruled the land,

All people lived as equals,

They lived with joy and harmony,

No one faced danger or harm.

I belong to a generation that grew up enjoying Onam and its playful celebrations like *onakkali.* On occasions like Onam my mind would be filled with those bittersweet memories of childhood years, an overwhelming feeling of saudade when memories of Achan, Amma, Anandam, my second eldest sister, my grandmothers, and all those family members who left us, that would fill my mind. Onam is a rare kind of festival, the festival of festivals, the festival of oneness that we always looked forward to.

The festivities last for fourteen days, beginning with *Atham* and concluding with *Uthruttathy,* the fourth Onam, in the Malayalam month of *Chingam. Thiruvonam,* the most auspicious day, falls on the tenth day. A key aspect of the celebration is the *Athapookalam*—beautiful floral carpets crafted with care and creativity. These are laid in the front yard, which is first cleaned and purified by sprinkling cow dung water, a traditional practice. Children, both boys and girls, joyfully take part in creating the floral patterns. Early each morning, they gather flowers from gardens, fields, and the wild. From *Atham* to Onam, a new *pookkalam* is made daily, with elders guiding and encouraging the children's artistic imagination. On *Thiruvonam* day, the *pookkalam* is adorned with *Onathappan*—three conical clay figurines symbolizing the spirit of King Mahabali. In earlier times, children would receive the *Onathappan* with loud *'aarppoo irrooo irooo'* and *kurava*—joyful shouts and traditional ululations.

The most important part of Onam celebrations would be the traditional *Onasadya,* the delightful feast consisting of a dozen or more different items, including *pappadam, pazham* and *payasam. Sadya* is a grand, full-fledged vegetarian feast, beautifully balanced by an array of tastes—the sour punch of pickles, the bitter edge of *pavakka pachadi,* the salty crunch of *pappadam,* the tangy zest of banana, and the sweet delight of *payasam* - a symphony of flavours served on banana leaf.

Onakkali is a traditional dance form that is inseparably linked to Onam. The dance is performed by men, women and children. The dancers would line up in a circle around the *Pookkalam* with a lighted *Nilavilakku* in the centre. The *Kali* involves forward and backward movements of each player around the circle. As it's performed in a circular manner, it is also come to be known as *vattakkali.* There is no hard and fast rule regarding the number of dancers that may vary from a few to a dozen or more. The songs of the *Onakkali* would be sung by the lead dancer, the *Aasaan,* that would be chorused by all others in the group. Normally *Onakkali Pattu* would be centred around stories from epics like Mahabharata and Ramayan. The melodious songs, accompanied by pound clapping and rhythmic movements lend extraordinary grace and beauty to *Onakkali.* As the tempo of the songs increased so the foot movements finally reaching its crescendo. The dance typically concluded abruptly with the ubiquitous verse: '*Tharikida Thimrita Thai*'. On Onam and following days, small troupes of *Onakkali* performers would visit middle class homes and performed for a meagre remuneration. When such *Onakkali* team visited us, Amma would send them off with a glass of hot black tea and fried banana chips apart from a small amount that would gladden those young boys and girls.

Puli Kali, the tiger dance, was another popular entertainment that was practiced only during the Onam days when some village youth, usually with gigantic tummy, would transform themselves into tigers with faces and bare chests painted beautifully and colourfully to resemble a tiger. The *kali* involved a hunter attired in hunter's dress complete with a fedora, pointing a gun try to shoot an elusive tiger, as someone would sing aloud *'Pulida vale panam ketty, pulithumbel panam ketty'*, and finally the beast falls to the hunter's bullets. The famous *Puli Kali* of Thrissur is held on *Naalaam* Onam, showcasing a spectacular parade of two-legged tigers prowling and prancing through the streets, dancing in rhythm with the vibrant beats of traditional drums. Crowds from far and wide flock to Thrissur to witness this electrifying celebration of the tiger dance.

The high point of Onam was the *onakkodi,* a new pair of clothes that every child of our generation longed for. I was fortunate enough to get two pairs, one from Amma and another from eldest brother-in-law. For the first Onam after their marriage, when I was hardly three, Valsala, my sister and Bahuleyan, brother-in-law presented me with a fantastic *Onakkodi.* It included a wonderful white terylene shirt and equally beautiful half pants. I vividly remember the shirt was embellished with embroidery that depicted a scenery of a coconut palm with a couple of birds flying beyond. It was a time when terylene has not become popular and was expensive too. He bought it from Mattancherry bazar where such exotic products were available in the grey markets. Wearing the new terylene shirt and shorts the day after Onam holidays I went to the nursery school of Unni *Aasaan.* My mood was upbeat and I imagined how my friends would welcome me in my new attire. However, contrary to my expectations their response was lukewarm that saddened me. Some looked at me with envy. In fact, those children from impoverished families could not afford a square meal and many wore old and faded clothes. It's understandable they'd feel envious or insecure when seeing peers with new clothes.

After the first, second, third, and fourth Onam, the celebrations would gradually draw to a close, much to the disappointment of both children and elders. As the festivities faded, a quiet gloom would settle in—the long wait for yet another Onam, and another set of *Onakkodi,* had begun.

42.

Small Screen, Big Impact: The Evolution of Television.

Till late seventies, I have seen television sets only in the old black and white cinemas where the gigantic television would be another gadget to show the upper-class opulence of the hero. The first television set in our locality was owned by Sudarshan, a wealthy gentle man who was the Regional Manager of a well-known multinational company. When Indira Gandhi was assassinated in 1985, people in the neighbourhood thronged his magnificent residence to watch the body of Mrs Gandhi lying in state, bedecked with flowers. To accommodate the crowd, he placed the TV in a vantage position in the sprawling veranda.

It was in late eighties that television programmes were started airing from Kochi, for which we should thank K Karunakaran, the then Chief Minister of Kerala and S Krishna Kumar, who was Minister for Information and Broadcasting from 1984-1989 in Rajiv Gandhi ministry. Though television broadcasting started in India in September 1959 Kerala had to wait long for over a quarter century to start Malayalam transmission. DD Malayalam was launched on January 1, 1985 by Karunakaran in Thiruvananthapuram. Malayalam programmes were aired through terrestrial transmission and programmes from DD Delhi Kendra through satellite transmission. Achan bought a brand-new TV of **Sony Orson,** the most reputed brand of the day. It was the only colour television set in our locality, that soon became a cynosure of all eyes. A few had B/W sets of **Keltron** and **BPL**. The heavy instrument was brought home secured safely on the carrier of an Ambassador car. The equipment was so heavy that it was brought inside the home with the help of a few neighbours.

Fixing the antenna in the right direction was a difficult task indeed. Attached atop a long metal pole and firmly fixed on the parapet wall, one would turn the antenna in all possible directions till a clear picture is obtained when someone from the floor below would loudly give direction to the one on rooftop. Unexpected gusts and rain would occasionally play spoilsport with the enjoyment as it would mar the clarity and picture quality with too much grains. We would curse the rains and winds for snapping our string of enjoyment. In the 1990s and early 2000s, government-imposed power cuts came as a shock to TV enthusiasts, disrupting their entertainment routine.

On Sunday mornings our modest drawing room would transform itself into a cinema hall, as children and women from the locality would gather there to watch *Ramayan* serial. Anticipating the crowd, Amma would serve breakfast earlier than usual time, while Achan would arrange a dozen steel chairs in the room. This has become our Sunday morning routine for the coming few years as when *Ramayan* ended *Mahabharat* started. In fact, Ramanand Sagar's *Ramayan* (1987-88) and B R Chopra's *Mahabharat* (1988-90) played important roles in the evolution of TV as a popular medium. These two epics had catapulted Ramanand Sagar to a space above Valmiki and Chopra was elevated to the place above Ved Vyasa. Such was the influence of them over a population of illiterate Indians. The *Ramayan* was one of the most popular TV serials in Indian television history. Arun Govil and Deepika Chikhalia, who portrayed Lord

Ram and Goddess Sita respectively, were idolized by millions of fans. Many uneducated villagers revered them as divine incarnations, worshipping them whenever possible. I recall an incident in the early 1990s when Deepika visited our city to launch a popular footwear brand. Chaos erupted as fans swarmed the location, and the police struggled to control the crowd. The serial's influence on viewers was so profound that they sacrificed their usual routines, including meals, festivals, and celebrations, every Sunday morning to watch it. They would sit glued to the TV, eyes fixed on the screen, and never miss a single episode. The electricity board even ensured uninterrupted power supply during the show's time slot, knowing that any disruption would invite widespread discontent. The Congress government at the centre aired *Ramayan* with the hidden agenda of capitalizing on Hindu vote banks. However, the TV serial unexpectedly turned out to be a blessing in disguise for the Sangh Parivar, which leveraged it to their advantage. In fact, the timing of *Ramayan*'s broadcast gave a significant boost to the Hindutva forces' campaign for Ram Janmabhoomi, revitalizing a previously feeble voice and creating a powerful rallying point. It's interesting to recall that in the early nineties, when I was working in Nairobi, Kenyan Television used to air *Ramayan* on Sunday evening, of course with sub-titles in Swahili, the national language of Kenya. Programmes like *Bharat ek Khoj*, a serial based on Jawahar Lal Nehru's epic literary work Discovery of India, R K Narayan's *Malgudi Days, Buniyaad*, the serial that had shot Shah Rukh Khan to prominence, Master Mind India Quiz by the celebrated quiz master Sidharth Basu (the audience listened in rapt attention his rapid-fire patter), Sports Quiz by Narottam Puri, the English news being read by Neeti Ravindran, Rini Khanna, Gitanjali Iyer, Saran Das and Bhaskar Bhattacharya , the poll analysis by Prannoy Roy and Vinod Dua; all popular programmes that captivated Indian television audience. In the early days of Doordarshan, interestingly, news bulletins consisted of the newsreader merely reading from a printed text, with visuals limited to a few photographs and videos being a rare luxury. *Bharat ek Khoj* was a coming-of-age serial that serialised the scholarly book of Jawahar Lal Nehru during the golden age of Doordarshan. Directed, written and Produced Shyam Benegal, the drama unfolds the 5000-year-old marvellous history of India from the beginning to the time of independence in 1947. The work reflected the Nehruvian hopes and aspirations of a 20th century India in which Roshan Seth enacted the role of Pandit Jawaharlal Nehru. News, however, were mere lip service to the ruling party and reflected its policies and often degrading to the level of the mouth piece of the party in power. Nevertheless, the emergence of private channels breathed in a whiff of fresh air as they tried to give a somewhat impartial picture of important political developments. **Asianet** was the first private owned Malayalam news channel, founded by Sasi Kumar and Regi Menon, that started operation in 1993. Then programmes started early in the morning and ended by eleven at night.

The broadcasting of Malayalam programmes marked a significant chapter in Malayalam television history. The weekend Malayalam films proved to be quite popular that was watched by thousands. In fact, the arrival of television has influential impact on the habits of the people. They rescheduled their routines like family prayers, the study time of students and even dinner times. The usually chatty dinners became silent rituals as family members sat around the dining table, their eyes firmly fixed on the screen. Under the spell of the mini screen, the elders often became oblivious of their health issues as they gleefully watched TV programmes. Tear-jerking serials have turned many active individuals into couch potatoes, as they become engrossed in shows with often implausible storylines and far-fetched themes. The influence of TV on children was astonishing, as they kept themselves away from their favourite games and sat in front of the TV in rapt attention, their eyes glued to the screen as they silently enjoyed the programmes.

Over the years television sets have undergone a spectacular evolution from the small-screen, heavy Cathode Ray Tube to slim LCD to sleek and gigantic LED screens to Laptops and handy Smartphones. The digital revolution has enabled customers to watch programmes they prefer at choicest time. Now programmes are available 24x7, and we have separate channels for news, sports, entertainment, business, wildlife and education.

When TV became a ubiquitous gadget with an overdose of programmes on mediocre topics round the clock, round the year, it lost much of its original charm testifying the old saying that even nectar is poisonous if taken in excess.

43.

Palluruthy Market: The Village Mall of Another Time.

The marvellous history of Palluruthy would be incomplete without mentioning the ancient Veli market, a one-of-a-kind marketplace in its time, where one could buy everything from daily essentials like salt to rare items like camphor—true to the Malayalam adage "*uppu thottu karppooram vare*".

Palluruthy boasted a vast, bustling market right in the heart of the village, beside the highway. This nearly century-old village market featured brick-and-cement, tile-roofed buildings on all four sides, enclosing a central square. Within this courtyard stood a large tile-roofed building with open sides, which housed the fish market. Around forty small shops were spread across the surrounding structures, occupied by traders engaged in various businesses. The nondescript shops had wooden ceilings and large doors made of multiple wooden panels, securely fitted into channels carved into the door frames, called *niarappalaka* doors.

At one end, near the western entrance, was the provision store of Parameswaran Chettan. For decades, this was our supermarket, where we procured all our groceries—rice, wheat, oil, and cattle feed—for an entire month. The benevolent Parameswaran offered us a rare credit facility, allowing purchases on the condition that payments were settled in full by the following month. This privilege was extended only to a select few in the village, the primary criterion being a steady income. After every purchase, he meticulously recorded details in his thick ledger, summarizing them in our pocket-sized *pattu pusthakam* with his superb calligraphy. This tiny booklet was essentially our credit card, requiring updates after every transaction.

People used separate containers for fish, vegetables and groceries. An oblong shaped, hand-crafted, woven basket made of thin bamboo reeds or cane with a round, narrow mouth fitted with a small handle (*meen vatty*) for keeping fish and clothes bags of different sizes for rice and other groceries. For coconut oil, we used a thick glass bottle and a used petrol can for kerosene.

At the beginning of each month, upon receiving a money order from Achan, Amma would prioritize settling the dues owed to Parameswaran. My elder siblings have vivid memories of shopping at his store. He was a tall, lean man with dark skin and a prominent Adam's apple. His sunken cheeks gave his face a sharp appearance. When in a joyful mood, he would boast—sometimes with exaggeration—about his wife's wealthy uncle.

The flour mill, located in the southwest corner, housed two grinding machines side by side. The larger one had a massive funnel-shaped hopper for grinding wheat and water-soaked rice, while the smaller one was exclusively used for grinding chillies, coriander, and turmeric. Only one machine operated at a time. The mill was run by a stout middle-aged man in a *kallimundu* and white *banyan*, presumably the owner, and a young assistant who handled the machine. Their voices were loud as they struggled to converse over the relentless hum of grinding. By the end of the day, both were covered in a fine layer of grain flour.

During twilight hours, women lined up at the flour mill with cloth bags full of grains. I remember spending many such evenings there with my sister Sheela, enduring mosquito bites and deafening sound.

Thuruthan's stationery shop stood in the eastern corner, catering to schoolchildren who came to buy notebooks and ink. Apart from Parameswaran's store, there were a few other grocery shops owned by Devadas, Thavarna family, and a store run by a Co-operative Society. Several tea shops were also part of the market—the food courts of an earlier time.

In the central courtyard, which functioned as the fish market, vendors—both men and women—gathered every morning and evening, displaying their fresh catch on the unkempt floor. Ice was unavailable in those days, and even when it became accessible, people refused to buy iced fish, assuming it was stale.

Vendors selling high-quality fish like *Karimeen, Kanambu, Aavoli,* and *Chemballi* occupied the middle section of the shed, while those selling cheaper fish like *Kilimeen, Mullan, Netholi,* and small unsorted fishes; clams, and dried seafood and *Chemmeen parippu* positioned themselves along the periphery. Back then, fish were sold in small heaps called *panku* (meaning "share") rather than being weighed. Each heap ranged between one and one-and-a-half kilograms. In the sixties, a heap of sardines cost 15 paise, and mackerel ranged between 25 and 40 paise, depending on size. Weighing fish became common practice much later.

A large well served the market's water needs. Nearby, the mutton stall was run by an elderly Muslim man, whom we affectionately called *Ikka,* alongside his son, a man in his early thirties. *Ikka,* always attired in a *mundu* and blood-stained Jubba, suffered from constant coughing and breathing difficulties. The sight of blood-dripping goat carcasses hung on hooks, alongside severed heads displayed openly, always made me shiver. *Ikka* would ask the waiting customer in his distinctive style, *"monikku enthu venam?"* ("what do you want, son"). Father and son shared a steaming glass of tea as they chopped meat into pieces and placed them on the balance. Had the young man contracted TB from his father through their shared glass? Who knows! In the late sixties, a Kilogram of mutton was priced at ₹4. Amma often bought lamb bones to make soup, which she force-fed me to rebuild my strength after recovering from pneumonia. Back then, two forelimbs and two hind limbs of a lamb cost 12 *ana,* equivalent to 75 paise, while a Kilo of mutton liver was priced under ₹5.

Mutton, liver, and other by-products were neatly wrapped in *chembila* and lovingly handed over by *Ikka,* while his son collected payments and kept them in a wooden cash box. Palluruthy market gained fame for offering every food item under one roof—from fish and meat to groceries, vegetables, fruits, and cooked food—a rarity at the time.

There were also shops selling clothes, stitched skirts, undergarments, glass bangles, and fashionable items for women. An exclusive shop sold earthenware like *chatty, kalam, kudam,* and *kooja,* owned by my classmate Ousepachan's father. A similar shop sold *kutta, murram,* screw pine mat, and bamboo-woven household items.

Opposite the mutton stall was a *pappadam*-making unit where an elderly man and his two sons tirelessly rolled out *pappadams* on wooden boards using rolling pins. Next to it stood Ramakrishnan's shop, packed with toys and countless miscellaneous items. I once bought half a dozen cowries and later a pencil cutter from his store. Any leftover one-, two-, or three-paise coins after shopping were spent on such simple treasures—approved by Amma.

Vendors selling jackfruits, tapioca, mangoes, and bulky produce traded in the open ground. Sellers of fresh-cut grass and jackfruit twigs - the staple food for cattle, *athar* (cheap perfumes), *ottamooli* (singular cures for incurable diseases), *mayilenna* (oil ostensibly extracted from peacock), and palmists also shared the space. Small-time traders, mostly women selling homegrown vegetables like spinach, long beans, and snap melons, happily coexisted. Occasionally, cotton candy sellers joined the crowd, fascinating children with the way sugar spun into fluffy clouds in manually rotated drums. One day, a snake charmer appeared in the market, much to the amazement of the children and women who gathered around his open bamboo basket to get a clear view of the serpent coiled inside. As the charmer gently and rhythmically blew his horn, the snake slowly extended its neck and swayed, displaying its fangs. Curious to know their future, the naïve villagers gathered around the fortune-teller. The ice-candy man, with a wooden box fitted on his bicycle, full of different coloured ice sticks, did brisk business.

The market's main building was flanked by a few structures of similar size, housing tailor Pavithran's humble shop, the Mahalakshmi Typewriting Institute, Chilanka Club, Kerala Pharmacy, Central Radios and Electricals, the radio showroom owned by Kalarickal Gopalakrishnan and Iris Studio.

On the opposite side of Veli Maidan, by the roadside, stood Nice Bakery—the only bakery in the locality—owned by

Sundaran. Back then, it was a far cry from today's well-stocked, elegantly arranged establishments. A dozen or so thick glass jars with equally sturdy lids lined the shelves, holding a modest selection: dried grapes, large irregular lumps of sugar (*kalkkandam*), rusk, buns, bread, and the ubiquitous *venna biscuit*—those small, fried butter buns beloved by all. Whenever we were down with fever, our survival often relied solely on black tea and the rusk procured from Sundaran Chettan's humble bakery. Remarkably, the bakery still operates today, maintained by his son—though extensively modernized to keep pace with others in the neighbourhood. I could almost smell the butter biscuits and hear the clink of those glass jars!

Majeed, the middle-aged man who collected vendor fees, had a rough appearance, his face scarred by smallpox. I found him intimidating, and the mere sight of him sent shivers down my spine. On Sundays the market would come alive earlier than usual as people from neighbouring places too visited searching for their favourite fish and choicest vegetables.

The market played an important role in the lives of generations, serving as a place they routinely visited to procure essential goods for their daily needs—unlike modern malls, where we stop by to buy a packet of tea and, a few hours later, find ourselves leaving with a gigantic TV set.

Sometime back someone tried to make it posh, but later abandoned his plans. Decades later, the market remains largely unchanged, except for minor modifications and new ownership. While the setting endures, the characters have changed. Parameswaran, Devadas, *Ikka* and his son, the miller, the snake charmer, and many other merchants were once flesh-and-blood figures with their own stories to tell.

44.

Remembering My Solo Whistle Concert.

During my younger days, I had a strong passion for whistling film tunes and folk melodies-I could whistle them with ease, with the songs reverberating through the air. In my journey to perfect the art of whistling, I was inspired by Joshy, my neighbourhood friend; who became my guru and trainer in this rare skill. Over time, I mastered different styles of whistling, simply by adjusting the size of opening and shape of my lips. My friends admired my talent, and often received their praise. However, elders in the family considered whistling an impolite art and never encouraged it. Whistling in the presence of elders were considered a sign of utmost disrespect and would be sternly dealt with. Whistling was then a male dominated activity, girls and women never attempted as it was treated as an unpardonable sin by the patriarchy. Friends' appreciation made me proud. The stern warnings and occasional disapproving glances from elders did not curb my enthusiasm. Amma always discouraged me as she feared whistling would aggravate my breathing problem. However, later my family physician suggested it along with a few other exercises to improve my lung power.

I used to whistle even at odd hours, when in a playful mood after finishing home works. However, Ammumma would frighten me with her fearful story.

One evening, as I was casually whistling an old film tune, Ammumma came and whispered in a hushed tone; "do you know what happens to boys who whistle at night?" she asked, her eyes glowing with a mysterious glow. I shook my head in the negative. Moving closer, she said, "if anyone dares to whistle at night, snakes would come out of their burrows and would coil beneath his cot". A sudden chill ran down my spine. I was overpowered by a strange sense of awe.

As I lay in bed that night, I kept my ear to the ground, searching for the hissing sound coming from beneath my cot. But I heard nothing. To reassure myself, I scanned the dimly lit corners of the room and looked under the cot and found only an old, dust-covered brass vessel (*chembu)* and a pair of worn-out chappals. That night I slept with my legs safely wrapped under the blanket. Tossing and turning on my bed, I fell asleep very late as my usual sound sleep eluded me. From that moment onwards I stopped my solo whistling performances during the serene night hours, wondering if Grandma was right-perhaps the reverberations were attracting snakes, just like in her story. Thus, the made-up story of Grandma had its intended effect. Whether it was true or not, I did not have the guts to test fate.

Grandma, like other village elders, had many scary tales up her sleeve shrouded in enigma.

Tail piece.

It's quite fascinating to note that many superstitions surround whistling, transcending countries, cultures, and civilisations. In many nations, there's a long-held belief that whistling at night is undesirable, as it's thought to attract evil spirits. In Indian society, whistling has never been considered a good habit, and whistlers are often viewed with contempt and aversion, damaging their reputation. Whistling indoors, especially after sunset, is deemed inauspicious in many cultures, believed to bring poverty and misfortune. The people of Turkey and China believed that nighttime whistling invited evil, a notion shared by the Japanese. Even in the UK, deep-rooted beliefs existed, such as the legend of the "seven whistlers" – seven birds or spirits foretelling death. Sailors were also prohibited from whistling onboard, fearing it would bring bad luck to the crew and ship.

What we fail to recognize is that whistling, like many other musical talents, is a creative talent requiring patience and skill to master. Whistling is an art that should be encouraged among the younger generation, not just as a pastime but also as a stress reliever.

45.

Rural Weddings: Celebrating Innocence.

In our contemporary society, marriages are celebrated in fanciful ways full of razzmatazz and panache. Even among the lower-middle class, marriages have become trending events and the occasions are used to showcase family wealth and affluence. The number of celebrities and political figures decide the weight and value of the occasion and have emerged as new benchmarks. Cutting across classes and castes, the extravaganza that accompany marriages has deeply infected the society as symbols of pomp and opulence. These days the marriages are preceded by many related ceremonies such as Mehndi, Haldi, save the date and bachelor parties.

However, till a few decades ago, marriages were solemn occasions, the event used to be celebrated with all the sanctity they deserved, in accordance with the customs and believes. Marriages of yester decades were wildly discrepant, a far cry from modern-day marriages. Then marriages used to be social events in which the people from the entire locality participated. Usually, celebrations would commence a few days before the function in which relatives, friends and neighbours participated wholeheartedly.

Celebrations would begin with *Kaalnaattu karmam,* the ceremonial planting of the first pillar of the temporary pandhal, a few days before the marriage. A make-shift pandhal would be erected in the front courtyard, using bamboo poles, and tarpaulin sheets. The erection of pandhal was carried out in an unprofessional manner in which youths would take the lead while the elders would direct them in the venture with advices and instructions. It would be then decorated on all sides with *cheenaveli,* a kind of bamboo grills painted in white, while the roof would be embellished colourfully with used bedsheets. The *manipandhal,* the small enclosure in the middle where the newly wed would be seated, would be profusely decorated with elegant frills using colourful silk sarees in accordance with the wild imagination and dubious skills of the youth who erect the structure.

A couple of days prior the event, the neighbourhood women would assemble in the house and would engage themselves in mediocre tasks like sorting dirt and stone pieces from rice and other grains. They would gather once again on the day before the function, this time to participate in the elaborate process of cooking, by peeling onion, potato and slicing vegetables as directed by the cook. It was a laborious task to de-husk dozens of coconuts and scarping them on wooden scrapers, a job accomplished by the neighbourhood youths. Extracting coconut milk required for curries and *payasam* was equally cumbersome. By late night the women would slowly withdraw from the scene and menfolk would take the centre stage. After gulping down a few pegs of their favourite brew, they would become energetic and engage in playing cards.

Thenge pattu, the blaring of old film and drama songs from horn-shaped 'Ahuja" speakers tied on top of coconut palms would begin by evening. As the stock of vinyl plates of records are exhausted, there comes the ideal time for the villagers to express their musical talents. This high decibel, unsightly musical performance in their harsh voice would continue till dawn, much to the discomfiture of the neighbours. (As a young boy, I had a passion for singing, but fear of judgement that what others would think, stopped me from singing in public. This persistent worry about *'what others might think'* has been a costly constraint, preventing me back from pursuing my passion. However, a few of my classmates sang in cultural programmes in school with ease despite their lesser talent. While I envied their ability to perform, I realized that their self-assurance often outshone mine, despite having less natural talent. It was a valuable lesson in how confidence can overcome obstacles and sometimes outweigh raw talent).

For Hindu marriages, a sumptuous *sadya* was the norm, that would include 15-20 various culinary items. For Christian marriages, meals with beef curry were indispensable. They would celebrate the evening before the marriage with a modest dinner with cooked rice, *pulisserry*, cabbage *thoran*, and *potty curry*, a unique and delicious preparation using the cleaned intestine of cow. The freshly butchered, blood dripping carcass of the beast would be hung in a corner of the make-shift kitchen, the *kalavara,* like a decorative piece. I have vivid recollection of attending one such pre-marriage evening in our neighbourhood. In the backyard, I happened to see the skinned and eviscerated body of a large cow, being hung down, while a few elders huddled around, gossiping and sipping an alcoholic drink. The sight of the bloody carcass had presented me with many sleepless nights. In Kerala Christian wedding, there is a charming pre-wedding ritual called *Madhuram Vekkal* that means offering sweet. This is a solemn occasion that is celebrated on the eve of the wedding in the homes of both bride and groom accompanied by family prayers, blessings by elder family members, merry making and songs.

For Muslim marriages, *Neychoru*, the delectable ghee rice was the choicest delicacy. In those days foods were served on the floor, as the guests sat on palmyra mats. Serving food, cleaning the pandhal after serving each group, to finally cleaning the huge *uruli* and *vaarp* and the dismantling of the pandhal, everything would be meticulously accomplished by the youth. Those were rare occasions of utmost friendship and camaraderie.

Quite interesting were the village customs. In those days, it was a familiar scene that near the pandhal a young man would be seated beside a table with a thick register. As each guest parted after the ceremony, he/she would give a modest amount as marriage gift- a custom referred as *osaaram.* The name of the donor would be written with the amount against the name. This ledger would be kept as a valuable document by the patriarch of the family and for marriages in the locality, he would meticulously scan this document to decide the quantum of gift money to be reciprocated. During his adolescent years, Rajiv, my elder brother had donned the role of recording such gifts. As he had superb calligraphy, the uneducated locals would accord him the task which he did with utmost dedication.

In those days only a limited number of people - the close relatives, friends and immediate neighbours, accompanied the groom to the bride's home. While groom's parents, uncles and other guests would remain in his house. Back then, in the houses of both the bride and groom a similar kind of vegetarian *sadya* would be served. In those times the last *panthy* (the group of gastronomes) would be earmarked for the poor, the destitutes and the labourers and was referred as "*Sarvani sadya*". For this the left-over meals would be served. What an irony that the working-class who toiled in our land and farms, who provided us with many valuable and unique services like mending fences, plucking coconuts and braiding palm leaves, were made to wait for their turns. In front of every marriage venue, long queues of those uninvited guests, patiently waiting for their turn for the *Sarvani sadya* were common. Such was the intensity of poverty.

Like marriages, the receptions too used to be simple celebrations. A modest "tea party" would be arranged in the evening as part of marriage function. Such "tea party" invariably had a set menu to which everyone in the village adhered to and no one ever attempted to modify the eatables till late seventies. A rectangular piece of Halwa, a Laddu, a Jalebi, and a spoonful of mixture- these were the quotidian items which would be served in a plate, of course a *Poovan Pazham* to complement the array of delicious eatables. A cup of coffee or tea would be served or in some cases Goli soda (carbonated water in thick glass bottles with a narrow neck tightly closed by a Goli). In one such reception I attended in our neighbourhood, we were served with bottles of "Crush" a brand of sweet, aerated drink much to the delight of the guests. For reception, the newlywed couple would be presented with simple gifts, and they would reciprocate by offering a return gift- usually a lemon and a *vadamalli*, (Bachelors Button) flower stuck on a small piece of *eerkkil*. What a simple marriage function? Those were rare occasions that the people made good use of to renew social contacts and friendships.

Koottamma and *Koottappan.*

Among Christians, when a girl was married in olden days, a couple would accompany the bride as she steps into her new home for the first time as a young, coy *manavatty*. The couple thus accompanied the bride are called *Koottamma* and *Koottappan*. As the name suggests they act as caretaker, friend and companion to the girl in the new, strange environment of the groom's house. They continue to be there for a few days as the bride is settled in her new surroundings. It was normally the *Koottamma* who answered to the questions of curious neighbours.

Adukkala Kaanal/Veedu Kaanal.

Adukkala kaanal, which literally means "seeing the kitchen," was an important part of the marriage ceremony. It involved an announced visit by the bride's parents, uncles, aunts, and a few close relatives—about a dozen in total—to the groom's house a few days after the wedding.

In those days, the bride's mother was not supposed to visit the groom's home during the engagement or wedding. *Adukkala kaanal* or *veedu kaanal* marked her first opportunity to visit her daughter in her new home and become acquainted with her in-laws.

For this much-anticipated visit, the mother would bring a variety of gifts, including sweets, bananas, and household items. The sweets and bananas were shared with relatives and neighbours.

As a child, I always looked forward to *adukkala kaanal* ceremonies in the families of our relatives and neighbours, knowing I'd get to enjoy a share of those delicious sweets.

I have vivid memories of the *adukkala kaanal* ceremony of Anandam, my second eldest sister, in the early seventies—a cherished memory of someone who left us far too soon. Amma accompanied by Achan and a few close relatives left for her home in Edappally. Apart from some house hold items and two banana bunches, three huge containers full of black Halwa, Laddu and Jalebi formed part of the gifts that were kept fastened on the carrier of an Ambassador car. Achan arranged Velayudhan Chettan, the expert sweet maker of the village who prepared the delicious sweets assisted by his son Mohanan. It took a day for them to prepare the three items which they cooked in a temporary kitchen, set up in front of our cattle shed. I caught a glimpse of the elaborate arrangements they had made for sweet-making, but Amma warned me I'd be late for school if I lingered. I left that day quite reluctantly, missing the chance to witness the making of my favourite sweets firsthand.

Village life was fascinating—full of unique customs and traditions

46.

The Vanishing Art of Banana Ripening: The Smoking Pit Technique.

Strange and quite interesting are the ways of village life. Many of the crude technologies employed in bygone decades may sound incredible and outlandish to the current generation. During my growing up years in our sleepy village, I had not only just witnessed but really enjoyed many such practices and procedures unique to village life. Now, I am delighted to share one such technique that was widely used in our village during fifties and sixties to ripen banana.

In those days banana cultivation was a common practice in the village. In the modest kitchen garden in our homestead, one time we had as many as two dozen plantains with fully formed bunches, thanks to the hard work and passionate caring of my second eldest brother Rajiv Chettan during his early adult years. He had also mastered the technique of preparing smoking pits and ripening banana- a procedure called *"kuzhi kachal"* in Malayalam. After harvesting banana bunches, he would embark on a laborious job of making smoking pits. Back then it was a team work, with his friends enthusiastically participating in the procedure and later sharing the bounty.

The laborious process begins with digging two side-by-side pits in the ground, each about two to two and a half feet deep and separated by a few inches. One pit is smaller, while the other is slightly wider and longer to accommodate an entire bunch of bananas. A small opening is then created between the two pits to allow the passage of smoke.

Next, dried leaves and hay are filled into the smaller pit, while the banana bunch is placed in the larger one, sandwiched between layers of banana leaves above and below. With preparations complete, the actual smoking process begins.

Chettan lights the dry material in the smaller pit, producing thick smoke that flows through the connecting channel into the larger pit where the bananas are kept for ripening. The ripening pit is then sealed with plantain leaves or coconut fronds to trap the smoke inside. This smoking continues for several hours, allowing the dense smoke to circulate and hasten the ripening process.

This pit-smoking method not only preserves the bananas but also enhances their sweetness, making them a delightful treat during hot summer months. The smouldering leaves release smoke containing ethylene gas, a natural ripening agent. The green bananas absorb this gas, triggering the ripening process, further aided by the warmth from the smoke.

Traditional smoking pits offer numerous benefits: improved flavour and texture, cost-effectiveness, eco-friendliness, and a completely natural process. However, over time, this age-old technique— *kuzhi kachal*—was gradually replaced by artificial methods involving harmful chemicals, leading to its decline.

Smoking pits have a long history in India and were widely used, especially in rural communities, for food and crop preservation. Though they have faded from common practice, they are still employed in some parts of Asia today.

47.

Kitchen Secrets of Kerala: Traditional Dishes for Body, Mind, and Soul.

This is the story of some unusual culinary delights that are unique to Kerala and I grew up savouring them. Kerala has a few traditional yet unique foods which have profound impacts on body and soul. Handed down generations, many such recipes are on the verge of extinction as there are few practitioners for such culinary delights. Nor any documented recipes are available as they passed through word -of-mouth along generations.

As we consider their health benefits, one would be astonished as most of such foods have health benefits as proved by investigations using tools of current science.

1. MANGO KERNAL SEED (MKS) APPAM (*KATTANDI* APPAM).

Several decades ago, when I was a kid of 5 or 6. Amma used to prepare a special culinary item using the seeds (kernal) of ripe mangoes. During summer months, the normal season of mangoes, we would collect the mango seeds, which are discarded after eating the sweet and fleshy meat, in a gunny bag. When the collection reaches sufficient quantity, Amma would embark on the preparation of this excellent dish. Separating the white and soft mango seeds from the thick and hard, fibrous shell husk was a laborious and time-consuming task which would be accomplished by my two elder sisters. The seeds once extracted would be given an initial washing in clean water and then would be ground into on a grinding stone to obtain a bitter, thick paste. The paste would then be wrapped in a fine cloth and the bundle would be hung overnight in a corner of the kitchen- a process to get rid of the bitter taste (*kattu*) due to the presence of tannins. This would take 10-12 hours. next day, early in the morning Amma would take the mango seed paste, by now the bitter taste would have dissipated, and would be blended with rice flour, scraped coconut, and jaggery. Using this rare dough mixture, she would make delicious Appam which we relished enthusiastically. When asked about the role of the mango seed as an ingredient, she expressed her ignorance and added that she was merely following a culinary practice that she had learnt from Ammumma, her mother. We savoured such tasty mango seed Appam till late seventies and after the marriage of my sisters, an ageing Amma found the task too tedious and thus the tradition of a rare kind of Appam became a memory.

However, later I used to ruminate on such olden days and wondered what would have prompted our ancestors to use mango seed as an ingredient of a common food of the land. I firmly believe that the seeds contained some chemical compounds that had a beneficial impact on health.

Recent findings by food technologists and nutritionists have revealed surprising benefits of mango seeds. They are indeed nutrient-dense and sources of micro-nutrients including Vit. A, C, and E and bioactive compounds like phenolic compounds and flavonoids. They are also a good source of protein, lipids, fibre and essential amino acids.

The many antioxidants help reduce cholesterol levels, thereby promoting cardio-vascular health, alleviate digestive issues like dysentery and diarrhoea by promoting the growth of beneficial gut flora, help in diabetes management and reduces blood glucose levels.

Eating mango seeds boosts immunity, reduces inflammation, supports liver health, improves respiratory health and bone health.

Next time, before throwing away a mango seed, think twice, you could be discarding a treasure trove of health benefits, all for free as it is a reservoir of many rare compounds which have health benefits. It can be used for making *Kattandi* Appam, a typical traditional evening snack- a food for body and mind.

2. *KARKKIDAKA KANJI.*

Also known as *Marunnu kanji* as it contains a number medicinal plants, *Karkkidaka Kanji* is a unique Ayurvedic preparation usually consumed during the Malayalam month of *Karkkidakam* as a rejuvenating food. It is an excellent example of food being consumed as medicine and also a medicine consumed as food.

During my adolescent years, Amma used to prepare this magic potion using medicinal plants collected from our homestead and neighbourhood compounds. Medicinal herbs such as *Adalodakam, Kayyunyam, Karinkuringy, Muyal cheviyan, Kattu thrithavu, Tulsi, Thumba, Kurunthotty*, and may more would be ground well and their juice would be separated. The bitter juice that contains many beneficial alkaloids and chemicals would be mixed with coconut milk, *Njavara* rice, a peculiar rice variety would be cooked in the mixture. Other ingredients include fenugreek seeds, cumin seeds, coriander seeds, and turmeric powder.

The ingredients would be cooked under low flame accompanied by frequent stirring in a *kalam* made of clay on a hearth fired by firewood. The preparation is a slow and time-consuming procedure. Every year Amma would serve 6-8 medicinal porridge every year that would be consumed with *pappadam* roasted in oil with chilli powder and onion. Pickle, *Chammanthy*, and *thoran* are other usual accompaniments. As an unwritten rule, the monsoon porridge is always consumed in the evening, substituting the supper. The *Kanji* would have a cleansing action on the digestive system as early next morning we would experience an easy motion.

Karkkidaka kanji is believed to have several useful effects on human body including boosting immunity, aiding digestion, and promoting intestinal health as a digestive aid.it is also a rich source of antioxidants. It is consumed during monsoon months when many infectious diseases occur.

3. FENUGREEK PORRIDGE (*ULUVA KANJI*).

Uluva kanji is another traditional Kerala rice porridge of immense medicinal properties and uses primarily fenugreek seeds as key ingredient. The preparation is less elaborate than *Karkkidaka kanji*. The ingredients apart from fenugrrek are *unakkalari,* jaggery syrup and coconut milk. The magic porridge is prepared by cooking raw, broken rice with soaked fenugreek, grated coconut, cumin seeds, Halim seeds (*assaaly*) and salt. Jaggery syrup is often added to mask the bitter taste of the porridge. The *uluva kanji* is served hot with *chammanthy, pappadam* or pickle.

Considered more as a food than a medicine, it reduces body's absorption of cholesterol from fatty foods. This apart, it possesses many potential health benefits such as blood sugar control, hormonal balance, testosterone control, reducing menstrual cramps and anti-inflammatory effects.

4. *PAZHAMKANJI.*

Several decades ago, when poverty and disease plagued many rural villages, even three meals a day were beyond reach for countless families. Food choices were minimal, and many survived on nothing more than rice gruel. Leftover *kanji* from the previous night would be sealed in an earthen pot, allowing it to ferment naturally overnight. By morning, this transformed into *pazhamkanji*—a humble yet nourishing breakfast. A pinch of salt, along with crushed green chili and shallots, made for perfect accompaniments. Energized by this simple meal, people would set off to their daily tasks—most demanding physical labour and stamina.

Many from older generations sustained themselves on *pazhamkanji*, and some credited their vitality to it. One such person was Cleetus Master, the father of Bellarmine, my childhood friend, who recently passed away at the age of 98. He often claimed that his long life owed itself to two things: his daily evening walks followed by quiet contemplation under the banyan tree near the Azhakiyakavu temple, and his unwavering morning ritual of *pazhamkanji*. In a conversation long ago, he shared that he had been enjoying it since childhood, swearing by its astonishing health benefits. Though he came from a modest middle-class background and could easily afford three hearty meals a day, *pazhamkanji* remained a cherished constant on his plate.

Interestingly, recent studies affirm what many like him believed all along—fermented rice gruel is a powerhouse of probiotics, essential for gut health and digestion. It also contains vital minerals like selenium and potassium. What was once seen as poor man's food is now being rediscovered as a nutritional gem.

Today, *pazhamkanji* enjoys renewed prestige, especially among urban food lovers. On a recent visit to a high-end restaurant famed for its traditional Kerala cuisine, I watched in amazement as a group of well-heeled youngsters, fresh from luxury cars, eagerly devoured *pazhamkanji* served in earthen *chattys*, accompanied by *chammanthi*, pickles, and *pappadam*. This once-humble dish has journeyed from a survival staple to a rare gourmet indulgence.

With its proven benefits for gut health, immune function, and metabolic balance, *pazhamkanji* deserves wider recognition as an ethnic superfood. However, caution is necessary—natural fermentation, when done in unhygienic conditions, can lead to contamination and health risks.

Today, the quintessential *pazhamkanji* of the past holds its head high on the menus of modern eateries celebrating traditional Flavours. Its story is a reminder that sometimes the simplest foods carry the deepest nourishment—of both body and memory.

5. FISH OIL APPAM.

Appam fortified with fish oil was yet another yummy food which I used to eat during my younger days albeit, reluctantly owing to its pungent and unpleasant odour.

During monsoon months, starting in June and extending through September, which are the peak season of *neychala,* sardine that contain oil along Kerala coasts. Amma would buy such sardines with lot of fats in their belly. Before making curry, or frying them, she would carefully remove the white fatty tissues from the belly cavity and would be collected separate.

The fish fat would be mixed with wheat flour, grated coconut, and leavened with onion, chillies, and curry leaves. The *meen appam* would be served as evening snack along with tea. The fish fat appam is a highly nutritious and flavourful traditional dish of Kerala. The crispy appam with a rich flavour was indeed a culinary delight. In those days both the rich and the poor savoured this nutrient-rich Appam as sardines were common and damn cheap. I'm clueless as to what prompted people to incorporate fish fat as an ingredient into their favourite preparation. Thanks to the recent advances in nutrition science and food technology, that fish is a unique source of a class of chemical compounds - poly unsaturated fatty acids (PUFAs), Omega 3 fatty acid being the predominant one. They have several health benefits as they support heart health, and improve brain function. For this reason, fatty fishes like sardine are described both as a brain food and a heart food.

6. BANANA PEEL CURRY.

Culinary innovations of our ancestors have always been mindboggling. This is the story of one such curry, made from an ingredient that's normally discarded as waste. Yes, I'm talking about the peel of unripe bananas.

On *Uthradom* day, our home would come alive with vibrant energy and noise as Amma and my sisters dove into the preparations for the grand *Ona sadya* the following day. After retirement, Achan too joined in with enthusiasm—scraping coconuts, peeling onions, and skinning raw bananas for making chips and *sarkara varatty,* those fried banana fingers coated in jaggery syrup.

Amma, ever resourceful, would turn the banana peels into a delicious *thoran*. She'd first chop the peels into small pieces and then wash them thoroughly. They would be cooked with green gram or lentils, along with a pinch of chilli, salt, onions, and a drizzle of coconut oil.

On *Uthradom* night, we'd gather for a sumptuous dinner. The banana peel *thoran* would take centre stage, flanked by samples of other *sadya* curries like *inchi curry, ulli curry, sambar, rasam,* and *pachadi*. The taste of the banana peel curry was simply wonderful—a once-a-year culinary delight that lingered long in our memories.

Today, we also know that banana peels are a powerhouse of therapeutic properties. Here are just a few:

1. **Stress relief**: Banana peels contain tryptophan and vitamin B6, both known to help ease symptoms of mood disorders and depression.

2. **Cancer prevention**: Packed with antioxidants, banana peels help neutralize free radicals that can lead to cancer.

3. **Digestive health**: Their high fibre content promotes smooth digestion and regular bowel movements.

4. **Eye health**: Rich in vitamin A, banana peels support better vision.

5. **Dental care**: Their antibacterial properties may help prevent tooth decay and infections.

I marvel at how our ancestors recognized the immense therapeutic value in ingredients like mango seeds, fenugreek, banana peels, fish oils, and countless other plants. Today, modern science is rediscovering the timeless wisdom passed down through generations. Science could be a key to unlock the many secrets of traditional knowledge systems.

48.

Afterthoughts.

On the opposite side of the nameless river was a tiny island and lush paddy fields beyond that stretched infinitely. A few people who belonged to the marginalised section of the society, inhabited there. They had dark skin and bright, sparkling eyes. They routinely visited our part of the mainland to collect drinking water from public taps. They would come in their tiny skiffs loaded with numerous earthen pots at unearthly hours to escape the wrath of the natives for infringing into their territory. They would come braving brackish wind and, downpour. They made a living by fishing and working as farmhands. I walked through the newly tarred road that leads to the bridge, beyond lies an emerging small town with a couple of schools, a few resorts, and shrimp farms on either side, extending endless. Most part of the day was overcast, preluding the arrival of monsoon. This time the summer was unkind. A light drizzle forced me to cut-short my evening walk. It was after a while that I took the stretch that passed through the end of Nambiapuram road. Adjacent to the road, construction works have been progressing at a fast pace for the residential complex meant for Coast Guard; apartment complex that appeared like carefully stacked match boxes. A number of high-rises along with a few seafood companies have transformed the landscape beyond recognition. I noticed that the tiny, tile-roofed building with a large wooden-panelled door, where Vakkachan Chettan once ran his modest tea shop, has vanished. Vakkachan died a few years ago and since then, the shop had remained locked. Till a couple of decades back, the shop used to be a landmark, that indicated the abrupt end of Nambiapuram Road and Cochin Corporation limit as well, that led to the small ferry. During its heyday, the teashop would be crowded with people. On the dark, soot-covered wall hung a faded, framed photo of Jesus, accompanied by a lit candle on a wooden stand. An aged ferryman used to ferry his customers back and forth the river, the youth often with their bicycles onboard. After refreshing themselves with a glass of hot, steaming tea from Vakkachan's shop, they continued their onward journey to the small-town, to their work places. A couple of decades ago, when the tiny island was connected to the mainland by a small bridge, the ferry along with the ferryman and his small wooden canoe fell into oblivion. Today the landscape reverberates with the echoes of the past.

The gentle breeze that once soothed the senses is now a rarity. The parrots that once nested in mango trees have vanished from the landscape. The enchanting scenes of croaking frogs and misty wetlands have vanished forever from our landscape. Gone too are the buffaloes that sought refuge in muddy ponds to escape the scorching summer heat and the flock of birds that flew under the clear blue sky. I looked out through the open window that afforded a view of the glowing twilight sky. Only a lone woodpecker is pecking at the deadwood of the coconut palm that stood in the neighbour's yard. The once-pristine waters of the river have been polluted, and the diverse fish populations that sustained the aquatic ecosystem and supported the livelihoods of many have disappeared. Where have the majestic jackfruit and mango trees, once abundant sources of fruit and shade, disappeared to? The carefree and naughty village boys who roamed the streets, sharing laughter and mischief, are no more seen. The older generation, who spent their twilight hours under the banyan trees in front of the village temples, with their colourful stories and gossip, that they recounted several times, have also faded away. The elders who served as our guiding lights and beacons of hope in our life have vanished, leaving us isolated like a rudderless ship in turbulent waters. In their place, a vast emptiness surrounds me. Instead, I'm met with crowded streets, overwhelmed hospitals, sprawling mansions with dwindling occupants, and homesteads hidden behind imposing gates, often locked and inaccessible. Amma's old *tharavadu*, her ancestral home, a weatherworn, tile-roofed building, remains abandoned by the side of the new highway, with a thick layer of creepers growing on its walls, the courtyard carpeted by falling dry leaves. Perhaps, the dilapidated building is reflecting on its glorious past when up to 26 members of the extended family lived happily there several decades ago.

A generation has retreated into itself, eyes fixed on smartphones, oblivious to the world beyond their screens. The recent surge in suicides among adolescents, often triggered by trivial reasons, is alarming. The involvement of teenagers in heinous crimes, such as the brutal murder of their classmates, is equally disturbing. They suffer a sort of social disconnect syndrome that have been accentuated by the COVID imposed lockdown and the digital revolution. In their age how innocent we were, roaming village paths, with paper planes in hands, playing hide and seek and similar innocent games, and blowing *Appuppanthadi*? It's hard to reconcile. The youngsters rebelled in teenage enthusiasm. Today's youth seem to mature at an accelerated pace, losing their innocence and charm by the time they reach their teens. This is a stark contrast to our own generation, who grew up in the 1950s and 1960s with a more carefree and naiver outlook. The pervasive influence of movies and television serials that glorify violence and narcotics-abuse are likely contributors to this disturbing trend. The Internet has made many Japanese and Korean web series which portray extreme violence, accessible to adolescent children. Today the age-old institutions of family and marriage are under threat as people aspire for a nomadic life, remaining as part of a floating population in mega cities. "God's Own Country", it seems, is slowly degrading into a God-forsaken land.

The insatiable greed of modern humanity has ravaged nature and depleted our natural resources. With bee populations dwindling, coffee may soon become a rare luxury. As bat populations decline, the natural pollinators of mango trees, mango juice may also become a scarce commodity in the coming decades. As Sarus cranes vanish from our wetlands, the fast-multiplying pests will affect the rice fields making our favourite plate of rice unavailable. Future generations, including our great-grandchildren, will likely learn about the once-abundant sardines and mackerels of Kerala's waters through AI-generated digital images, a consequence of the overfishing that has depleted our seas. The anthropocentric focus has shifted our attention entirely to human-centred development, with scant consideration for an ecocentric world. In this ecocentric perspective, development prioritizes the larger ecosystem, recognizing the interconnectedness of innumerable flora, fauna, and abiotic components that are essential for the planet's survival.

A future awaits where Artificial Intelligence (AI) dominates the universe, shaping the nature of our future, relegating humans to a subordinate role, stripped of their creativity and their capacity for intelligent decision-making, and reduced to a state akin to that of animals. I fear such a world being controlled by AI may turn out to be a Frankenstein's monster, creating more problems than it can solve.

As I look back on a boisterously enchanting past, I feel a deep sense of sadness. Although the landscape has changed for the better in terms of material comforts, many virtues that we once held dear - love, sympathy, compassion, empathy, honesty, patriotism, integrity, and social bonding - have taken a backseat, as we gave them scant regard. We were chasing a world that promised instant gratification. The fast-paced life and its inevitable hectic schedules took a toll on our social lives. I apologize to future generations for my inability to leave the world a better place than the one I inherited from my ancestors. I regret having contributed to the degradation of our fresh air, pristine water, fertile soil, lush forests, and the innumerable natural gifts that have been bestowed upon us. The atmosphere has grown hotter and more humid than ever, harming the diverse plants, birds, and animals that once coexisted peacefully. The ecosystem has undergone a drastic transformation for the worse. I feel as if I'm writing an elegy for a bygone era of timeless beauty and profound human connections.

From the highest point of Thoppumpady bridge- a structure that connected not just two land masses, but two cultures-, I gazed out over the tranquil lake, its surface dotted with floating islands of water hyacinths. Upon these flotsam's, majestic white cranes stood motionless, with their eyes closed, as if in contemplation, while the water flowed lazily beneath. The city as usual was bustling with people and vehicles. Slowly I walked down the crowded path with the firm steps of a truth-seeker, wading through recklessly moving humanity- an adventurous task indeed. Life is getting pretty hectic for the citizenry. As I slowly merged into the crowd, I felt like a fish out of water, gasping for air. I felt as if I were isolated in the crowd, a loner among the milling masses. Two silent tears clung to my lashes, echoing the tenderness of a time now gone.

****